MW00790310

THIS NEVER HAPPENED

Also by J.B. Manheim

Strategy in Information and Influence Campaigns: How
Policy Advocates, Social Movements, Insurgent Groups,
Corporations, Governments and Others Get What They
Want

THIS NEVER HAPPENED

THE MYSTERY BEHIND
THE DEATH OF
CHRISTY MATHEWSON

A Novel By J.B. Manheim
Illustrations by John Payne

SUMMER
GAME
BOOKS

This book is dedicated
to Jonah, Eli, and Asher
and to their fields of dreams

Contents

THIS NEVER HAPPENED

Some History, and a Conundrum

Baseball's claim to popularity is built on myths, legends, eternal truths, passing fancies, long collective memories, and tall tales. The sport takes great care to develop and preserve them. The long-accepted origin story of the game itself, that it was invented by Abner Doubleday in Cooperstown, NY, in 1839, we know today was woven out of whole cloth by Albert Spalding, an early star player and later sporting goods purveyor, to give the game American roots in the face of claims that its origins traced to England.

Another well-known foundational story has to do with Christy Mathewson. Mathewson was a crucial figure in rendering baseball, hitherto known as a sport of drunks and ruffians, as socially acceptable, even respectable, circa 1900-1910. Mathewson was prominent, college-educated, devoutly Christian, and seen as a true gentleman who chose baseball as a career and became what many still regard as one of the best pitchers in its history. His combination of personal traits and success was key to baseball's development into the "national pastime."

When the United States entered the Great War in 1917, baseball players were initially exempted from military service. But in 1918, as the war continued and the draft bit deeply, this status became politically untenable. The Secretary of War removed the exemption, and the government pressured organized baseball to encourage players to join the military. Mathewson became a symbol of patriotism when he volunteered to serve in the Chemical Warfare Service working on a daily basis with poison gas. Another prominent player, Ty Cobb, volunteered for the same. Both were recruited to the military by baseball executive Branch Rickey, best remembered today as the man who brought Jackie Robinson up to the major leagues some thirty years later.

The prevailing story is that Mathewson and Cobb joined the Army as Captains sometime after August 1918, shipped out to France, and were involved there in a training accident that exposed both to poison gas. Mathewson got the worst of it, and, his lungs weakened by the incident, died prematurely of tuberculosis in 1925.

Lately, some researchers have begun pointing to evidence that calls this account into question. One 1920 affidavit from a divisional surgeon, for example, claims that Mathewson's exposure to poison gas occurred elsewhere in France and only after the war ended. Similarly, General Amos Fries, who became the second commander of the Chemical Warfare Service, claimed that Mathewson was never exposed to more than an occasional whiff of the innocuous gas used in training, and Rickey himself said he was with Mathewson throughout the training in France and denied that an accident ever occurred. Meanwhile, Mathewson's wife, Jane, attributed his contracting of tuberculosis to a case of influenza he caught when he first arrived in France, and to his having inhaled poison gas. Finally, it is worth noting that Mathewson's brother, Henry, died of tuberculosis in July 1917, giving rise to speculation that Christy himself may have contracted the disease as early as 1914, though it had remained undiagnosed until 1921. Adding to the difficulty of parsing these competing explanations is the fact that about eighty percent of the military records of those discharged between 1912 and 1960 were destroyed in a 1973 fire at a St. Louis storage facility of the National Archives.

Yet, there *are* some surviving records of the period, and they are not entirely consistent with the delivered history of Cobb's and Mathewson's military service. Nor are they accounted for in the extant critiques.

The records in question are those of Ordnance Depot Company No. 44 at Camp Hancock, Georgia, dated June 1918. Ordnance companies at Camp Hancock, and in the military generally, tended at that time to be staffed, in the words of one newspaper, by "men of the highest intelligence, men who are either under or above the draft age and who gave up responsible and profitable positions to enter this branch of service." The papers show that Mathewson was the lieutenant commanding the unit, and that Cobb was a corporal in it. The unit also included seven other then-current or retired professional baseball players, among others, all but two of whom were also later named to the Baseball Hall of Fame. This seems very clearly to have been a "show" unit, an exercise in propaganda, one that was set up by the Army to encourage volunteers for the military, and for the Chemical Warfare Service in particular, even as its members performed real and dangerous work.

These facts have remained generally unknown. Even the archives of *The Augusta Chronicle* (Camp Hancock was just outside of town, and Ty Cobb was essentially a "local") are silent as to the presence of these very prominent athletes in the area. More to the point, the other newspaper in town, the *Augusta Herald*, perhaps coincidentally, produced a special issue featuring

Camp Hancock during the very time the players were assigned there, but made no reference to their presence. In fact, on two occasions the paper published the roster of the Camp Hancock baseball team, which played a game against the team from the Charleston Navy Yard while the major leaguers were in camp, and none of these players was listed. It is as if they were not there.

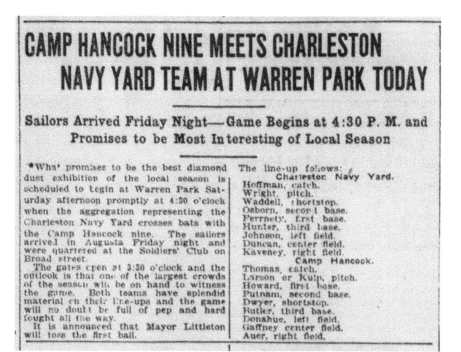

CAMP HANCOCK NINE MEETS CHARLESTON NAVY YARD TEAM AT WARREN PARK TODAY

Sailors Arrived Friday Night—Game Begins at 4:30 P. M. and Promises to be Most Interesting of Local Season

*What promises to be the best diamond dust exhibition of the local season is scheduled to begin at Warren Park Saturday afternoon promptly at 4:30 o'clock when the aggregation representing the Charleston Navy Yard crosses bats with the Camp Hancock nine. The sailors arrived in Augusta Friday night and were quartered at the Soldiers' Club on Broad street.

The gates open at 3:30 o'clock and the outlook is that one of the largest crowds of the season will be on hand to witness the game. Both teams have splendid material on their line-ups and the game will no doubt be full of pep and hard fought all the way.

It is announced that Mayor Littleton will toss the first ball.

The line-up follows:
Charleston Navy Yard.
Hoffman, catch.
Wright, pitch.
Waddell, shortstop.
Osborn, second base.
Ferrnety, first base.
Hunter, third base.
Johnson, left field.
Duncan, center field.
Kaveney, right field.
Camp Hancock.
Thomas, catch.
Larson or Kulp, pitch.
Howard, first base.
Putnam, second base.
Dwyer, shortstop.
Butler, third base.
Donahue, left field.
Gaffney center field.
Auer, right field.

From the Special Edition on Camp Hancock, *Augusta Herald*, June 8, 1918, page 3.

In 1918 the Army was greatly concerned about maintaining public support for the war, even going so far as to cover up large-scale outbreaks of influenza in its training camps near urban centers, with the effect that the then-deadly disease was able to escape into the general population and spread rapidly. Indeed, George Creel, the driving force behind that decision and the remainder of the nation's wartime propaganda efforts, had a special appreciation for the usefulness of professional baseball, in particular, as a conveyor of important social and political messages. In 1915, just two years before his appointment by President Wilson to head the so-called Committee on Public Information, the nation's first propaganda agency, Creel, then serving as publicity chairman for the Men's League for Woman Suffrage in New York State, organized an effort in which the suffragists purchased 8000 tickets and one hundred twenty-five boxes for a Cubs-Giants game at the Polo Grounds in New York, filled them with movement supporters, and decorated the park with their banners. Creel later applied that same propagandistic spirit to military recruitment efforts, of which, it seems, Ordnance Depot Company No. 44 was to be a prominent element. The idea was to demonstrate that even famous athletes were willing to take on this dangerous work.

And yet, *no one has ever heard about this unit.* It appears in no baseball histories, no press accounts, no histories of the Great War. It is as if the unit never existed.

Why is that? And how can it be that this special unit, apparently designed and recruited expressly with propaganda in mind, has remained a secret all these years?

This Never Happened is an imagined answer to that question, a pure fiction, a what-might-have-been. But if this is a fiction, one is left to wonder: What is the fact? If *this* never happened, what did?

Charlie Chaplin once commented that one is more likely to find valid facts in works of art than in history books. Perhaps he was correct.

First Pitch

Max Tomhoff looked out over the room with a wary eye. It had been years since the Marbury House auction master had seen such a crowd for sports memorabilia, and that was the day they had sold off the only known pristine T206 Honus Wagner baseball card for just under three million dollars. For a cardboard square! Today's prize was so much greater. And so was the buzz in the room. A very different crowd from Marbury's more frequent fine art auctions, a little less polished, a little more... rowdy might be the word. But then, this was a different game, an auction of sporting memorabilia. And the more he thought about it, the more he appreciated the import, and the pure sweetness, of the moment he was about to initiate.

It had been quite a week. Because of their value and their delicacy, these papers had been afforded very special treatment. The seldom-used six-foot mahogany display case with the special UV-resistant art glass top had been brought over from storage, and outfitted with custom display mounts topped by acid-free archival fabric. These were used for the letters and, as importantly, for the two century-old military documents. Arrayed between them were the notebooks, only one of which lay open, and the typescripts arrayed in a fan-like display. The notebooks themselves were particularly fragile, and Marbury House management had ruled that they could not be opened for further inspection while on exhibit. A small plaque had been installed atop the frame of the case stating the obvious, that Marbury House had performed its customary due diligence and guaranteed the authenticity of these items. A custom security system protected the lot, and a special video feed served the needs of both Internet viewers and the in-house team monitoring the area. And, should a bona fide bidder wish a closer examination of a signature or even the paper itself, whether with a jeweler's glass or with the assistance of her own expert consultant, a gloved attendant was on standby to assist.

The phone banks to his left were fully staffed, as were the three computers beside them monitoring the online action. And both the lines and the secure website had been awash with pre-open bids. He had a number in hand that he knew would awe the crowd and, not unexpectedly, limit the number of real players in the room. Max thought he knew who might win the bidding today, as any experienced high-end auctioneer who knew his clientele might. He had even tried to arrange a private sale several weeks ago, but his colleague Frederick, over in acquisitions, had simply done too good a job of persuading the seller of the high ceiling of an auction sale for this collection. So here they all were.

Now it was Max Time, a moment he had come to cherish.

A hush fell as the spotlight hit the next Lot, and he stepped to the podium.

"Lot 21-143B7. Pages 16 and 17 in your catalog. A collection of baseball memorabilia. This one-of-a-kind collection was lost for almost a century, then rediscovered in a barn a few months ago. As indicated in the catalog, certain of these items have been authenticated by Bonomo Sports Authenticators. Others have been reviewed by historians and document specialists commissioned by this House, and deemed period-appropriate and in accordance with certain known facts, though the potential value of this collection lies in the extent to which it *extends* our knowledge of the history of baseball during the period of World War I beyond previously known facts. The provenance of the collection has been confirmed. The collection will convey with full Marbury House certification.

"Included in the Lot are the following items: A pay roster covering the period June 1 to June 30, 1918, for Ordnance Depot Company Number 44, Camp Hancock, Georgia; an assignment log covering the same period and the same military unit; a personal letter from Branch Rickey to Christy Mathewson seeking to recruit the latter into the military unit he was to command; a personal letter from Ty Cobb to Jane Mathewson expressing his regret at Mathewson's death; and a manuscript and fourteen handwritten notebooks, attributed by credible provenance to a prominent sports writer of the era, JT Willett, detailing post-war interviews with members of Ordnance Depot Company Number 44 and others."

Tomhoff had to admit to himself that he loved the understated accuracy of this description.

"Lot 21-143B7 carries a buyer's premium of twenty percent."

Wait for it.

"Bidding will open at... $3.7 million. Do I hear $4 million?"

Six paddles virtually flew into the air at once, cell phones sounded around the room as distant bidders instructed their proxies and urged them forward, the website flooded with online bids, and the house phones lit up. To start the action in the room, Tomhoff recognized the bid of Roger Constance, a Marbury House regular.

"I hear 4, do I hear $5 million?"

The cell-phone chatter swelled, though as the news of the opening bid spread, Max could see several of the devices drop into the laps of their holders. Wheat from chaff. Five paddles split the air, together with one raised arm from the phone bank. At least for the moment, the online bidders went silent.

The drive north and west from Albany seemed to take forever. Much longer, Adam thought, than when he had first made it so many years before headed in the opposite direction, an escape route from the life he had been born into and the only available path he could see to a hoped-for future. Now, even that future was mostly behind him.

The call had come from his oldest friend, Jason Drumm. Jason had never taken that drive, or at least not with the same purpose. They had kept up by letter, phone, or eventually email, and had caught up with one another a few times over the years – the upstate farmer and the downstate writer – and still exchanged Christmas cards most years. But however many slow miles or streaming electrons might link them together, the gulf of experience and ambition remained as wide as ever. Jason had never moved away from the family farm along the Oswegatchie. When both of his parents were killed in an auto accident – on this same road – he had simply taken over the operation and carried on. That was Jason. Adam, on the other hand, had returned to DeKalb Falls only twice, once to bury his own father, and a second time to move his mother into a senior living facility in the city when she could no longer look after herself.

So, Jason's phone call was not without precedent, but still, it had come as a bit of a surprise. Really, it was less a call than a summons. "Come," he had said. "You need to be here. I won't tell you why. But you need to be here."

"Who died?"

"Actually, my grandfather. In 1957. You need to be here."

"Wait. What? That makes no sense. That was sixty years ago. What'd the old boy do, have a second family that's claiming the farm?"

"Don't be an asshole. Have I ever asked you to come up here before? Actually *asked* you? In like, what, fifty years? I know you're not doing anything these days except sitting on your terrace and looking at the lights. So, get your bony ass in the car and come up here. I promise you: you won't regret it. Pack a bag. Plan on staying a few days. Maybe longer."

"Damn it, Jason. If that farm hand of yours – what's his name, Melvin? If Melvin left and you need help running things, just hire a new Melvin. I am not your guy. I am *still* a look-at-the-lights guy and not a watch-the-corn-grow guy, retired or not."

"I'll expect you on Tuesday."

This was Monday. Adam couldn't help himself. His bony ass was in the car – and starting to ache just a bit from the ruts and the potholes – as hour after hour of pine trees and abandoned factories drifted past. Miles of nothing. Ah, the glories of Upstate New York. What the hell, he wondered, am I doing?

It was dusk when the lights of DeKalb Falls finally came into view, and as he made his way through town, in the growing darkness, he had to fall back on old memories to find his way to the farm. Once or twice they failed him, but eventually the familiar outline of the house and barn rose out of the night as his headlights hit the big rural mailbox. "DRUMM FARMS," it declared. He was, he thought, not exactly home. But he was somewhere close by.

Jason was on the front porch of the house with three or four others, and as the lights of the car turned down the drive, he rose with a welcoming smile and a wave. "Man! I thought you were lost or fell in the river!"

"Don't go there. Just put a drink in my hand and a cushion under my butt and tell me what the hell I'm doing here."

16

"I can take care of the first two easily. But let's hold off on the third for a while. I have some folks I'd like you to meet. You remember Melvin, of course..."

Adam had to smile. He would not be running a combine after all. "Melvin, how are you? It's been years!"

"I am just real good, Mr. Wallace. Real good."

"And these young lovelies," Jason injected, pointing to his other guests, who appeared to be in their middle years and well-tended, "are Jenna and Elaine. Ladies, meet my oldest bud, Adam Wallace."

Jenna and Elaine, it turned out, were Jason's first cousins, the daughters of his father's younger brother, Paul. They had grown up on the adjacent farm - literally across the road. But they had no interest in farming, and when their parents passed away, Jason had bought them out lock, stock, and llamas. The llamas were a distant memory now, but Jenna and Elaine, who still lived in the farmhouse, had stuck around, investing their newfound capital in a pottery shop and health food store in town. As Jason put it, they catered to the six local hippies and the dozen or so tourists who passed through each year.

Adam detected only a small wince between the two when he said this. Obviously, it was a line they had heard before.

"Ladies, very nice to meet you."

"Adam is the big New York writer I was telling you about. Only person I know who got out of the Falls and stayed out."

"Good for you," Elaine exclaimed. "You'll have to tell us how you managed that. We've all been here forever. Never found a way out. But you know that story."

"What do you write?" This from Jenna.

"Not much these days. I'm pretty much retired. But I used to do a little of this, a little of that. I'm kind of permanently between projects these days, though I will confess that I'm always on the lookout for that one book that cries out to be written."

"Adam is being modest," noted Jason. "He's done a book or two, some short stories, and a lot of writing for some really important magazines. Won some awards, too, haven't you?"

"Well, some. But where's that drink?"

Jason slipped a two-finger portion of perfectly-aged Green Spot into Adam's hand, but he wasn't yet done praising his friend, who might have been the only marginally famous person he knew. "I saved out this clip one time. Really liked it," he said, taking a folded and yellowed paper from his shirt pocket. "Listen to this." And he proceeded to read.

Whaling Songs of the American Southwest

By Adam Wallace
Special to *Science in Our Age*

The umber sky was a stark contrast to the white and pink limestone striations of the Mogollon Rim, and a thing of beauty in its own right. Here we were in Northern Arizona, where God the Historical Geologist, using wind, sand, and water as instruments, had shaved away layer after layer of the underlying sandstone to carve the earth, revealing the history before history, the history almost before time itself.

Here, in the growing dusk of a desert night, sat the base camp of Dr. Suzanne Rodriguez Jones, archaeologist, paleontologist, Earth historian.

Her team of graduate students and trained volunteers had been digging below the base of the Rim for the last four or five years, far below the era of human habitation, though some evidence of that did emerge from time to time in the detritus of natural erosion that lay all through these sandy canyons. But their objective was far older, far deeper in time, far below the layers of the Rim itself. They were in search of new evidence testing the age of the vast inland sea that once covered all these lands and more, and of the life they were sure it had sustained. It was, they hypothesized, a life of small creatures struggling to survive as all creatures do.

I was on hand because last week they found that evidence, but it was not what they had expected. Yes, they had found fossilized fish. Yes, they had found fossilized crustaceans. But they had found something else. Under layers and layers of sandstone deposited over too many eons, they had found teeth and bones that could only be those of a whale. Actually, a whole pod of whales. Where they should not be. Where they could not be. Where they had lain at rest for all of the ages there were.

What's going on here? How did a pod of whales come to be buried hundreds of feet under the Arizona desert – at a time when whales of any kind did not exist? Or so thought the brightest of minds. That's the question that has more than one scientific discipline buzzing, and Dr. Jones answering questions from the media....

When Jason's voice trailed off, it was Jenna who broke the silence. "You sure didn't learn to write like that around here!"

And from there the evening progressed. Jenna and Elaine told stories of growing up female in DeKalb Falls, an experience like Adam's own, yet different. They seemed content. Jason went on about the joys of farming in the twenty-first century, all of which, Adam had to admit, escaped him altogether. Melvin sat quietly and drank, then was the first to excuse himself. By the time the cousins left, Adam could barely lift his lids.

"Tomorrow," Jason said. "Get some sleep and we'll talk tomorrow."

One day and a few hundred miles down. And for what?

Jocko Drumm was a hanger-on. He played a little ball, and a lot of poker. He rode the rails hard, and his friends easy. He served his country, and he served himself. But mostly, he talked. He talked about growing up in rural Indiana, or was it Kansas? He talked about high cotton and low water. He talked about fighting Kaiser Bill so much you'd have thought he beat the man himself, single-handed. He talked about the ladies of Paree, and the women who met the boats. He talked about where he'd been, what he'd done, and whom he knew. If you could think it, he could talk about it. Thing was, about ninety percent of what he said was, well, made up. But no one really knew Jocko, and no one really knew the real from the rest.

He was, in short, a lot of fun to be around.

And even as he talked, he knew how to listen, how to smile, and how to take from your stories and experiences those parts that he could weave into his own. A rascal? Perhaps. A scalawag? Perhaps. Today one might think of Jocko Drumm as a phony or a con man. But he really was not out to con anyone out of anything. After all, a con is just a dream someone else chooses to believe is real. Not a lie, exactly, but just an expression of what might *possibly* be true depending on what might *possibly* be the facts. No, he was in the game simply because it was there to be played. America during the Depression was like that. It was the place and the time and the circumstance in which he found himself, and he was determined to make the most of every opportunity life offered.

And yet, Jocko Drumm could get into trouble. Sometimes it was the ladies, usually those who were, in the parlance of the times, already spoken for. Jocko was, when he could afford it, a bit of a rake. Sometimes it was the whiskey, for which, truth be told (and this was a known and witnessed truth) he had a certain weakness. Jocko was, when he could afford it, generally a happy drunk. Sometimes it was one or another of the over-sized pockets in his well-worn cloth jacket or his trousers that might give way from the weight of goods before he was able to exit a mercantile. Just so he could afford it, you understand. Sometimes it was merely his mouth. That, he could seldom afford.

This was one of those times. All of them. Yes, he'd had a little too much to drink. And yes, he'd gone into the James Mercantile with a great hunger and a light fortune. And yes, he had placed a few objects in one of his pockets - on credit. And yes, in his altered state he had been a bit ambitious, and yes, while still in the store the bottom of his pocket split, spilling merchandise noisily at his feet. And yes, the aforementioned James had noted the clatter and reached for the scattergun he kept behind the counter for just such exigencies. And yes, on Jocko's necessarily rapid exit from the mercantile, he had run headlong into a young lady on her way into the establishment, knocking her ass over tea kettle. And yes, even as he showed his chivalrous side by apologizing and helping the lady to her feet, grasping what purchase on her person he could for the purpose, he could not help but comment, quietly, on the charms of her physique. And yes, his comment was not so quiet as to escape the hearing of her companion, a burly fellow with large fists but a slow wit, who took umbrage and moved to pummel him. And yes, he took off running with the brute chasing behind. And yes, he lost his pursuer by the expedient of jumping aboard the last car of the 10:15 for Boston, which, fortuitously, was running exactly one hour and thirty-seven minutes late.

Vintage Jocko.

It took some moments to catch his breath and take inventory. First and thankfully, he was still breathing. A bit too rapidly, in fact. Second, he still had what little money was left when he had pushed away from the bar a mere, what, fifteen or twenty minutes ago? Third, he was not sure where the train that had rescued him was headed, though truth be told, it mattered not, as he did not know anyone in Boston. Never been there. But fourth, and perhaps most important, no one on the train knew – could know – of the circumstances that placed him in their company. He was, in sum, a free man on a roll.

Jocko stood up, steadied himself against the exaggerated rocking motion of the trailing car, took a breath, opened the door, and walked into the carriage. Ah, he thought. That's more like it.

Luck was with Jocko that day. Once the train had started, the Conductor, expecting no fresh stowaways, had begun his long march toward the engine, clip-clipping tickets in that secret binary code of the Brotherhood that sorted the scofflaws from the paying passengers, stashing each ducat in the appropriate seatback. By the time Jocko joined the party, he was long gone. Not only that, the carriage itself was at least half empty, empty enough that no one had chosen to sit in any of the rear-facing seats. There was no one in a position to see him enter. Nor did anyone seem to notice the clatter as he opened and passed through the rear door. Just another humdrum, routine rattle as the train bumped over the switches on its way out of town.

Jocko took a seat three or four rows behind the rear-most passenger and settled in. He figured he had at least fifteen minutes before the Conductor returned, if he did. Best to wait until the train was at full speed before moving forward to relative safety.

Jocko had not considered the size of the city, nor the fact that it spread mainly to the north and east. So, by the time the train finally cleared the urban landscape and began to gain speed, he was becoming just a little bit nervous. But the moment finally arrived, and he stood as if to stretch his legs and walked slowly, calmly forward. One car. Two cars. Punched ticket now in hand, courtesy of an unknowing fellow traveler. Mind if I sit here? Help yourself.

And he did.

It was a long way from there to Boston, and travelers had to find ways to pass the time. They slept. They read. They looked out the window. And sooner or later, they talked to one another. Now, Jocko Drumm was wide awake and not much of a reader, near as anyone knew. And watching life pass him by at fifty or sixty miles an hour had limited appeal. But as we already know, Jocko was drawn to door number three like iron filings to a magnet. Fortunately for him, the rather dour grey presence seated across from him seemed in a talkative mood himself.

"Jocko Drumm. How d'ya do?"

"Name's Willett. Nice to meet ya. Headed for Boston?" As he laid down the copy of *The Sporting News* he'd been reading, Jocko noticed a string of photos on the cover of some baseball player arguing with an umpire.

"Appears so. I decided to get on a train and go where it goes. Guess this one goes to Boston."

Willett smiled at that. He'd met a lot of men in his time. Loners. Travelers. Ambitious men. Talented men. Losers. The occasional lunatic. He could usually tell when entertaining conversation was to be had, and this had the look of one of those times.

"Yourself?"

"Yeah, Boston. Just got done chasing some guy halfway across Indiana. Boston's next."

At the reference to his new companion being in the business of chasing people down, Jocko's heart skipped a beat. Smiling, but cautious, he pursued the offering. "You a cop of some kind?"

"Nah," replied Willett, deciding in that instant that he would not reveal his true self to this fellow. "Nothing so romantic. I'm a salesman. Wholesale, really. I sell fixtures to stores – you know the kind of thing.

Counters. Signs. Lights. That's my sample case up there." He nodded toward the overhead rack. "Help people get set up in business. Everything's on credit these days. Nobody has any money, but people still need to make a buck. Damn Depression can't last forever.

"Guy in Indiana stiffed me. I set him up in this nice little shop in Chicago. Dry goods, lace, that kind of thing. Even took some time to help him put the store together. Don't usually do that, but I took a liking to him. Seemed like an ace. Well, that joker couldn't make a go of it. Stopped paying. Not my problem, right? But the guy I work for, he's a mean son of a bitch, and he says to me, 'Willett, you picked that guy. You gave him credit. He don't pay up, you do. Make a choice.' Well, it ain't no choice. So off I go to Chicago.

"Took me almost two weeks to find him. Emptied the store and left Chicago with the goods. And that's how I found him. I tried every whistle-stop and weed patch south of town. Ever see this guy? Make it worth your while. And you know, he was as dumb as they come. No wonder he failed. He left a trail of shirts and lace and ladies' private garments straight from Chicago to Indianapolis. Financed his trip by selling off some of his stock. And then he set himself up in a little store front in Indy. He still had some of my damn shelves and signs, by god! And that's where I found him."

"Well, what happened?" Jocko was fully engaged in the tale by this point. "Did you brace him? Is he still walkin' around?"

"Oh, I braced him alright. I walked into that little store one bright morning – day before yesterday, as a matter of fact – and you could see the blood drain from his face. He knew what he did, and he knew I had him dead to rights."

It was about that time that the Conductor passed through on his way to the back of the train. Jocko could have sworn that he did a bit of a double-take and paused in his rolling gait as he neared the pair of men so deep in conversation. But the ticket on the back of Jocko's seat was good to Boston, better, if perhaps less legitimate, than the Conductor's memory for faces. He moved on.

"Well, look who finally decided to roll out of the sack!"

Adam propped open a lid and glanced at his watch. "What the hell, Dude. It's seven thirty in the morning!"

"You forget. This is a working farm. Been up since 4:30 or so. Can I fry you an egg? Still warm from momma."

"You can pour me a cup of that coffee I smell and tell me what was important enough to drag me up here to the middle of Upstate. It surely isn't to eat farm-fresh eggs."

"Fair enough." Jason poured the coffee, sat himself at the old wooden table, and began.

"I don't think you ever met my granddad, Jocko. Truth is, I'm not sure I remember him myself. He died pretty young – sometime in the 50's. What I know about him, I know mostly from my dad's stories, and some of them were wild. It's pretty clear old Jocko was a character. Ran away from home as a kid. Hoboed around. Worked now and then. Got himself in trouble from time to time. But I never was sure what was real, and what my dad was making up. And he got it all from Jocko himself anyway, and Jocko wasn't exactly reluctant to embellish things. So, who knows?

"Anyway, somehow Jocko ended up here. DeKalb Falls. He was the one that started this farm. Don't know how he got here. Don't know where he got the money. Don't know if he already knew how to farm, or just picked it up as he went along. But he settled down, got the farm going, met my grandma somewhere in town. My dad said he won her over with a wolf whistle. I remember her a little, and it wouldn't surprise me. She had a little of the devil in her herself. But who knows?

"Seems to be the case around here, and maybe everywhere, that people who lived through those hard times came to appreciate little things. And by appreciate, I mean they kept every little thing that came into their hands. You never knew, I guess, what might be useful someday. I'm not sayin' they were all pigeon feeders and cat ladies, but by the way we think today, well, they were just a little bit crazy. And that was granddad. 'Course, he may have been a little bit crazy to begin with.

"I kind of figured this out a couple of months ago. Melvin and I were trying to economize a bit, and we started lookin' around the place more closely than we ever had before. And there was this old barn off behind

24

the one my dad put up before he died. That's the one we use now. And off behind the sheds where we keep some of the equipment and do a little work on things. All tucked away and literally forgotten. Or at least never really noticed.

"You'll see it. Place is almost ready to crumble down in a heap. Roof leaks. Walls are standing out of inertia, pure and simple. Just too much work to fall over. I'm sure it was the center of a booming society of raccoons over generations, and that's not to mention the hornets. No wonder we left it alone all those years.

"Well, me and Melvin got to thinking that old barn wood might actually have some value these days. Some hotsy-totsy New York City decorator type might pay a few bucks for that, especially for a whole barn's worth. So, we decided we'd pull it down. First thing, though, we had to see whether anything was inside.

"Scary moment. I knocked the rusty old lock off the door and swung it open, and I thought the place was about to collapse right then and there, with me under it. Whole thing shifted toward where the door had been. And then, Jesus, bunch of birds flew out into the light. Obviously been nesting in there. Scared the living shit out of me. And there's old Melvin, layin' on the ground and laughin' so damn hard I thought he was gonna pee.

"Then we looked inside, and we both had the same thought. Crap! That barn wasn't standing up because it just *wouldn't* fall over. It was standing up because it just *couldn't* fall over. It was full of stuff from wall to wall and floor to roof. And when I say "stuff" I mean just stuff. Wood stuff. Metal stuff. Mechanical-looking stuff. Stuff under so much dust it looked like rocks or just lumps of who knows what. Right away it became pretty clear. We might reclaim all that old barn wood, but not without a fight. Might have been Jocko's rainy-day fund, sort of. But for us, it was going to be a major pain in the ass.

"So, we thought about what to do. The easiest thing would be to hook up a tractor to the corner of the place and start pulling. Bring the barn down on top of the pile of junk, then just pull out the usable wood and bulldoze the rest into a ditch, or just leave it there to rot. Melvin was all for that, and I have to say, I was almost there with him. But some buzzing in some dark recess of my brain told me not to do that. Probably just a hornet that got in through my ear, but I listened. And decided to do it the hard way."

"Okay," Adam said, having long since drained the last of the coffee. "So, you found something, right? What the fuck was it?"

"I'm gettin' to that. You were always in such a damn hurry. But this is my story, and I intend to milk it for all it's worth. Pun intended.

"As I was sayin'," he droned on, slower than necessary and just to make a point, "I decided to do it the hard way. Me and Melvin, we banged some stakes in the ground and tied them to the building wherever we could find some piece of wood that would hold a hook. And just to be safe, we propped up the walls with some 2-by-4s. Not much we could do for the roof from outside, so we pulled out some hard hats and got to work.

"It was pretty slow goin', digging though that pile, but we started moving everything outside into the light and sorting through it. You'd be amazed. Rusted away parts of cars we don't have. A beat-up old gas pump. Chains and gears and rotted old rope and little bits of rotted hopsack seed bags that the raccoons had missed. Old signs. Broken dishes. Some kind of fruit peeler. Scale weights, but no scale. It just went on and on.

"And there were boxes. Old, rotted cardboard boxes mainly, but a few wooden ones. And every one of them was just chock full of more crap. And we dug through it all.

"After a couple of months, we had a pile outside of stuff that I wouldn't take to a flea market. Waste of effort. But we could see the floor nearly wall-to-wall. That left just the corners. We figured that whatever was in the corners was what was really holding up the building, so we left all of that for last.

"Now, jammed into one corner was a big old wagon. Horse-drawn type of thing, and we figured that might have some value. Over in another corner was a pile of bricks and cement blocks maybe four feet high. Probably left over from building one of the farm buildings back in the day. The third corner was packed tight with a bunch of old oak farm furniture. Antique dealer's dream. Tables, desk, chests of drawers. It was covered with an old tarp, and it was in surprisingly good condition. Somebody in town'll want that to sell to the tourists, and I'm sure we'll get something for it."

At this point, Adam was out of patience. "Let me guess...."

"Yep, corner number four is the reason you're here today. It wasn't real big, or even real heavy. But it was wrapped in several layers of oil cloth. Obviously, something my grandpa had gone to some considerable trouble to protect. And likely as well, to bury. I confess that, when I saw it, I was curious. Naturally, I unwrapped it and opened it up. That was Sunday. That's when I called you. I knew you had to see this. Follow me."

The talk went on for hours, it seemed. Jocko was like that, and it appeared that Willett was the same. They traded stories, one or two of which might have held some gem of truth. They played a little rummy. Willett shared a cigar - a rare treat in those days for Jocko, who, nonetheless, was able to produce the requisite match. Both drifted in and out of sleep as the train rocked eastward toward Cleveland, Buffalo, Rochester, Syracuse, Saratoga Springs, Albany, Springfield, and any other excuse to stop it could find on the winding way to Boston. It was sometime after Rochester and before the Springs that Willett awoke with a start, opened his eyes wide, and slumped in his seat. As in dead. Jocko had seen dead before, knew it when he saw it. And this was dead. Nice guy. Too bad.

Jocko also knew opportunity when it bumped up against him. And this was opportunity. He looked around the speeding railcar, taking quick stock of everyone and everything. As fortune had it, he was the only one awake. The only one who knew that one stranger among the many would not be departing the car of his own volition. Boston be damned.

Jocko reached carefully into the breast pocket of Willett's well-worn jacket, the one where, he had long since noted, his erstwhile companion carried his wallet. That was the first surprise. He thought briefly of that poor, anonymous shopkeeper in Illinois. Then he thought maybe the store fixture wholesaler business must be pretty good, Depression or not. Then, being Jocko, he came to the realization that no shopkeeper and no salesman had this kind of money. Whoever Willett really was, he was clearly a man after Jocko's heart.

He removed most of the money from the wallet and jammed it into his pants pocket, being careful to leave behind about twenty dollars, enough in 1936 to make it appear that Willett had not been robbed by a fellow rider whom some might recall having seen in his company. Next, he reached up to the overhead rack and grabbed Willett's suitcase. The one thing he knew by then that he would *not* find in it was a bunch of salesman's sample store fixtures. Beyond that, the mystery would have to await a solution. Carrying the bag before him, he moved as quietly as he could out onto the back platform of the car, taking care to avoid a nasty swipe from the swinging safety chains. All he had to do was wait until the train slowed for some reason – a hill, a crossing, an approaching town, a water tank. It really didn't matter. Jocko had mastered the drop and roll long ago, though it might be a little tricky with the suitcase hugged to his chest.

———————————————————

When in Rome.

In this case, Rome, New York. That's where the train slowed enough to let Jocko effect his escape. A far cry from Boston, but the sun was coming up, and daylight would sooner or later reveal poor Willett's true state to Conductor and passengers alike. A hue and cry. A stop at whatever the next town might be. A doctor. A policeman. Obviously, a natural death. No sign of foul play. But where is that stranger he was traveling with? Probably just got spooked.

So, there was Jocko, standing on a road just outside Rome, New York, suitcase in hand, shivering a bit in the morning chill, and looking for all the world like just one more poor soul carrying all his earthly goods and hoping for something better. He fit right in to his times and his place, and Jocko knew the part well.

Curiosity finally got the better of him. After all, he had been clutching that suitcase for what seemed like hours, and he had no idea what was inside it. Time to find out. He slipped off the road and into a small clearing in the woods, sat himself down on a log that happened to be handy, and went to work on the lock. Gently, he thought, because if he was lucky, he might need that lock to be working himself.

Some clothes. A pair of shoes. Both good as gold in that time and place, of course, but neither would qualify as a treasure. Then, oddly, there was a kind of small, portable typewriter. And there were papers. Lots of papers. A few looked official, one way or another. A few looked like letters. There was a bunch of typed pages. And there were some notebooks filled with a chicken scratch that Jocko assumed to be Willett's handwriting. Shit.

Then Jocko looked a little closer. Read a little of this paper, this notebook, a little of that one. And a light came on. These were names he knew. A few of them at least. These were... worth carrying along with him for a few miles more. He tied the various bundles back together, kept the clothes and shoes, which, he found, fit him reasonably well, and headed back to the road.

Jocko hitched a ride here, walked a narrow road or a forest path there, worked a few days in one town or another, or on some farm, borrowed an apple or a tomato to get along. And he headed north. Canada was up that way, and if he had done something truly and seriously wrong, he knew he could slip across the line almost anywhere. But Jocko was not running from anyone. No one missed him. No one sought him. No one cared if he was around at all, and some probably wished he had never been. No, Jocko wanted something else. He wanted solitude. And if there was one thing far Upstate New York could offer in bunches, it was solitude. It was the land of the map-dot. The land that time would have forgotten if it ever knew it was there in the first place.

Jocko Drumm had landed in DeKalb Falls, Willett's money in his pocket and Willett's suitcase in hand.

John Tyler Willett the younger joined this world in a modest apartment above the family's tavern in Trenton, New Jersey, a few years after the end of the Civil War, a second-generation County Cork-American. Named for his father, who was in turn named for the President of the United States when, in the 1840s, his progenitors had made the journey from Kinsale on the South Coast to Jersey City on the East, he was tending bar by the time he was ten, and playing winning hands of twenty-five in the back room of the tavern by the time he hit his teens. Clever to the point of audacious, he earned a reputation as a risk taker.

Among those who frequented the family's establishment was one Michael O'Farrell, who had recently been named by Pope Leo XIII as the very first Bishop of Trenton. A bit of a sportsman himself, Bishop O'Farrell knew the back way into the place, better to avoid the prying eyes of local parishioners. And he took a particular liking to young JT, as he preferred to be known. Just what he saw in the young fellow is not clear, but for whatever reason – and there were those wags who suggested at the time it was as a "favor" to JT's still attractive mother – the cleric made a place for the lad in one of the parish's schools and did his best to make sure JT attended regularly.

It is doubtless true that JT learned his letters and his numbers at school, as both of his parents were illiterates. All of that would stand him well later in life. But his real education came closer to home. Behind the bar. At the card table.

By luck or by divine intervention, the Willetts' little tavern sat on the informal boundary between the central business district of Trenton, then a town of about four or five thousand, and the various offices and chambers of the state government, which it served as capital. And it sat there at the very time when the Irish population of New Jersey was booming. Translation: Trenton was filling up with a growing number of Irish-American politicians seeking drink, seeking entertainment, and seeking back rooms where they could meet with the kind of people who preferred to do business in twilit corners. The Willetts offered all three, with the added benefit of their convenient location. And young JT was right in the middle of it. He quickly came to know everyone who was anyone in New Jersey, and learned to be at ease with the prominent and the powerful. Quiet as a child, he became gregarious. Reticent as a child, he became outgoing. People liked John Tyler Willett, Jr.

By the time he was twenty, JT Willett was an influential young man in his own right. Need an introduction? JT could arrange it. Need to know the status of some bit of legislative legerdemain? Or where the Governor would be next Tuesday afternoon? JT could find out. Life as a political fixer and man about town beckoned.

But JT wanted something different. He wanted a bigger stage. He wanted a bigger audience. He wanted a kind of fame, a degree of fame, that Trenton could never offer.

Now, where did a kid from Trenton, New Jersey, go to find fame and fortune in the closing years of the nineteenth century? The question almost answered itself: New York City. So, to the surprise of few who knew him, to the surprise of many who only thought they did, and to the dismay of his parents, who had come to depend on him in the running of the tavern, JT saved up some money, bought himself a ticket on the Pennsylvania Railroad to Exchange Place in Jersey City, as close to the City as trains ran in those days, and on the railroad's ferry service across the Hudson to Courtland Street – reversing the very path of his immigrant grandparents – and headed east. An hour on the train; a lifetime of difference.

They say that timing is everything in life, and for young Mr. Willett that surely proved true. He did not know a soul in the City, but he could read, he could write, and he could talk to just about anyone in any station of life. He settled on a career that was just then coming into its own. JT would be a journalist.

The 1890s were a time of ferment in New York journalism. The population was expanding. More and more people were going to school, learning to read. Suddenly, there was an audience for newspapers that had never existed before. Those people still did not have much money, but the combination of new, cheaper paper made from wood pulp instead of rags, and automated type-setting machines that reduced labor costs and sped up production, meant the news of the day could be published on a large scale and sold to a mass audience. The emergence of the first true advertising agency, N.W. Ayer, in Philadelphia in 1892, and the imitators it soon spawned in the City, provided a growing revenue stream for those who would do the publishing and meant that the news could be sold, literally, for a penny a paper.

Still, that wasn't quite enough to set off a boom in readership, because even if they could get the newspaper and read it in numbers never before imagined, people did not have any reason to do so. There was no precedent, anywhere, for the mass of citizens of this or any other city to be consumers of the news. And no reason for an ambitious fellow like JT Willett to seek a career in journalism.

Except.

At first, JT did not realize that he had stumbled into a unique moment in the history of journalism. It was the moment when two marketing geniuses – Joseph Pulitzer and William Randolph Hearst – recognized the potential to make money selling news to the masses, and set out to best one another at doing it. The new style of journalism they created, known as "yellow journalism," with its emphasis on crime, corruption, sex, drama, and large personalities, opened the door to JT's future. He just happened to be standing in front of it at the right time.

Pulitzer, the son of a wealthy Hungarian merchant, was educated in private schools in Budapest. At seventeen, he tried to enlist in the Austrian army, but was turned down for reasons of health. His efforts to join Napoleon's Foreign Legion and the British army, in both instances for overseas colonial service, led to the same result. But the Union Army in America, engaged in the bloody Civil War, had no such qualms, accepted Pulitzer as a paid substitute for a draftee, and in 1864 shipped him off to Boston. Though he reportedly jumped the ship once it arrived in port, he did serve a year in the Lincoln Cavalry. Later, he made his way to St. Louis, where he worked in various jobs – muleteer, baggage handler, waiter. And he spent many hours in the city's Mercantile Library, where he studied English and the law.

There he met by chance two editors of a leading German-language daily newspaper. The pair engaged Pulitzer in a conversation that ended with a job offer as a reporter. He accepted, and four years later, in 1872, wound up with a controlling interest in what was by then, alas, a failing enterprise.

That was the first in a series of transactions that led Pulitzer in 1878 to merge two newspapers to form the *St. Louis Post-Dispatch*. In short order, Pulitzer married well, began to dress elegantly, and came to feel at ease in the elite stratum of St. Louis society. Circulation grew, and the newspaper became a success. But in 1882, one of those random events of life occurred. Pulitzer's chief editorial writer shot and killed one of the newspaper's political opponents - in the paper's newsroom. It was probably the first time that a newspaper had ever "cancelled" a subscriber.

The newspaper lost more than a thousand readers almost overnight, and its standing in the community began to slip. So, too, did Pulitzer's own health. To escape, and to recuperate, in 1883 Pulitzer and his wife set off for New York, the gateway to a planned, physician-ordered European getaway.

Before boarding the Atlantic steamer, however, Pulitzer met with rail magnate Jay Gould, who controlled the financially troubled *New York World*. Pulitzer decided to buy the newspaper from Gould, cancelled his tour, and set about remaking the New York paper. He took on corruption, sensationalized the writing, pioneered the extensive use of illustrations, and even staged stunts and special promotions, including one that raised the money to build the pedestal in New York harbor on which the Statue of Liberty would be mounted. It all worked to perfection and by the early '90s the *World's* circulation exceeded half a million readers, the largest circulation of any paper in the country.

But competition was on the way.

William Randolph Hearst, was a Californian of Ulster Protestant stock who traced his American roots back to the 1760s. While it might not be said that he was born with a silver spoon in his mouth, it was not long before such utensils were commonplace in the Hearst household. For while William was a boy, his father was traipsing through the west, where he became a partner in three massive mining successes: the Comstock Lode in Nevada, the Homestake Mine in South Dakota, and the Anaconda Mine in Montana. Wealth and power quickly followed, as did one of the Senate seats assigned to the Golden State.

By his teen years a son of privilege, not to mention of a U.S. Senator, William was enrolled at Harvard University, but not for long. He had a penchant for contrarian humor and practical jokes, some of which lay within the boundaries of the day - Hasty Pudding Club productions and the *Lampoon* - and some that fell well beyond. After going too far once too often, Hearst was expelled from Harvard.

Disappointed, but seeing an opportunity to help his errant son mature, George Hearst pressed William to take over management of the family's far-flung holdings in mining and ranching, but William would have none of it. Instead, he focused on a small newspaper, the *San Francisco Examiner*, that his father had accepted in 1880 as payment for a gambling debt. In 1887, George acquiesced, and William Randolph Hearst became owner and publisher of his first newspaper.

It turned out that he was good at this. He invested in new equipment and talented writers and turned the *Examiner* into a window on corruption, public and private, titillating the public with dramatic coverage. He pulled in an audience, and built the paper into dominance of San Francisco journalism.

But San Francisco for Hearst, like Trenton for Willett, was too small a stage. He needed something more. And in 1895, with his mother's support, he found it. He purchased a failing New York newspaper, the *Morning Journal*, and took his ambitions and his model for success eastward. Hearst decided to take Joseph Pulitzer and his *World* head on.

Once again, Hearst hired top writers and he lured away Pulitzer's own Sunday staff, not least the inventor of the color comics that had given yellow journalism its name. Hearst offered pictures, advice to the lovelorn, and sentimentality; favored unions at a time when they were not granted much legitimacy; and reflected the widespread attitude of racial superiority of the day, particularly on the question of Asian immigration, or the so-called "Yellow Peril." But he knew he needed more. He needed new blood. He needed new ideas.

Hearst needed, as it turned out, John Tyler Willett, Jr.

Perhaps it was Willett's Irish blood that appealed to Hearst. Perhaps it was his roguish character, his swagger, his evident ease in conversing with one so powerful. Perhaps it was his ambition, his energy. Whatever it was, when Willett fought his way into Hearst's office to ask for a job, the outcome must have surprised even him. Hearst took an instant liking to the young man. He was hired.

But he was hired with a challenge. Find a new niche. Make a place for himself. Build the newspaper in some new direction. Find a new reason for readers to buy it. Or go back to Trenton.

Things did not go well for JT in those early days. He knew Trenton like the back of his hand, but he felt as if the back of the hand was exactly what he got from New York. He knew no one who was anyone. He knew nothing of the city's politics or its social establishment. He had no pals, no network to point him toward stories. He was adrift, without any sense of direction. And he knew that Hearst was watching. Always watching.

After one especially bad morning, JT just had to get away for a while. It was summertime. It was pleasant. He needed a walk. He needed one of the city's newest amenities. He needed Central Park. He grabbed his bowler and started walking north.

It had been a long time since Willett had been out walking, and he found that he really enjoyed it. The summer air of the park cleared his lungs of urban New York; the walking cleared his mind. So, onward he walked as in a trance, mindless of the time, or even where he was. The park ended, the walk uptown continued. Harlem, with its rich and fragrant mix of Italians and Eastern European Jews, its new Opera House, and the noise of the elevated trains. Washington Heights, where the woods that had long sheltered the opulent villas of the city's wealthy were being clear-cut to build housing for those whose fortunes existed only in their immigrant dreams. This was new territory to a kid from Trenton.

There was a sound in the air, of a crowd somewhere nearby. Where was that? Off to his right? Over near the river? Willett followed the trail of sound, a detective in search of the telling clue.

So it was that JT Willett found himself face-to-face with his future, standing in an area known as Coogan's Hollow, at the gate to the Polo Grounds, the third and newest incarnation of an open space once devoted to that eponymous and most upper class of sports, but later rededicated far down the social spectrum, to baseball. These new playing grounds occupied a stretch of bottomland wedged between the shore of the Harlem River, which forms the northern boundary of Manhattan Island, and a promontory soaring 175 feet above the river, known as Coogan's Bluff. Fans could watch the games from on high without taking the trouble to purchase a ticket, and over time, baseball writers, probably following the lead of Willett himself, came to refer to the Giants' baseball home as Coogan's Bluff.

Though he had heard of the sport, which had been around long enough to be a favorite means for soldiers of the Union Army to get their minds off the carnage of the Civil War, he had never attended an organized game of baseball. Not really surprising, since the main professional league at the time, the National League, had been in existence only since 1876, and Trenton was pretty well off the beaten path of professional athletics. Plus, he had spent his youth mostly indoors – behind the bar or playing backroom games of a different sort. Curiosity, some sunshine, and truth be told the prospect of finding some shade, led him through the gate. And there it was.

Larger than life characters. Hundreds, perhaps thousands, of jacketed and jacketless men, young boys, and even a scattering of women, shouting with enthusiasm. Intercity rivalry (against Philadelphia, yet!), with a robust team, the Giants, previously known as the Gothams, *representing* all of metropolitan New York – or at least Manhattan, the part that counted. Drama. Eccentricity. Exaggeration. Emotion. The scene screamed *New York Morning Journal* in full voice.

JT Willett, *baseball writer*. No newspaper, or at least none that he knew of, had a dedicated baseball writer. Hell, he thought, except for reporting some scores, almost no newspaper covered baseball, or for that matter, most sports other than horse-racing and boxing, much at all. Not the way JT could. Willett knew in an instant. *This* was what Hearst was looking for.

The challenge was how to report the game when he barely understood it himself. But for that one, JT had a ready remedy. In fact, it was right down his alley.

Though with some notable outliers, professional baseball players as a group were not known as towering intellects, college professors and doctors and lawyers and architects drawn away from their mundane lives to apply their skills at throwing a smallish hard sphere, hitting it once thrown, catching it, and managing all of this without drooling great streams of tobacco juice onto their uniforms. The pay was hardly an incentive; they barely received any. With a few exceptions (Cap Anson, who attended high school for two years at the University of Notre Dame and then enrolled at the University of Iowa before being expelled for bad behavior, influential future evangelist Billy Sunday, and, of course, Christy Mathewson himself among them), they were mainly school dropouts, refugees from the farm, blue collar workers, misfits, local bullies and toughs – all drawn together by a very narrow and specialized set of skills and by the fact that they really could not do much else very well. Most were illiterate, at least in the earliest days, because almost everyone was. Many were immigrants within one or two generations of arriving on these shores, again because almost everyone was. Like everyone else, they drank, they smoked, they gambled, and they consorted with others who drank, smoked, and gambled on their deeds. And like everyone else, they needed places to do that, places near the parks where they played, places near the row houses and tenements and rooming houses where they lived, and places where they could be surrounded by their social equals and ethnic brethren and hangers on. They needed neighborhood taverns that in every way resembled the one Willett had known as long as...as long as he had known anything.

JT set out to find those places, to talk with those who frequented them, to learn the game and its nuances from those who played it at the highest level. And that is just what he did.

Flanagan's. O'Leary's. Shay's Lounge. The Dump. There were more than 7,000 establishments licensed to sell alcohol in New York City in those days, and that was only counting the legal ones. And yet, JT knew just where to start. He began attending the Giants' games, and followed the players home afterward, always at a distance. As often as not, heading home included stopping off for a beer or a whiskey at some favored spot, sometimes alone, sometimes with fellow players or with friends they ran into along the way. Within just a few weeks, JT had mapped the terrain and developed his plan. He was ready to make his pitch to Hearst.

In the event, it was an easy sell. Hearst already knew the game well. As JT discovered in that conversation, it turned out that his San Francisco paper, *The Examiner,* had been the first to publish the emergent poetic anthem of baseball, Ernest Lawrence Thayer's "Casey At the Bat," just a few years earlier. In fact, Thayer was actually one of Hearst's Harvard classmates. It took him only an instant to see the possibilities. A natural in every way. Why, Hearst wondered aloud when this nervous young fellow Willett stood before him, didn't I think of that myself? Sex, corruption, crime, and now baseball - they could all sell papers. And in that instant, JT Willett, twenty-something refugee from Trenton, New Jersey, became the chief baseball writer - in truth, the only baseball writer - for one of the most important newspapers in New York City.

Arts and crafts. Baseball at the professional level was a craft. Its practitioners were adept at using their hands to shape the game. And the game was played within the lines. Balls, strikes, outs, hits, runs, wins, losses, standings - baseball was addition run wild. The numbers added up, and the team with the best numbers at the end of the game was the winner, at the end of the season, the champion. But interesting as that might be to those who closely followed the sport, and integral as it might be to reporting on it, JT came quickly to realize that this basic arithmetic would not extend to newspaper circulation. Few new readers would subscribe to the *Journal* just to read statistics. He knew he needed more, and he found it, almost without trying.

The players of this game were men of interest in themselves, and some of them in quite outrageous ways that matched perfectly with the style of the paper. JT befriended them, told their stories, made them famous. The communities where they lived were the collective essence of the city itself, especially its ethnic enclaves, and they were filled with prospective subscribers. JT told their stories as well, through the players who became their heroes and their symbols of acceptance and achievement.

And then there was the game itself. Not exactly cerebral to the casual observer. But as JT came to understand the basics, he came as well to understand that there were stories behind the basics - who stories, how stories, and especially why stories - origin stories, stories of friendships and personality conflicts, funny and sad stories based on players' experience, and above all, stories of strategy and of the mental game within the game - all of which he set out to tell, even where (in the great tradition of the *Journal*) he had to make them up. Yes, JT could be very inventive. And the funny thing was, his inventions, his made-up strategic explanations and tactical applications actually found their way into the game. Players, owners, and especially team managers were reading JT and learning new ways to think about their own game. Power of the press. Self-fulfilling prophecy. Call it what you will, JT Willett was making a lot of money for William Randolph Hearst, and in the process becoming an icon of the game in his own right. Everyone in New York, and everyone in the world of New York baseball, knew his name, and many knew the man himself. If baseball was a craft, JT Willett became the artist who painted its portrait.

It wasn't easy at first. True, JT had a way with words. But putting those words on paper - and in the paper - was difficult for him at the beginning. One early effort tells the tale. "Some English writer once said," Willett wrote in an early column, "that if you changed the color of a rose, it would still be the same when it hit your nose, or something like that. Obviously, the English don't know baseball, and that writer never spent a moment in the Giants' dressing room after a mid-summer game. Nothing smells the same after that." Or this one: "It was a dark and stormy night, not just under the moonless Manhattan sky, but in the dressing room of the New York Giants, where the lightning and thunder came from the gaze and the growl of the Little Napoleon, manager John McGraw. The Giants had given another one away, and Mugsy was blowing hot and hard as a hurricane." But eventually JT overcame his love of clichés and perfected his craft. He learned to stand to the side and let the stories tell themselves, and as he did, he developed his own unique style, and quite a following. More importantly, Hearst could see that JT was selling papers.

Local fame is a wonderful thing for those who seek it, and New York local fame is about as big as local fame gets. But there are larger stages still, and there came a day when JT was offered exactly the kind of opportunity that might catch his eye. It was while he was traveling with the Giants on a road trip to Chicago and St. Louis that JT happened to run into Alfred Spink, a baseball man, but also a publisher. A few years earlier, Spink had begun a new weekly newspaper that he called *The Sporting News*. The newspaper covered horseracing and professional wrestling, but its real focus was going to be baseball. Indeed, *The Sporting News* eventually so dominated feature coverage of the sport that it soon became known as "The Bible of Baseball." But that moniker was still in the future, and JT Willett would have no small role in bringing it about. He read the paper from time to time, of course, but had never before met Spink. Indeed, he wouldn't know the man if they passed in a narrow hallway. And that fact alone makes clear that this impromptu meeting was nothing of the sort. Spink sought JT out. He had an offer to make.

"How would you like to be the lead baseball columnist for *The Sporting News*" a Spink wondered over a couple of Jameson's, neat. Spink knew just how to appeal to the Irish in Willett, even in what was predominantly a German town. "More money," he said, "no deadlines, freedom to write about whatever you like, a travel budget, and best of all, a truly national audience. Every player will want you to tell his story. Every fan in every Podunk corner of America will read you every week. And hey, you know Charlie Conlon, right? Well, don't say nothin' to nobody, but we're talking to Charlie about taking pictures of all the players that come through New York, from all the teams, and we're going to publish a bunch of those. Think of it, player profiles by Willett with accompanying photos by Conlon. And you know what? We're also talkin' to Ban Johnson about the state of the game – all the drinking, the gamblers, beating up the umpires when a call goes the wrong way. We're thinking about starting up a new league where none of that is allowed. And you'd be on the inside of that, too, to tell the story like nobody else could. Whaddaya say? Huh? Whaddaya say?"

A few years earlier, JT would have tossed his head back, laughed, and made some punkish comment about Spink and his little weekly. (Then, of course, he would have tracked down Ban Johnson to get the rundown on this new league, and probably also told Hearst about the plans for Conlon and his camera.) But these days, the pressures at the paper were building. No matter how many readers they had, Hearst wanted more. And there was always some financial crisis, some need to cut back, some demand to write more columns, some new editor to please. Baseball writing was still fun, and he was the best at it. But baseball writing for the *Journal* was no longer fun at all. If timing was everything, Spink had it down.

When JT told Hearst the news, his boss fussed and fumed and threatened to shut down *The Sporting News* or, better yet, to buy the damn thing just so he could fire Willett. And yet, JT had done a lot for the *Journal* in his years at the paper, so in the end the two men parted as friends. Hearst was a good friend to have, and not a good enemy, and JT was smart enough to know that. So, over the years he made sure the *Journal* sports page got some juicy leads – as long as he was not going to pursue them himself. And he made sure Hearst knew where they came from.

Hearst seemed to have needed the help. After JT left, he cast about for replacements. Sam Crane was one, and he was okay in JT's book. At least he knew and respected the game. But by 1905, Hearst had even taken to hiring comedians and poets – *poets* – to cover baseball. Maybe Willie Kirk knew everything about Hamlet's suicide, but he didn't know squat about a suicide squeeze. Consider his "story" on a supposed insult Giants' manager John McGraw tossed at Pirates owner Barney Dreyfuss – calling out to him by his first name, apparently a violation of protocol at the time. McGraw was suspended for 15 days in the incident, and Crane and the Giants campaigned hard for his reinstatement, including a petition signed by about 10,000 Giants fans, something of which JT wrote approvingly in his own columns. But Kirk? Here was his after-the-fact "coverage" of "The Dreyfuss Incident."

The shades of night were falling fast,
When toward the Giants' club house passed,
A magnate with a new spring suit–
Suddenly came this flip salute:
"Hey, Barney!"

His brow grew stern, his jaws were set;
Said he, "Vat's dis alretty yet?"
And still from the veranda came
That slogan, spoken just the same.
"Hey, Barney!"

"Ach, himmel!" said the Pittsburg [sic] chief,
"Such nerf iss quite peyond pelief!"
Again that salutation raw—
'Twas from the lips of Muggs McGraw:
"Hey, Barney!"

"Be careful, Muggs," a rooter cried;
"You're injuring little Barney's pride."
Another fan said, "Cut it out!"
But still arose that ringing shout:
"Hey, Barney!"

Now Muggs is fined—a measly shame;
Fined and ejected from the game.
But fans for many years to come
Will keep that war cry going some:
"Hey, Barney!"

A class act to be sure.

It was at *The Sporting News* that JT became truly legendary among sports journalists, and a household name among baseball fans. Not only did he continue to tell the story of the game and its players, to devise strategies and tactics and somehow convince real baseball men that they had come up with those notions themselves – individual strokes of genius that created reputations for the ages – he came up with whole new ways of measuring the game. Earned run average? Henry Chadwick gets the public credit for thinking that one up back around 1900. Despite their great age difference, Henry and young JT were often seen in one another's company at the Giants' games, deep in conversation. Henry got the idea from JT. Slugging percentage? From a 1908 Willett column about Ty Cobb, one of the greatest hitters of all time. Four-bagger, a slang term for a home run? JT Willett, 1925.

In 1908, JT Willett was among the founders of a new organization, the Baseball Writers' Association of America (BBWAA), that set out an agenda including standardized scoring and limiting access to the press box to actual writers (read: exclude the gamblers). Willett was offered the presidency of the group, but turned it down in favor of a good friend, Joe Jackson of the *Detroit Free Press*. In 1936, JT was instrumental in creating the very first *Sporting News* Player of the Year Award, which went to Carl Hubbell of the Giants. The award was decided by a vote of the players themselves, and remains prestigious to this day. Without JT's connections with all of the players and the clubs, it is difficult to see how the award process would have ever gotten started.

In the way we think about and talk about baseball today, JT Willett's influence on the game he learned to love lives on.

From the early 1900s well into the years of the Great Depression, JT Willett crisscrossed the country, following the players, the teams, and above all the stories of the sport that became, in no small measure as a result of his writing, our national pastime. He was there, behind the scenes, in 1903 when *Sporting News* editor Arthur Flanner helped write the National Agreement - really a peace treaty between the old-line National League and its upstart and surprisingly successful (at stealing its players as well as its fans) rival, the American League - that led to creation of the World Series. And he was at every World Series game, from the first, unofficial one in 1903, when the Boston Americans of the American League, behind the pitching of Cy Young, defeated the Pittsburgh Pirates of the National League, and again every year from 1905 onward.

JT even had the backstory - the real backstory - of the World Series that never happened, a 1904 matchup that would have pitted that same Boston team against his old crew, the New York Giants. At that time, and notwithstanding the National Agreement, a team's participation in the post-season series was purely voluntary, and the Giants declined to play. Their owner, John T. Brush, said the American League was so inferior to the National that the game served no purpose. His manager, John McGraw, went even further, declaring that his Giants were already world champions because there was really only one major league. As one can imagine, this was a somewhat controversial stand, especially in Boston, where more than one wag claimed that the real story was clear: After the Boston victory in 1903, the Giants were afraid of being embarrassed. In New York, the most widely credited story was a bit different: Brush had long opposed formation of the American League, and he had a strong personal dislike for the aforementioned Ban Johnson. It was Johnson, after all, who was the prime mover in forming the new league and in reforming the game itself in ways that Brush found objectionable, even offensive.

JT knew better. It wasn't that. Any of it. It was far more personal, and it wasn't Brush, or McGraw. At least not really. It was Hearst and it was Hearst's revenge... against JT Willett. Hearst knew that Willett's newspaper had played a major role in establishing the World Series. And he knew that Willett himself was the ultimate Series insider, the man through whose writing the entire country would follow the Series. No series, no Willett competing with his own sportswriters, at least for a week or two. And it was the Giants! Willett and the Giants had history – a history Willett himself had written on the pages of the *Journal*. Hearst's *Journal*!

William Randolph Hearst knew how to make things happen in New York, or in this case, not to happen. In many ways, the *Journal* had *made* the New York Giants. Without Willett's columns and the interest they had generated across the city, the Giants would have been just another failed franchise, just another club team. Why, the New York Highlanders would have owned the city. Hearst knew this, and he knew that Brush knew it as well. JT had it on good authority – and when it came to the Giants JT had the best authorities – that Hearst and Brush had shared a clubby little lunch where it was decided: The Giants would decline to play in the World Series, and the *Journal* would continue to favor the team in its coverage. Everything else was eye-wash.

Hearst, obviously, knew the real story, but wouldn't tell it. Not even to Crane, and certainly not to Kirk. Couldn't you just picture *that* poem? And if you bet Pulitzer's *World* didn't have the real story, you'd win hands down. If those guys knew what JT knew, or even suspected it, they would have been on Hearst like a pack of mad dogs.

It was the only time in his entire career with *The Sporting News* that an editor ever spiked a column by JT Willett. Not only will we not publish this story, he was told in no uncertain terms, but you must never tell it to anyone. This story would ruin the game, and if the game is ruined, this newspaper is ruined. And if not, you can bet that nasty son-of-a-bitch former boss of yours would find a way to do the job. Fifteen years later, when the Black Sox gambling scandal hit in the wake of the 1919 World Series, and when JT had the story and was ready to break it, the paper was far less squeamish about the fate of the game or its own survival. But then, Charley Comiskey, whatever his proclivities, was no William Randolph Hearst. JT put his story in print, the baseball world shook, and life went on.

By 1936, JT was into his seventh decade, and you might think he'd be slowing down. He was feeling his age more and more. An ache where he didn't used to have aches. A pain where he didn't used to have pains. The wear and tear of time was inexorable. But for him, baseball was something of a fountain of youth, and he kept up a prodigious pace of travel and writing, secure in the knowledge that there would always be another story tomorrow. In 1936, it was a big one. There was a fellow up in Cooperstown, New York, a hotel owner by the name of Stephen Carlton Clark, whose business was suffering along with so many others during the Depression years. But Clark had a big idea: he announced he was going to build a Baseball Hall of Fame near his hotel to honor all of the great participants in the game.

A Hall of Fame. Official baseball loved the idea and went along. In fact, though the facility Clark was building would not open until 1939, baseball had decided to begin selecting members three years ahead of time, which is to say, in 1936. The selections were to be made, as they still are, by a vote of members of the BBWAA. In that first year, the vote was delegated to a select committee chaired, of course, by America's premier baseball writer, JT Willett. Members of that first class included Ty Cobb, Babe Ruth, Honus Wagner, Christy Mathewson, and Walter Johnson.

This was big, as sports stories go, and JT wanted to give the story the Willett treatment. While others satisfied themselves with pictures, statistics, and the canned biographies distributed by the two leagues, Willett set out on a journey across the country, determined to produce a complete story about each inductee. He would talk with the players themselves, if they were still alive, and with those who had known them best and longest. Family, friends, teammates. The one challenge would be Mathewson, for the pitcher many regarded as the best of all time had passed away prematurely about ten years earlier. That one would require more work, but he was sure he could pull together a great story. Mathewson, after all, was not just a baseball hero. The man was a genuine, bona fide war hero as well.

As he had so many times before, he went off chasing a big story. Another JT Special. What he found instead was the story of a lifetime, a story that would change everything about the Hall, everything about the game, perhaps even everything about America. JT Willett was on the trail, and back on the trains.

Jason pulled the bundle from the corner out into the middle of the room, where there was a stream of light from the doorway. Together he and Adam carefully unwrapped the layers of oilcloth. What they revealed was an old leather suitcase with a rusted metal clasp of a lock that yielded to gentle persuasion.

"Wait," said Jason. "Let's take this into the house where we can get a good look at what's inside."

Less than five minutes later, they were standing over the opened case, which was resting on a wooden farm table. The case was perhaps ten or twelve inches deep, and whatever remained inside was covered with one of those suitcase dividers, well preserved, which also appeared to be of leather, this stretched over a wooden frame. Out it came.

The first thing that caught Adam's eye was a black case about ten inches on one side, perhaps twelve on the other, just a bit larger than a sheet of paper, and about five inches high. The case bore an embossed label, "Royal," and sure enough, inside they found a miniaturized typewriter. It was black, had four banks of keys, a well-worn platen or roller bar, and, stretched between two spools, a ribbon that even the layers of oilcloth had been inadequate to preserve well. The platen had lost any rubber-like qualities it might once have possessed, but retained the evidence of many thousands of ancient key strikes. If there were any doubt of the find, a panel across the back, the paper rest, bore a company logo and, in large capital letters, the name "ROYAL," and a second label was painted across the front right-hand side of the machine. It read, "ROYAL portable."

Adam turned to Jason. "I think what we have here," he noted rather drolly, "is a Royal Portable Typewriter."

"Thanks for clearing that up. I knew I had invited the right guy up here."

Adam lifted the typewriter and its case out of the suitcase and placed it to one side on the table. "Thing actually weighs more than you'd think. Maybe six, seven pounds or more. Whoever was carrying that puppy around must have really liked to write."

"How old do you figure?" This from Jason.

"I don't know that I've ever seen an old one that small. But looking at the way it's put together – the two-level typebars and the old white printed letters and symbols under glass on the keys – this thing has to be close to a hundred years old. Maybe the twenties or the thirties, I'd say. But that's just a guess. You could always have somebody look at it if it's that important to you. But I don't think these things have much value these days."

"Well, maybe." Jason again. "But you haven't seen everything."

"Fair enough." And both men turned their attention to the remainder of the payload.

"Well look at that!" Adam could barely contain himself. "It's a stack of papers, and, oh my goodness, there's typing on them!"

"You're gonna make me sorry I invited you up here, aren't ya." This was not a question.

"Okay, Okay. Sorry. Let's see what we've got."

What they had was a manuscript of sorts, or more correctly, several pieces of a manuscript that each looked to be two or three pages long. Each one had a numbered label on the first page, as in Part 1, Part 2, and so on. And there were titles after that. "Casey at the Bat." That sort of thing. Seemed pretty clichéd to Adam's eye. Could have been chapters of a book, something like that. On the top of the stack was the answer to at least one question: Whose papers are these? The title page read:

DOWN IN FRONT

By JT Willett

The paper was thin and lightweight. Adam recognized it as onionskin, which you did not see around much anymore. It was meant for typing, as in using a typewriter, completely useless for laser and inkjet printers. And that fit with the suitcase. It was just the sort of paper some traveling writer might use, especially if he had to haul around seven pounds of typewriter. The remarkable thing about it, though, was that it was pretty well preserved. The ink had faded a good bit simply with age and with being pressed tightly against the pages above. Or maybe the ribbon had been dry to begin with if it was used a lot. But the combination of sitting under the typewriter and being protected by oilcloth for the better part of a hundred years seemed to have done as well as some museum conservator of that earlier era could have done.

"If you're really interested in the age of the typewriter, maybe the paper could help. You know, if it's rag paper or pulp paper, and watermarks. That sort of thing. There have got to be some paper nerds somewhere that know all about that kind of thing.

"Want to read it?"

Jason considered for a moment, but suggested that they finish unpacking the suitcase first.

The rest of the space was filled mainly with small notebooks, each maybe four inches by eight, made of cheap paper and once bound at the top with a glue that had not survived as well as the remainder of the trove. They were all falling apart to the touch, though the paper itself still had some integrity. And they were filled with notes in what looked to be a man's handwriting. Pen and ink, some in pencil. On the cardboard cover of each notebook was a name. Sometimes more than one. Mathewson. Cobb. Ruth. And so forth.

"Now *that*," Adam observed with a bit more energy than he had thus far demonstrated, "*that* is interesting."

"Isn't it?" responded Jason. "Now you see why I thought you'd want to make the trip up here."

Gently, the two lifted the notebooks out of the suitcase. They were fourteen in number. And that is when Jason saw something else, something that he had failed to notice the first time he'd opened the case. Not surprising, because it was large, flat, and brown, and had been completely covered up by the notebooks themselves.

"Adam," he said. "Check this out."

What lay on the bottom of the case was a large brown envelope, flat and not very full. Jason lifted it out, undid the string clasp that was holding the flap in place, and peered inside. Then, ever so gently, he slid the contents out onto the table and spread them out.

The pair bent low to get a good look at their find.

"Holy Shit!" Jason.

"Holy *Freaking* Shit!" Adam, as a professional writer, was far more facile with his adjectives.

There was only one possible first stop – Saranac Lake, New York. JT had known Big Six for years. He was still covering the Giants quite a bit when Mathewson had come up, and even though Matty was a college guy – he was actually president of his class at Bucknell back in the '90s – and smart as a whip, he and JT got along well from the moment they met. JT had met Matty's wife, now widow, Jane, even before the two became engaged, and he was an usher at their 1902 wedding. Matty was a true gentleman, and a hell of a pitcher. He played fourteen years for the Giants and three for the Cincinnati Reds, and he won an amazing 373 games, including 79 shutouts. Never pitched on a Sunday, the Lord's day, but that didn't seem to stop him. JT had covered it all and knew his stats by heart, but it was a heart that in the end was broken. Like many a good American lad, Mathewson had gone off to war in 1918, and he had come back much the worse for it. He was in the Chemical Corps, not the best place to be, but typical Matty. Mustard gas accident did him in, not in Flanders fields where he was exposed in 1918, but up at Saranac Lake, where he had gone to seek treatment for the tuberculosis that infected his gas-weakened lungs. That was in 1925.

Mathewson had a special place in the game – he had made it respectable. Educated. Religious. Upstanding. Nice. And he had a special place in JT

Willett's pantheon of athletic gods. He was an honest man through and through, and even after the war, when he was having his own health problems, he had helped JT map out the gamblers behind the Black Sox scandal of 1919. He did his own writing as well – a play, a children's book, some columns (JT did not fear the competition – hell, he'd even helped commission some of them for the newspaper), and even his own memoir. Christy Mathewson was the proverbial gentleman and scholar, and a hell of a ballplayer.

Mathewson was without a doubt the premier member of the first class of inductees for the Hall of Fame – sort of the class president all over again. And JT's first stop had to be a visit with Jane. He had not seen her in the ten years or more since Matty's funeral, but he remembered her warmly and hoped she would remember him the same way.

"John Tyler Willett! Is that really you? My lord you look old!"

JT immediately remembered what he liked best about Mathewson's saucy widow.

"Jane, you look terrific. Time has been truly good to you. And how's Junior?" Junior was the couple's only son, who by then would have been in his thirties.

"He's had a hard time, JT. Got married about four years back. He was a flier, you know. Well, he took his bride up for a ride just two weeks after the wedding, and the plane crashed. She was killed, and he lost a leg. It's been very hard for him ever since." She paused to collect herself.

"Now, what brings you to my door after so many years?"

"Jane, you know about the new Baseball Hall of Fame. And of course, Matty is going to be one of the first five to get in. First, as far as I'm concerned, and as far as a lot of others are as well. The Hall is a wonderful idea – a chance to remember these players forever. And I want to help make the first class really special. I am going to write up the life stories of all five – not just the usual statistics and baseball stories, but who these guys really are. Or in Matty's case, who he really was. And I had to come see you first."

"That's so sweet, JT. It truly is. Sweet that you'd want to do that for Chris, and sweet that you thought to pay me a visit. You know, I don't see too many people from the old days anymore. It's a young man's game, I guess. And I don't think they feel comfortable dealing with the fact that Chris is gone.

"But yes, I did hear about the new Hall of Fame, and the neighbors here were all excited that Chris was getting inducted. But you know, I haven't really paid a lot of attention myself. You said there were five getting in? Who are the others."

"Oh," he replied, "about the ones you'd expect. Cobb, Hans, Ruth, Big Train. It's pretty fast company. But there'll be more. Been a lot of great players over the years."

"Cobb. You mean Ty Cobb?" Jane appeared startled, or really more taken aback.

"Yeah, of course. Ty and Matty were always close. In fact, Matty may have been one of the few guys in all of baseball who actually liked Cobb, or at least could stand to be around him."

"You know they were in the war together, right?"

"Well, I hadn't really thought about it. But, yeah. Lot of the players went in for a while. They almost had to after what's his name – Newt Baker, that old asshole... sorry – said baseball was not a, what was the term, an essential industry – and said the players could all be drafted. There must have been a hundred or more volunteered. Why, were they in the same unit?"

"Oh, yes." Jane paused for a long time, then seemed to make a decision. "I have something you should see."

Spread before them was an array of documents.

"Look at this!"

"I'm looking. I'm looking!"

The object of their immediate attention was a letter dated October 10, 1925. It was handwritten, one page, and signed by Tyrus Raymond Cobb.

"Is this for real?" Adam.

"What's it say? Can you read this chicken scratch?" Jason.

October 10, 1925

Dearest Jane;-
I don't have the words to say how sad I felt
Today, when I heard about Matty's passing. I
will try to come up in time to be there with you
for the funeral.
Jane, I don't know what you heard over the
years, or what Matty has told you. I can only
say that I loved the man like a brother. He was
a true Christian, and has forgiven all. I don't
know how, as it is not something I could do if
our places were reversed, But bless him, and
bless his memory.
I am sorry, So sorry for your loss,

Tyrus Raymond Cobb

"What the hell?"

Adam pondered only for a moment. "Wow. This is really something. You have a handwritten letter from Ty Cobb, probably the best hitter that ever played baseball. And if I am reading this right, it's a letter to the newly widowed wife of Christy Mathewson, who some people think was the best pitcher who ever lived. If it's real, this thing could be worth a million dollars!"

Jason weighed that one for his own brief moment, then just exhaled. "Whoa! But what on earth is he talking about?"

"I'm not really sure," Adam replied. "But that's what the Internet is for. We might be able to figure it out. Got a connection?"

Jason looked at Adam with that I'm-just-an-old-country-boy look that usually serves as a warning to watch your wallet. But in this case, Jason was, in fact, just an old country boy. "You know," he said, "we just can't get anybody to run a wire out here. I can send emails on my cell phone – you know that. But no. Believe it or not in this day and age, there are still places in Upstate New York that don't have the Internet.

"But I do have a solution. You remember Jenna and Elaine? Well, they do Internet stuff for their store in town. When I need to use it, I just head in there and they always let me do it. We can go down there later on and see if we can figure anything out. What is that thing... the Wiki?"

"Wikipedia. Wikipedia. Not always right, but always there with something to say. We'll see what we can find out.

"In the meantime, what else have we got here?"

JT read Cobb's letter, then he read it again. "Jane, what is this about? What did that old miscreant do?"

"You know all about Chris and the war, right? And how he got accidentally gassed over there in France, and after he recovered he came back a hero? Well, he was a hero, but not the same way that everybody thinks. There was a lot more to it."

"I'm listening."

It's all that old Mr. Rickey's fault, when you get right down to it."

"Branch Rickey?"

"Of course, Branch Rickey. Back after the war started and, you remember, how the government was putting all that pressure on baseball – calling the players unpatriotic and all that?"

"I remember."

"Well one day Chris gets this letter from Mr. Rickey. Personally, I think that hypocrite Wilson put him up to it, but that's just me talking. You remember how Wilson was the first President to throw out a pitch at a World Series game? Big baseball lover, right? Then he turns around and has the Secretary of War basically call out baseball and challenge all the players to get in the fight. I mean, what is that?

"Anyway, Chris gets this letter. And it says Branch is going to be an officer and he wants Chris to come and serve in his unit. I've got that darned letter here somewhere... Here!" And she handed JT a second document. "Now, he didn't say right away what that unit was. And you know Chris. He always wanted to do the right thing. Loved the country, and he loved the game. So, Chris writes back and he says yeah, of course I'll join up. Now I'll tell you, JT, I begged that man not to do it. I pleaded with him. But I never had a chance.

"So then, just before he was ready to leave, Mr. Rickey tells him what they'll be doing. Defusing bombs and cannisters of mustard gas, teaching soldiers to use gas masks – as if they were experts themselves. Can you believe it? Well, I hit the roof. But Chris, he just smiled and said Janie, somebody's got to do that work. Guess it's me. And off he went."

Seeing the tears welling up in her eyes at the memory, JT decided he had to say something. But he didn't want to interrupt her narrative. Best he could do was to gently encourage her. "I knew some of this, or had heard rumors or gossip, but never the real story. What happened after he left?"

Branch Rickey, Esq.
Attorney at Law
St. Louis, Missouri

May 1, 1918

Dear Matty:

By the grace of our Lord, I hope this letter finds you well and in good spirits. As you can see, since I was let go by the Browns club, I have resumed my law practice. Life is changing, but good, on this end, and I still hope to get back into the game in some capacity.

I need not tell you what a challenging time this is for the country we both love, and for our game. The war in Europe is taking a toll on all of us, and as it goes on, it is bringing baseball and our fellow players into the shadow of disrepute.

As a Christian like yourself, I have come to the personal belief that we must do something to address this. Accordingly, I have accepted a commission as a Major in the National Guard, and have agreed to form a new unit and recruit members for it. I am turning to old friends and others to help me in this endeavor. I believe this is the best way we can serve our country and the game we love.

In a short time, we will be mustering at Camp Hancock, just outside Augusta, Georgia, for training. You have the respect of your fellow players, and the respect of the entire country. I would like very much to appoint you as an officer and my second in command. I hope I can count on you to join me. If so, I will promptly send you all the details.

For God. For Country. For Baseball. Bless you.

Branch

"No. Before I tell you what I know, you've got to go down to Georgia and find Abner. I only know what I know because Abner told me.

"When Chris died it was big news. And I guess down in Georgia, when they heard about it, some of the old ball players - a lot of them came from down there in the old days, you know - well the newspapers were full of comments and remembrances from a bunch of them. Anyway, I gather that our friend Ty was all over the press talking about Chris this and Chris that and how wonderful he was and how he'd died for his country, even though it was a few years later, and what good friends they were. You can guess.

"Well, Abner, he still lives down there. Or he did back in '25 anyway. I hope he's still alive. Probably so. I remember Chris had told me about him, or at least mentioned him. So, I knew who he was. He was younger than the others. Anyway, a month or so goes by and I get this letter from Abner, and he says, Missus Mathewson - it was pretty formal, as we'd never met. Plus, Chris was an officer and all. He says, Missus, I been reading all of this from Mr. Ty Cobb down here in the papers, and I'm just madder'n I can be. 'Cause I know what really happened, and when and where. I know I promised never to say nothin'. But this ain't right. And, he says, I don't want to do you (meaning me) no hurt, but I have been thinking on it for a long time now, and I think you should know the truth. And he proceeded to tell me the truth, or at least to spin a pretty good yarn.

"I hate to send you chasing around now, JT. But if you're interviewing all these Hall of Fame players, you'll be interviewing Cobb and some of the others. You're going to have to go down to Georgia anyway. While you're there, I do believe you should look up old Abner."

Jane gave him Abner's full name and a town or two to start the search, but would say no more.

Considering the information on how to find Abner, JT asked the obvious question.

"JT, I have no earthly idea."

"Jesus, Jason. Look at this. Branch Rickey, for God's sake. I always think of him as an old man, like in Brooklyn. Jackie Robinson and all that. I never connected him with guys like Mathewson. But obviously they knew each other."

"Appears so. And if he had already been running the old Browns in 1918, when this letter seems to have been written, then he must have been really old by the '40s. Maybe we ought to find out more about him? At least check the signature, see if it's real."

"Well, put it on the list. But there's more stuff here. Look at this thing."

Adam had picked up what looked like a paper sandwich, some kind of really old, brown document protected by that same onionskin from the typing, one piece on either side. It was thin enough to see through, but not to read through. And the writing inside was faded and full of what looked like notes or corrections. Adam carefully peeled back the covering sheet of paper. Inside was some kind of a form that had been filled out.

Scrawled across the top in relatively good penmanship it read "Pay Roll of Ordnance Depot Company No. 44, Camp Hancock, Ga." And was dated from June 1 to June 30. No year was specified, but it was an easy guess for the pair of amateur detectives seated at the table.

"This has to be from World War I, 1918 for sure," Jason declared. "Shit! Look at the names on this thing!"

"Were these guys all in the Army together? Man, how'd you like to be playin' in *that* intramural league!"

PART 1 [ED: REPLACES ORIGINAL #1]
CASEY AT THE BAT
SPECIAL TO *THE SPORTING NEWS*
By JT Willett

"Oh, somewhere in this favored land the sun is
shining bright
the band is playing somewhere, and somewhere
hearts are light,
and somewhere men are laughing, and somewhere
children shout;
but there is no joy in Mudville – mighty Casey
has struck out."

There is not a baseball fan alive, nor, perhaps,
will there ever be one, who could not recite at
least some part of Ernest Lawrence Thayer's classic
ode to the sport, and to its ability to stir the
emotions in man, raise them up to the highest high,
and then drop them to the lowest low.

Many ~~cities~~ towns have earned the Mudville
moniker in the last half century, and your Correspondent has probably visited them all. Many players have claimed the role of Casey, and your Correspondent has probably interviewed them all. Few
were true heroes; all had their ~~faults~~ flaws. But in
all that travel and all that talk, your Correspondent must confess, he had never felt he had truly
located Mudville on the map. Until now.

,or was,

Mudville is^in Richmond County, Georgia, a
short distance outside Augusta. Its real name was
Camp Hancock. Local folks say it was a town of
nearly fifty thousand souls, so no slouch as towns

go. It existed for just three innings, from 1917 until 1919.

Camp Hancock was one of those dozen or two mobilization and training camps the government set up to get troops of the Army National Guard up to speed before shipping them off to fight in the Great War. And to die. The local paper in Augusta said they spent almost six million dollars to set the place up. You'd think they could have found a better location than a giant mud-flat in the middle of the Georgia clay. But this is the government we are talking about. So, that's where they put it.

Your Correspondent never visited Camp Hancock, but he has seen ~~photos~~ pictures, and they tell a tale. Row after row of tents, lined up as only the Army can line up tents. About two thousand acres worth of tents, if you can imagine that. And they all had two things in common. On the inside, they were crammed full of America's best young men, ready to do their duty. And on the outside, they were connected by nothing but that good Georgia clay.

You may have heard the rumors that it rains a lot in Georgia? Your Correspondent can attest: It rains a lot in Georgia.

Camp Hancock truly was Mudville, more days than not.

Camp Hancock was a serious place for serious
times, and it was home^plate for the 28th Infantry Division. Those boys were in the thick of it in France, and a lot of them didn't cross the plate when the game ended. But before they headed off to France, they needed training. Welcome to Georgia.

Of course, you can't train all the time. Every so often you need some diversion. What better than the National Pastime? So, like American military outposts everywhere, the boys at Camp Hancock played a little ball. A big, flat open space in Georgia may not be good for luxury living, but it is surely good for baseball, and there were several diamonds.

There was also a baseball league of sorts. One unit against the others. That kind of thing. Great for building what the military likes to call "unit cohesiveness." You or I, we'd just say morale and camaraderie among fellows who knew they'd be facing the hardest of times together before long.

For at least a month or so around June of 1918, these little games were not exactly fair fights. Those were the games where some poor group of farm boys and factory hands was up against the team from Ordnance Depot Company Number 44. If there was a loudspeaker at the games, you could just hear the starting lineup being announced:

"Starting for Company 44: Batting first, the shortstop, Ordnance Sergeant John Wagner. Batting second, at third base, Corporal Frank Baker. Batting third, in center field, Corporal Tyrus Cobb. Batting fourth, in right field, Corporal Max Carey. Batting fifth, and playing left field, Corporal Davy Jones. Batting sixth, the first baseman, Private Frank Chance. Batting seventh, the catcher, Private Will Simpson. Batting eight, at second base, Private Herbert Stone. And batting ninth, the pitcher, Private Ed Walsh. The manager of Company 44 and coaching at third base, 2nd Lieutenant Christy Mathewson."

> You may recognize some of those names. Three
> of them (Cobb, Mathewson, Wagner) you will know, if
> you've been reading this column – or just breath-
> ing American air – are about to be enshrined in the
> brand new Baseball Hall of Fame. And it's a pretty
> sure bet that several of the others will follow.
> What on earth was a roster full of major leaguers
> and future Hall of Famers doing playing ball with
> a bunch of soldiers out on the plains of Georgia?
>
> Therein lies the tale, and this Column will
> be telling it in this series of Special Reports.
>
> # # #

"Look at the names on this pay list." Adam was enthralled, and trying to grasp the import of what he was reading. "Jeez. Ty Cobb! Max Carey! Frank Chance! Ed Walsh! Frank Baker... That's Home Run Baker! And I'd put dollars to donuts that the John Wagner guy up on top was Honus Wagner. I think his real name was Johann or something like that. Probably the Army couldn't pronounce that, and if you think about it, I'd imagine a lot of guys wanted to anglicize their German-sounding names at that particular time. Shit, man. That's six guys in the Hall of Fame. Maybe one or two of the others. Just don't recognize the names."

"Was there a Hall of Fame back then?" Jason wondered.

"Actually, I don't think so. Didn't they start that right after the Black Sox Scandal in 1919? Trying to restore the reputation of the game? Sounds like the sort of PR some of those old owners would try."

"So, let me get this straight." Jason always sought clarity in a complicated world. Probably the reason he stayed a farmer. Rains, or it doesn't. That sort of thing.

Page 1 — Pay Roll of Ordnance Dep't Co No 44. Camp Hancock Ga

NAMES, PRESENT AND ABSENT, AND RANK	WHEN ENL'D	ENL. PER.	ARMY SPECIAL NO.	WAR RISK ALOTS. CL. A COMP	CL. B VOL.	INS PREM. C&D	ARMY ALOT. F.R. WR 2nd	CL. E. LIF LOAN ALOT SecTr 3rd	ALL OTHER ALOTS
1. Wagner John (Ord Sgt)	1/6/18	1st	968363	15 00		6 65			
3. Cobb. T H (Corp.)	1/6/18	1st	109808		15 00	6 60			
5. Carey Max (Corp)	1/6/18	1st	500350			6 60			
7. Chance Frank (Pvt)	1/6/18	1st	604951	10 00		6 65			
9. Jones Hendrick (Pvt)	1/6/18	1st	720952			6 60			
11. Jones Davy (Comp Pvt)	1/6/18	1st	604253	12 00		6 65			
13. Simpson Will P. Pvt	1/6/18	1st	784354			6 60			
15. Stone Herbert X Pvt	1/6/18	1st	304688			6 65			
17. Walsh Ed Pvt	1/6/18	1st	600356			6 60			10 00
19. Baker Frank Corp.	No data given.								
21. Armstrong J. A. III Pvt.	Transferred June 5-1918					Pd 5-0118.			
23. Less.									
24. Armstrong J.A. III Pvt.									

H.F. Barnum
Co A

"Let me get this straight. We have this document here that looks to all the world to be some kind of legitimate Army pay sheet from someplace in Georgia. We think it's from 1918, but we aren't sure. And we think – this is the part I'm having a hard time with – we *think* that more than half of the names on the list are major league ballplayers who, at some later date we haven't figured out, got into the Hall of Fame. Do I have that right?"

"Jason, I think that is indeed what we have. But I can't say it makes a lot of sense to me. What were all of these guys doing in an Army unit down in Georgia in June? I mean, that's the middle of the baseball season. Think they all got drafted and ended up together by accident?"

"Maybe it was an Elvis kind of thing?"

"Huh?"

"You know, like when Elvis Presley got drafted when he was at the top of his fame. A lot of people didn't like his hip-wigglin' and such. Next thing you know, he's in the Army and shipped over to Germany or someplace. Sure did put an end to rock and roll, they did!

"Anyway, maybe this was something like that. I don't know about the rest of these guys, but everybody knows that Ty Cobb could be a real SOB. Lots of people had bad things to say about that man. Maybe this was a collection of bad boys, and the Army thought it was doin' society a favor by packing them off to Georgia."

"Well...," Adam paused to ponder. "That might make some sense. Of course, if that's what they were doing, it worked about as well as the Elvis thing. The Black Sox scandal hit the very next year. Gamblers. Throwing the World Series. Not what I'd call a successful strategy. But then, I'm a stickler."

They both had a good laugh at that.

"But I don't actually think that's the deal here. Yeah, everybody hated Cobb. He was apparently a real piece of work. But I'm not so sure about the others. I remember reading about Ed Walsh for some reason years ago. He was with the White Sox, so that would fit. But I think he was long gone by 1919. These others. Some of these are names every kid would hear when we were growing up. And I don't remember hearing anything bad about any of 'em.

"Of course, it's possible that Cobb just sucked the bad out of any room he went into, and didn't leave any for anyone else. But still.

"I think there's more to this than we can guess. Just something else to put on the list. The Mystery of Jocko Drumm just grows and grows."

"Guess so. But that's getting to be some list. How old is the typewriter? Was the onionskin paper from the same time? And how about the paper and ink in the notebooks? Then there's this whole Army thing.

"What the hell do we have here, Adam? And for goodness sake, if Jocko knew – and he must have known – that it was something of value, or at least interest, why did he hide it away without any word of explanation? It all just makes no sense. It makes no sense."

"Well, that's all true, and it's a conundrum. But if you think about it, we have barely scratched the surface here. Maybe we ought to take a look at what's actually in that manuscript, if that's what it is, and those notebooks. Chances are there's an answer in there somewhere, and if we stay lazy, we are never going to find it.

"But look at the time. How about a beer and some lunch? Even Ferraris don't run on fumes."

As he walked the long stretches of the road that would eventually lead him to DeKalb Falls, Jocko had a lot of time to think. He knew instinctively that he had a problem. It was not long before he came up with a solution. That left ample opportunity for the real task: developing a plan.

The problem Jocko had was in the suitcase he was carrying. He had not delved especially deeply into the papers it contained, but he had read enough to know that someone, somewhere might value them. Problem was, those papers had the name of another man all through them, and that man was dead. Not in any way by Jocko's doing, unless he had at last talked some poor fellow to death. But dead just the same. And he had begun to figure out just who this fellow Willett was, and that he might be missed. How, he wondered, could he dispose of the treasure he carried, if treasure it was, without somehow being implicated in some crime, when all he had done was borrow a suitcase from a stranger who no longer had use for it.

The solution was in a deep and carefully re-stitched pocket in his trousers. He had cash. He had, for those days, quite a lot of it. Same source, of course, but in its way far less problematic.

By the time he reached DeKalb Falls, more a point of timing and convenience than an actual destination, since, like the rest of the nonresident world, he'd never heard of the place – and so much the better – he had his plan.

Just as it was a commonplace of those years to see a man like Jocko toting his life's belongings along a country road in search of something, anything better, it was equally a commonplace for many of the farms and businesses such a man might pass to be abandoned, often with a big sign indicating which bank had foreclosed on the mortgage and now owned the property. So it was that, just as he drew closer to the next town, Jocko noticed a large farm, or perhaps two, as it or they spanned the road. The fence lines, if any there were, were not in sight, but the same sign was nailed up on both his left and his right.

> # POSTED
> # NO TRESPASSING
> # PROPERTY OF FIRST BANK OF DEKALB FALLS
> # INQUIRE FOR PURCHASE

There it was. The Plan. Jocko would use his newfound wealth, or some part of it, to buy the farm, and use the farm to buy time while he figured out the rest.

As he neared the town, Jocko took himself off to the side of the road and, after a brief patch of forest, he found a small, isolated clearing. There he took advantage of the one other asset he had acquired from the unfortunate JT Willett. It would not do, after all, for some itinerant beggar to wander into the bank, plunk down a wad of cash, and ask to buy a large piece of property. That sort of thing was sure to arouse suspicion. But Willett had been no itinerant bum. He was, instead, a seasoned and apparently rather affluent traveler. And Jocko had his clothes, right down to a fancy pair of shoes. The sizes were close enough, and within minutes of having disappeared into the roadside scrub, Jocko Drumm emerged a new man, a man of means. The eyes never lie.

He knew he ought not walk into town in his new persona, so he waited by the road, and soon enough a motorcar approached. True it was only a Ford, but it was not, thank goodness, a truck. Style points be damned.

Two good things happened right away. The first was that the Ford slowed to a stop, its driver no doubt influenced by the obvious class of the would-be hitchhiker, what with his nice clothes and shoes and his expensive leather suitcase. "Help ya out?" he asked.

"Thank goodness you stopped. My car broke down off on a side road back a while and I have been walking for miles. Could I trouble you for a ride as far as town?"

"Sure, hop in."

"You from around here?" Jocko was conducting a crucial test. "I don't recognize you. Headed for DeKalb Falls?"

"Nah, on my way further north. Is that the next town on this road, DeKalb Falls?"

This was the second good thing.

"Yeah, it's a little bump in the road, but we like it. You can just drop me when we get to the edge of town. It's an easy walk from there, and I'll get some help with the car tomorrow. I appreciate it."

And that is how Jocko Drumm, successful entrepreneur, made his way into DeKalb Falls without being seen by any nosy roadside residents, found what he hoped would be a safe place to stash his suitcase for a short while, stepped out onto Main Street, or whatever it was called there, and cool and collected, walked into the First Bank of DeKalb Falls, which was, as he knew it would be, at the very center of town, sharing an intersection with the local church, a small squat building bearing a sign indicating it was the town hall, and a mercantile.

"Can I help you, sir?" This from a combination guard and greeter.

"Yes, yes you can. I am interested in buying some property that I believe is owned by this bank. Would you be good enough to direct me to an officer?"

Now in 1936, small town banks were, well, small town. They were not terribly large places, and they were not terribly crowded. Savers, and there were still a few, tended to come in clusters on pay day or at harvest time, while withdrawers, if that's a word, tended to come in on market days.

Those who had loans and could not pay them had long since given up, their properties no longer their own, and moved on, which left the bank officers with a lot of free time on their hands. And almost no one came in looking to buy land.

No surprise, then, that before the guard/greeter could untangle his tongue and point in the right (and obvious) direction, Jess Moreland perked up, rose to his feet, and tried not to appear too eager as he walked over and introduced himself to the visitor.

"Jess Moreland. I'm the president of the bank. And you are?" Moreland offered, extending his hand.

"I am John O'Connell Drumm, sir. Pleased to make your acquaintance," Jocko replied, using his true name for the first time in many years, and accepting the proffered handshake.

"And how can I help you today? Please. Come have a seat. Did I hear you say you were interested in purchasing some property?"

"Yes, I am. These have been difficult times for so many people, and I do feel a little guilty about it. But I have been more fortunate in life. Alas, the misfortune of some creates the opportunity for others. As a banker, I'm sure you understand. And if one does not seize one's opportunities, well, there is a higher power to answer to about that."

Moreland felt the blood rushing to his face. It had been a very long time since he had had a conversation like this. In fact, he could not remember one. Oh, my. Banking had started out as a lark, but these days it was a tough, tough business.

"Was there a particular property you had in mind?" he queried.

"Actually, there is," Jocko replied. And he went on to describe as best he could the property he had seen an hour or so earlier.

"Oh, I know where you mean," confirmed Moreland, mentally rubbing his palms together. "That's the old Forbes place. Sad story, really. You know, all this land around here used to be owned by the DeKalb family. This was their town. They had farms, a big saw mill, great big furniture factory up in the hills, and owned just about everything else. One of them even started this bank, back in the day.

"Well, over the years the family just grew and married and grew and married, and every generation was entitled to some part of the land or the business. Old Tom Forbes, he was maybe third or fourth generation through one of the DeKalb girls, but somehow he managed to keep hold of quite a bit of land, plus he got control of the mill and the factory. Had a really sweet wife and one son, Jared.

"Jared was running the mill for Tom, and one day there was a terrible accident. I'll spare you the details, but Jared, he got real careless and there wasn't much left by the time they got the works stopped to where they could try to help him. Now Tom took it hard, as you can imagine, but it like to killed Bess. In the long run, probably did. After that, she wasn't ever right in the head, and one night she just wandered off. They found her face down in one of the creeks the next morning. Said she must have stumbled and hit her head, but who knows.

"That was September 1929. Around here, we all remember it like it was yesterday. And you know what happened in October. Now, if Tom had been himself, he was a smart enough man that he would have figured out a way through, even as bad as things got over the next year or two. But of course, he wasn't himself. Shut the mill. Just couldn't stand the thought of running it. Lost the factory because they didn't have the lumber from the mill and had to buy it from outside. Changed the whole deal. About a hundred men lost their jobs that day, and old Tom just settled in to farm. Out on that land you saw. But the prices collapsed, of course. Probably shouldn't say that, but you already know. And he couldn't make a go of even that. We held off as long as we could, but banks are businesses, and there was only so much we could do. After that, Tom just sort of disappeared. I don't know anybody's heard from him in quite a while.

"So yes, there has been a bit of misfortune around that land. But it's still good land, and prices are coming back a bit. Not sure I ever liked him as Governor, but old Franklin seems to have some idea of what he's doing down in Washington. 'Course, he was tough on us bankers, too, back at the start. But it's better now. You planning to farm the land?"

"I am. Looked like there were some useable buildings out there, with a little fixing up. City life has its pleasures, but it can get to a man. But if you can make your fortune there and then live a country life without too much worry, well that's the best of both, I guess.

"Of course, that depends. Just how much are you asking for the land?"

Moreland did a quick mental calculation, based partly on the money the bank had invested in the property, partly on the chances that another buyer would cross his threshold any time soon, and partly on the prospect of bringing in a new and clearly prosperous customer for the bank. They settled on less than Jocko had in his pocket, and the banker's delight at seeing actual cash, and not some letter of credit, sealed the transaction. The paperwork took about an hour, and together they walked across to the town hall to file it. From there, at Moreland's invitation, they had lunch at Miss Sally's, the best restaurant in all of DeKalb Falls and probably the entire county, and also the only one.

And that is when Jocko's carefully thought out plan ran asunder.

Miss Sally, it turned out, was a matronly sort with a real talent in the kitchen. But she was kept pretty busy with her pots and pans, which meant either the patrons had to serve themselves - and that did happen sometimes - or, if they were lucky, they would be served by Miss Sally's one and only waitress, her daughter Julie.

This was one of those lucky times.

"Julie, let me introduce you to the fellow who just bought the Forbes farm - all of it - and plans to start it back up. Mr. John O'Connell Drumm. John, this is Miss Sally's daughter, Julie."

"Jocko, please!" as he offered his hand.

"Julie Krebs. Pleased to meet you." The usual small talk followed, along with some food that Jocko, truth be told, never tasted. Miss Sally might have her name on the place, but it was clear that Julie was Queen of the May and, through some slight fault of her own, the center of attention. Julie was a bit of a tease, he thought.

It wasn't that he had never seen a prettier young woman. He surely had. And it wasn't that he had never met a sassier young woman. Done that, too. But he had never met a young woman who was fairly pretty, sassy as hell, and had a smile like that. He knew she was trouble right away, and Jocko always ran toward the flame.

For her part, Julie was intrigued. Here was this stranger - at last, a man who's *not* from DeKalb Falls and apparently is not just passing through - and judging by the way Jess Moreland was fawning over him, even buying him lunch, a fairly important man as well. Interesting.

Well, one thing led to another, and not too long after Jocko had settled in at the farm and gotten things going, the two began courting. That lasted all of two months, and before he knew it, Jocko had a wife and, soon enough, two young boys to help around the farm. Loved them all to death.

He didn't see that coming, and it did, in fact, mess up his plan. He'd had it all worked out in his head. Buy the farm and get known as an upstanding citizen of this little town, all the while taking a more careful inventory of the contents of his suitcase, learning as much as he could about who this JT Willett fellow was, then, when enough time had passed and the right opportunity came along, selling off what he could from the cache.

He used his first weeks at the farm, when he could, to study the documents, and he came to realize that Willett must have been a pretty important guy. He had access to baseball players even Jocko had heard of. I mean Ty Cobb? Christy Mathewson? Wow! And he was obviously some kind of writer. And he'd been interviewing a bunch of people who might remember him for a long time. This was like stealing a jewel that was so famous you couldn't fence it. He'd have to be very careful indeed, or he would get in trouble for what was, in his view, just a run of good luck. Selling would be taking a chance.

But then, with marriage to Julie, and first one son and then another, he realized that he, Jocko Drumm, who'd always lived by his wits, and lived quite well as often as not, could not take that chance. He had a family, and they needed him to stay right where he was. Forever. And to his continuing amazement, he understood that he needed exactly the same thing.

Still, he had something of value. Perhaps, someday he'd find a way.

So, Jocko took the suitcase, and he wrapped it in layers of oilcloth in the hope that would help preserve the contents, and he stashed it in the back corner of his barn, deep into the darkness where no one would ever think to look, and where the boys would be too frightened to explore. And there it stayed.

Then he did a remarkable thing. Jocko thought ahead more than a week or a month, more than a year or two. And he realized that someday his good fortune might come to an end, whether gradual or abrupt. And he realized that such a thing could as easily happen tomorrow as ten or twenty years out. It would fall to the boys, Robby and Paul, to cash out his treasure. How could he tell his boys what he had left them, and at the same time not give away the secret to just anybody?

He pondered that for a good long while. And it came to him.

Best laid plans, and all that.

While they had intended to grab a beer, wolf down some lunch, and get back to work, Adam and Jason spent much of the afternoon in idle chitchat, taking some time to catch up on one another's lives in the way that old friends separated in time and space will do. It was mid-afternoon when Jason's phone rang. Jenna and Elaine, with an invitation to come into town for dinner at the pizza place, and bring that cute Adam fellow with him. Jason smiled at that, and Adam did the same a few minutes later when he heard. Clearly, they were not going to be reading a word written by Mr. JT Willett today. But then they had a flash of inspiration. Jason called Jenna back and asked if they might come in a little early and use the computer at the store for a little Internet research. Google, Wikipedia, drinks, dinner. Sounded like a fun evening.

So off they went in Jason's pickup, mental list in hand, so to speak. And when they arrived a few minutes later at the store, they bundled themselves off to the office where an aging iMac awaited. Jenna and Elaine kept themselves busy out front, organizing shelves and serving the occasional customer.

"Let's start with the typewriter," Adam suggested. "If it was an early one, that tells us one thing, newer tells us another. They Googled "Royal Portable Typewriter," and, sure enough, there was a typewriter database that showed all of the Royal models. They scrolled down the page.

"Damn! There it is! A Model P. And it was the very first portable they made!" Jason was as much surprised as pleased. Then he had a bright idea. "Let's check the serial number. I saw it on the back and I have it written down here somewhere. Maybe we can figure out how old it is."

"Let's see.... P969... Here it is. 1928! Everything fits."

"Guess that's early enough. And it looks like this was one of the smallest mechanical typewriters they ever made. So, that would fit, too."

"Try the paper."

Adam Googled "onionskin paper."

Wikipedia came through. "Look at that," Adam muttered as he read the brief article. "Doesn't help us with the date any, but it does say they used it with typewriters and it was durable and lightweight, so good for portability. Looks like old JT knew what he was doing. And it says onionskin had a lot of cotton content. Maybe that's why it held up. Who knows.

"But look here. It also says onionskin was popular because, being so thin, it was good for making carbon copies."

"Well," Jason observed, "we didn't find any carbon paper. Of course, we don't know if that's something old Jocko would have kept, or if he would have gotten rid of that right off the bat. But it does raise an interesting question."

"Yeah," Adam chimed in. "Does anybody have a carbon copy of that manuscript, or whatever it is? Did they ever? Is it still around?"

Then, continuing, "How about that Army camp. What was it called?"

"Camp Hancock."

"Oh, yeah. Let's see what we get."

This time they ended up at something called "fortwiki.com," and sure enough, there it was.

"Check this out. Looks like Hancock was a mobilization and training camp for the First World War. Check. In Georgia. Check. Damn, that was a big place. Can you imagine 50,000 guys living in tents? Hey. Here's a photo."

"Shit. That looks like fun."

"Speaking of fun, let's see what we can find out about those guys we thought were ballplayers. Let's take an easy one for starters. Ty Cobb."

Adam keyed the name into a search box, and after a click or two ended up on a page run by Major League Baseball that looked to be an index of every player who ever put on a uniform.

"Mother Lode!" he shouted.

They started down the list. Wagner. Cobb. Carey. Chance. The two Joneses, one of whom was a direct hit, while the other turned out at least to have the same name as a fellow who had played all of three games as a kid in 1890. Walsh. Baker. It took some checking back to Wikipedia to confirm some given names and a few random facts. But there they all were. Well, almost all. No telling who Will Simpson and Herbert Stone were, but it was clear they had never played in the majors. Of the others? Six Hall of Famers. Count 'em, six.

"Okay," Adam said. "We really need to know who this guy JT Willett was. He ran in some pretty fast circles." He let his fingers do the walking, or in this case, the Wiki-ing.

> **John Tyler Willett, Jr.** (circa 1875-1936), better known as **JT Willett**, an American journalist and sportswriter, is widely believed to have been the first of his profession to style himself a "baseball writer." He was an innovative thinker, and is credited with creating not only several statistics (e.g., slugging percentage) and terms of description (e.g., four bagger for a home run) still in use today, but also basic strategies and tactics employed in the sport.

Willett was born to Irish-American parents in Trenton, New Jersey, and in his early years was well known to, and respected by, the politicians and other prominent citizens who frequented the tavern owned by his parents. He was educated in a local Catholic parochial school under the personal tutelage of His Excellency, Michael O'Farrell, the first Bishop of Trenton.

When he was approximately twenty years old. Willett moved to New York City to pursue a career in journalism. He was hired personally by William Randolph Hearst, publisher of the New York *Morning Journal*, where he began to chronicle the fortunes of the New York Giants baseball team. It was

during this period that he developed his rather unique style of presenting the sport, with an emphasis on personalities and back-stories. He became a favorite of players from a number of teams, but was true to his calling as a window on the Giants.

In 1900, Willett moved to a new position as principal columnist for *The Sporting News*, a weekly that was devoted largely to coverage of baseball. He remained in that position for the remainder of his professional career, interviewing baseball players, managers, and owners, profiling teams, describing games and stadiums around the country, all in his personal column, "Down in Front," a title he thought indicative of both interest in the people and events he covered and a willingness to demand the access he craved.

In 1936, Willett was found in Utica, New York, seated in a rail coach, dead of an apparent heart attack or stroke. Co-workers at the time indicated he was at work on what he had described as the story of a lifetime, but no one knew what that story was, and no evidence of that work was ever found.

Just then, the "girls" lost their patience and cracked the door. "What's all the hush-hush stuff going on back here?" Elaine wanted to know.

"Let's go eat," urged Jenna, who always seemed to have an appetite. "Tell us over pizza."

They closed up the store, which had emptied of customers a good half hour before, and walked the block and a half to Sal's, making small talk all the while. Orders were placed, a pitcher and chilled mugs were delivered, and silence fell.

"So?" Jenna and Elaine, almost in unison.

By the time Jason and Adam had finished telling the story of Jocko's secret suitcase and the seeming treasures it held, of the ballplayers and the interviews, and the manuscript – none of which, they reminded themselves, they had even read yet – and of the apparent celebrity writer of the 1920s and

1930s that none of them had ever heard of, well, by then the second pitcher was empty, the pizza mostly gone and partly gone cold. It was time to call it a night.

"Now that," Jenna said, putting a period to the evening, "that was some story. Who'd have thought grandpa would be involved in something like that?"

And off they all went, the sisters to the farmhouse on the left, Jason and Adam to the farmhouse on the right. Tomorrow was another day, and it promised to be an interesting one.

Thursday dawned a workday, as it usually did.

On one side of the road, Jason was up before dawn, as was his custom. He and Melvin had their daily chores to do, and after all these years, they had their rituals to observe and natural rhythms to honor.

On the other side of the road, Elaine woke a few hours later, washed up, and went to make breakfast. Jenna was nowhere to be found, but that, too, was normal. Jenna was in charge of inventory for the shop, and several of the farmers and jelly-makers, and even some of the potters, who were their main suppliers were early risers with their own routines to follow, and preferred to get their deliveries out of the way long before the place opened for customers at ten.

But when Elaine arrived at work around a quarter till, she was surprised that nothing new or fresh had appeared on the shelves, and Jenna had not even cleared up the pile of receipts they had left by the register the evening before. But then she noticed that the light was on in the office. Mystery solved.

"What are you doing, Jen? I thought you'd probably come in to meet Sam or Hattie for new stock."

"Actually, I was just really curious. You heard that line of bullshit the guys gave us last night. You can tell Adam is a writer. Who else could make up something like that on the fly? I figured the two of them were probably back here playing some video game.

"But like I said, I was curious. So... I went up on the Internet, and I traced back through the "History" listing of all the websites they had visited.

And damned if they weren't serious. They spent all that time looking up Army forts and baseball players and this guy Willett. I don't know just what they have out there, but it must be something good.

"I kind of figured Jason must be trying to work out what it might all be worth. You know how he is. I don't know how you'd put a price on old papers, even about Babe Ruth, or if they had autographs, or what. So, I decided to look at the prices of really old baseball cards. I was just getting to that when you came in.

"You can get some of those old cards on E-bay for ten bucks, and some for a hundred or less. But then, look at this. There's a Ty Cobb card that sold for a million dollars. A few years ago, somebody bought a Honus Wagner card – isn't that a name they mentioned? – for more than two million."

"Wow! Who'd have thought? It didn't sound like they had found a bunch of baseball cards. More like stacks of papers. But if those guys came across anything even half as valuable, that's still really something. It makes me wonder what's actually in all of those papers."

Down the road a few miles, Adam was wondering the same thing, and anxious to get to work himself. He'd slept off the beers and managed to rouse himself around nine, but Jason was still hard at work somewhere on the back forty, or the front forty, or some forty somewhere. It was a damn big farm. Adam scrambled himself a couple of eggs – they *were* fresh! – burned some toast, and poured himself some cold coffee from the pot Jason had left. He was impatient, eager to dig into the notebooks and the manuscript, but he kept telling himself: "These are not mine. Wait for Jason."

It was close to ten when Jason finally rolled in, and more like half past by the time he had cleaned up and changed clothes. He sauntered into the room, showing no signs of hurry, and made as if he wanted to sit down with the local weekly newspaper, which had shown up as usual that morning. Adam was nearly apoplectic. Until, that is, he saw the up-turned corner of Jason's lips and knew at once his friend was playing him.

"Want to get to work?" Jason asked as he broke into a full smile.

PART ±̶ 2

WAR GAMES

SPECIAL TO *THE SPORTING NEWS*

BY JT Willett

The Great War was hard on everyone, not least the thousands and thousands of young American boys who went off for a great adventure and came home in coffins, or in pieces, if they came home at all. And their families and friends and loved ones, of course. It was hard on factories and their workers who found themselves sidetracked if the goods they made were not essential to the war effort. It was hard on the women who found themselves filling difficult and dangerous jobs that had been vacated by volunteers and by draftees. It was hard on the children, who grew up with half-empty homes and new kinds of fears the world had never known. So, to say that the Great War was hard on Baseball seems nothing short of trivial.

And yet, the Great War <u>was</u> hard on Baseball. And we are talking here about Professional Baseball, because the sandlot version of the game not only endured during those years, but prospered as it was carried by our boys around the world and found new fans.

But on the home front, the pressure was building. Here you had j̶s̶u̶t̶ a game – a mere game – that was being played in full view of the public by young and virile men who, were they in any other line of work, would be joining others of their generation in France. There were arguments in f̶l̶a̶v̶o̶r̶ favor of keeping things as they were, of course. Watching or following Baseball was a form of release, a way for common folks to take their minds off the troubles of the day, if only for a couple of hours at a time. Baseball produced true American heroes, role models like Christy Mathewson, to stir the imagination, and it produced as well its share of villains, hard men like Ty Cobb, who could symbolize evil (unless you were a Tigers fan). The Romans had the Coliseum; Americans had the Polo Grounds. And what if Kaiser Bill was able to get his hands on some of these American heroes, throw them in prisoner of war camps or worse? How would that feel?

As more men shipped out to ^Flanders to dig and die in trenches, the contrast became ever more stark. Who were these men of privilege, these Baseball Players, that they should be exempt from serving their country. At a time when all industry was turned to the war effort, and when nonessential industry was deprived of workers and supplies that could be usefully diverted elsewhere, why should Baseball remain on a pedestal?

There was, after about a year of war, something of a hue and cry over this, and teams made a few efforts to appear patriotic. Who can forget the pre-game close-order drill exercises, with players wielding bats in the place of rifles? But that contrast only seemed to stir the flames of resentment. And when Secretary of War Newton D. Baker, on July 1, 1918, issued his famous "work or fight" order, requiring all draft-eligible men working in jobs deemed non-essential to the war effort had to either sign up for war-related work or face the draft, and yet Baseball was given an exemption, the pressure became nearly unbearable.

Everyone knew the President himself was a fan. Why, he had been the first of our leaders ever to throw out the first pitch of a World Series game. Of course, as some will recall, he did arrive quite late at the stadium, forcing a delay in the start of the game. But he was a fan.

Woodrow Wilson, though, was also a moralist, and perhaps that above all else. He had committed the nation to a moral agenda when he finally chose to enter the war, and he was determined to be consistent in his style of leadership. No one, he felt, should ever be able to accuse him of hypocrisy. No surprise, then, that within a month, Baker had revised his assessment of the game and withdrew the exemption. Baseball, he ruled, was not essential, and its players would have to serve just like anyone else.

So Baseball men fought, and some died, in the Great War. Those who perished are, alas, little known and little remembered. The first major leaguer to die in battle was Eddie Grant, who had recently retired from the game after ten seasons with the Phillies, Reds and Giants. He was killed by an exploding shell during the Meuse-Argonne offensive. Larry Chappell, who played outfield for several teams, joined up as a medic, and died of pneumonia after contracting the then-rampant influenza. Harry Chapman, a catcher who suffered the same fate. Ralph Sharman, shortstop for the Phillies, who drowned in a training accident the year following his rookie season.

Others were ~~luckier~~ more fortunate. Home Run Baker, Max Carey, Frank Chance, Ty Cobb, Davy Jones, Christy Mathewson, Branch Rickey, Honus Wagner, Eddie Walsh, and many more players and Baseball men, famous and obscure, did their part for the war effort. Shall I go on? Grover Alexander, Eddie Collins, Jocko Conlan (yes, even umpires did their duty), Larry MacPhail, Rabbit Maranville, Rube Marquard, George Sisler, Tris Speaker, Casey Stengel, and on and on. All served their country. Fortunately, when the war ended at the famous eleventh hour, most returned safely home. Baseball could get back to normal, its reputation restored.

Before you knew it, the year was 1919, and there was a World Series to be played. A new beginning beckoned.

# # #

On Deck, and In the Hole

Georgia would have to wait. There might be a story down there like Jane said, or there might not. But if only as a matter of convenience, George came before Georgia. And George was in New York.

George Herman Ruth, Jr. The Babe. The Bambino. The Sultan of Swat. Far as JT was concerned, he was the Sultan of Squat. What a lummox. He could barely stand the man. JT had been around the largest personalities in the game for nearly twenty years by the time Ruth came on the scene – John McGraw, Cobb – he'd known them all – but he had never met any man so full of himself or such a glutton – really no other word for it – as The Babe.

Every school kid knew Ruth's story. He was born in 1895, right around the time JT had started at *The Journal*, in Pigtown, a section of Baltimore over near the B&O yards, so-named because it was the city's center for butchering hogs. Pigtown. JT mused that that would have made one more appropriate nickname for the man, and maybe the most appropriate of all. One thing he and The Babe did have in common – when Ruth was about six, his parents moved farther from the pigs and closer to the tracks when his father bought a saloon and the family moved in upstairs. But there the similarity ended. JT had used the saloon as a schoolhouse of life. Ruth, on the other hand, was sent away just a year later, at age seven, for reason or reasons unknown (but heavily speculated upon), and lived for the next dozen years at St. Mary's Industrial School for Boys, a combination reform school and orphanage, where by most accounts he was regarded as "incorrigible." While there, he learned three basic skills, as a tailor, as a carpenter, and as a baseball player. When he was eighteen, in 1913, Ruth's luck turned, and he was signed by the Baltimore Orioles baseball club, a minor league team, as a pitcher. When the Orioles owner fell on hard times in 1914 and needed to raise money, he sold Ruth's contract to the Boston Red Sox for around $10,000. It was the next to the last time that Ruth's contract was sold. After a minor league stint with the Red Sox affiliate in Providence, he was named to the Boston starting rotation in 1915. The next year, he faced off five times with the Washington Senators' star pitcher, Walter "Big Train" Johnson, winning four of those games. The rest, as they say, was history, much to the eventual chagrin of the Red Sox and the eternal joy of Yankees fans.

So much for the mythical Babe. Far as JT was concerned, his true self began to emerge in full view the next year, 1917. In one game that summer, when the home plate umpire called the first four pitches to an opponent's lead-off hitter as balls, Ruth walked off the mound and punched him. And later that year, as players were drafted for the war or volunteered to serve, Ruth, ever the opportunist, noticed that this created vacancies in the Boston lineup and pressed for chances to play in the field so that he could bat every day. Eventually those chances came his way, and it was then that he began to develop into the game's most prodigious home run hitter, and by no small margin. Babe Ruth made the home run fashionable, expected, in a game where such things had been rarities. Then, after the World Series ended in 1918, he took a nominal job with a Pennsylvania steel plant, an essential war industry, which allowed him to avoid the military even as his principal responsibility was playing ball for the company team.

Ruth married early, in 1914, while still in his teens. But marriage meant little to The Babe, and he became a notorious womanizer, as well as a loud drunk. His appetites were enormous, as JT could attest from first-hand observation. Many was the club or bar that Babe Ruth closed down in the wee hours before a game day. The man was a lout, an oaf. His first wife left him, citing his repeated infidelities, and though they did not divorce, it was a mere three months after her death in a fire that he married for a second time. Made no difference. And when he was asked by one of the Yankees owners to clean up his act, Ruth had told him, "I'll promise to go easier on drinking and get to bed earlier, but not for you, fifty thousand dollars, or two hundred and fifty thousand dollars will I give up women. They're too much fun." That owner, Till Huston, had passed the quote along to JT himself, though Willett had chosen not to use it. Ruth was too important to the game.

Toward the end of his career, he basically became a bit of a barnstormer, a dilettante of sorts, sometimes freelance and sometimes with the Boston Braves. But in 1935, The Babe retired from baseball for good. Just couldn't do it anymore.

Well, that was just last year. And JT could not help but think that this whole Hall of Fame thing sprang up for that very reason. This guy up in Cooperstown - I mean, *Cooperstown?* - was stuck out in the middle of nowhere, hour or so west of Albany, which was itself out in the middle of nowhere for folks from the City, and he probably saw a chance to cash in on The Babe. I mean, if you were going to have a baseball Hall of Fame, and you proposed it in, say, 1935, and you were going to build it (next to your hotel) in, say, 1939, would it shock you if Babe Ruth was named to the first group of inductees, no matter how they were chosen? Maybe Yankee Stadium was the House that Ruth Built, but it was a good bet that Cooperstown was the Hall.

Still, the man had agreed to an interview. Hell, how could he resist? *The Sporting News* doing a feature on the first players elected to the Hall of Fame? That was Babe all the way.

"Looks like this guy was doing some kind of story about the start of the Hall of Fame," Jason observed as they read their way through the manuscript pages that lay before them on the table. "I don't think this was a book, do you? We know now that Willett was a columnist. These look like a whole set of columns he was working on about the Hall and the first players who were getting in."

"Yeah. I agree." Adam had a quizzical look on his face. "But I don't get that. According to his bio, Willett was working on some big story that he thought would have some kind of impact. But the Hall of Fame? That was no secret. I mean, they took votes and everything. And people must have known they were building the thing, too. Every sportswriter in the country would have had that story, and every kid in Wisconsin would have known all about it. Where's the story?

"And then there's this. What the hell does any of this have to do with some Army camp in Georgia? Probably just doing some background on Wagner and Cobb, showing they were war heroes and such. I guess if I was doing profiles for a newspaper, I'd want to lock down some proof, too. But I don't think this was any secret, either. I mean, you'd think they'd have been proud of that and everyone would know. Unless there was more to it. Maybe it was all for show, or something."

"Well, let's keep reading. Maybe he wrote it all up and it's here. But if so, it'd better come soon, 'cause we're running out of pages."

PART ~~2~~ 3
SAY IT AIN'T SO, JOE
SPECIAL TO *THE SPORTING NEWS*
By JT Willett

For the country, 1919 was a tough year. ~~The country~~
   Americans were
~~was~~ ^still shaken by the death toll of the previous
year's influenza pandemic, uncertain as to whether
it had truly passed. Whether from disease or from
more direct impacts of the War, a lot of men did not
make it home, leaving behind them broken families.
A lot of other men came back broken themselves,
some of them looking to take back their old jobs,
others living on the streets. A lot of women, who
had been doing jobs in factories and stores, often
for the first time, were forced out to make room for
the returning veterans. Some were glad to return
to life as they had known it, others not so much.
Rampant public drinking among the returnees, among
them no small number of major leaguers – just one
of the favored avenues to forgetting the horrors
they had experienced – became a part of daily life.
That, in turn, led to a resurgence in the temper-
ance movement, and the German brewers, important
partners of Baseball, especially in the Midwest,
who had successfully held this movement at bay before the war, were now weakened by their very Ger-
man-ness, hardly an asset at that moment.

     Not all of those who wanted jobs, of course,
could get them. The end of the war also ended the
wartime push for production of tanks, guns and other
war ~~stuff~~ materiel. Factories had to be retooled,
money got tight. And of course, the Bolsheviks and

anarchists started sending bombs around to public officials and setting them off on Wall Street.

Americans looked to Baseball for reassurance. The attendance figures bear it out. In 1916, just before the war, about six and a half million people watched a major league game. That dropped to four and three quarters million in 1917 and under three million in 1918. No surprise. There was a war on. But in 1919, Baseball was back. Over six and a half million fans, just more than in 1916, passed through the ballpark turnstiles. The Chicago White Sox trailed only the Giants and the Tigers in attendance, drawing 627,000.

You'd have thought things were pretty good for Charley Comiskey and his bunch. Perhaps they were for Charley, but his bunch was disgruntled. There is no red-blooded American male alive who doesn't know what happened next. A couple of gamblers offered to do what Charley would not – pay his players for their performance, or in this case, their nonperformance. The money never showed up – or at least so we are told – but the Sox players, being honorable men, held up their end of the deal, and a sure winner of a team came out on the short end.

Blackened were their white sox, and blackened was the reputation of the sport they all claimed to love. By the time the Prohibition Amendment passed the next year, there was not much left for a thirsty fan to believe in.

It took a while to get things going again, not just in baseball, but in the country. We know now that the Twenties were about to roar, but at the start of that decade, nobody really knew what was going to happen. Would the jobs come back? Would the government get control of the anarchists and Reds? Would the American troops who were still fighting against the revolutionaries in Russia come home? As you might remember, nobody knew.

Now, back before the Great War, Presidents had started tossing out baseballs on Opening Day down in Washington. Taft started it all in 1910, and Wilson was happy to keep it up until 1916. Didn't seem the right thing to do during the war, I guess, and by 1919 Wilson couldn't have thrown out a ball if he'd wanted to.

In 1921, Warren Harding, whatever we might think of him now, decided that this would be a good thing again. Perk the country up, so to speak. And maybe help Baseball a little, too. So, he went out there Opening Day and tried to jump-start the whole deal.

It was another fellow, though, who really
   the ball rolling
got^ ~~things going~~, flying actually, for Baseball, and captured the imagination of the whole country. A Baseball Man. The Babe. The Sultan of Swat. The Bambino.

Babe Ruth came to the Yankees from Boston in December 1919, famously traded for the cash to fund a Broadway show. And he was an instant sensation. It was The Babe who knocked the rust off the game with his prodigious longballs. It was The Babe who showed the country how to enjoy life again with his outrageous behavior off the field. It was The Babe who stirred the imaginations of men and boys and women and girls, brought them back to the stadiums and the sports pages, and shook the moralistic cob-webs loose on so many levels. Harding was a crook and long dead; Ruth was a scoundrel and alive in every sense of the word.

Coolidge kept calm and carried on. But it was Murderers Row - the heart of the 1927 Yankees line-up built around Ruth and Gehrig - without a doubt the best we have ever seen on a field, that dominated the game. The Yankees - love 'em or hate 'em - were at the center of the baseball world.

1926. 1927. 1928. Yankees. Yankees. Yankees. In the World Series in the first of these, and winners in the next two, four games to none each time. Boom! It was exhilarating, especially if you lived and worked in the City, places like Broadway or Wall Street. And then, in October 1929, the Yanks were cast aside by Connie Mack and his Philadelphia Athletics. How could this happen? New Yorkers were depressed. The whole country was about to be.

# # #

So they kept flipping through the stack of onionskins, looking for treasure but finding only what Adam concluded was the newspaper columnist's equivalent of B-roll, the background imagery that contextualizes a story but does not tell it. If JT had something, it was becoming clear to the pair, he was in no hurry to tell it. Or he wanted to be very sure everyone understood why it mattered when he finally did.

"So," Adam wondered, "what have we learned - really pinned down - so far?"

"First," Jason listed, ticking on his fingers as he went, "we know whose suitcase this is... or rather, was. We don't know how Jocko came to have it. Probably something nefarious. But we know that it belonged to this JT Willett.

"Second, we know that Willett was a real person, and by some lights, a fairly important one. Certainly at the least well-known. And well-enough connected to the people whose names show up in these papers to have known them all, had access to them, and probably interviewed them lots of times. They would have talked to the guy if he asked. That means all of this stuff is almost certainly legit.

"Third, we know the typewriter he carried was time appropriate, and just the sort of thing you'd expect a traveling writer to haul around. And the onionskin was the right sort of paper. So, that all fits.

"Fourth, we know – if we can believe Wikipedia – that he was off on a mission to write some big story, but nobody knew what it was.

"Fifth, we know this pile of papers is probably not a book, and that 'Down in Front' was actually the name of his column at the newspaper. So, all these sections are probably just columns for different days, and the numbers make them part of a series he was working on. Obviously, too, he was moving them around as he went, trying to 'see' the whole series, I'd guess.

"Sixth, we know the story has something to do with this old Army camp in Georgia. Otherwise, why was he carrying around that forty-year-old pay sheet and the other stuff? We don't have a clue what all of those guys were doing there, unless it has something to do with the letter from Branch Rickey to Christy Mathewson. Again, why else would he be carrying *that* around the country?

"Seventh, we know that, even though onionskin was especially suited to making carbon copies, old JT probably didn't do that. Maybe he didn't trust anybody with it. Or if he did, it got lost somewhere. Because again, nobody at the newspaper seemed to know anything about whatever story he was working on.

"Eighth, we can't be sure. But most of these player biographies we've been looking at tend to talk about wives and kids and brothers and sisters, but there were no references like that for this guy. Chances are, he was a loner, unattached.

"How'm I doing?"

"Pretty damn good, I'd say. You've been paying attention. But now the fun begins. What the hell was he on to? Where's this big story of his? I think we are going to have to look at the notebooks."

Next up on JT's itinerary was Big Train. JT had interviewed Walter Johnson a couple of times over the years, and the two had hit it off pretty good. Unlike the audience that Ruth had granted him, JT was looking forward to this chance to catch up with the former Senators pitcher – maybe the only truly great player that sorry excuse for a ballclub ever had. Guess somebody had to hold up all the other teams in the standings every year. What was the old saw? Oh, yeah. Washington was always first in war, first in peace, and last in the American League. JT smiled at that, remembering the day his old pal at the *Morning Journal*, Chuck Dryden, had run it by him before he put it in the paper. Back in 1924, Johnson had actually led them to a Series win over the Giants when he was already baseball-old at 36, and to the American League pennant the next year, but after he retired in 1927 the team basically disappeared at the bottom of the standings. Sort of the Atlas of baseball, holding up all the other teams. He remembered having once written a column about them after the manner of a wanted poster. Reward! Anybody seen the Washington Senators? He still chuckled over that one.

The problem with getting an interview with Big Train wasn't getting his agreement; it was getting to him. The guy grew up on a farm in… Kansas, was it? Family lost that, and he ended up working in the oil fields out in Southern California after his folks moved out there for a fresh start. His big arms came from all of that physical labor, but his big hands were God-given. Guess God was looking for a place where he could hide a baseball and nobody could see it. The Senators heard about this kid out in California who was throwing peas nobody could hit, and they signed him up. That was 1907, if JT remembered correctly. Team stayed deep in the cellar after that, but the kid was learning his craft.

The legend of the Big Train got started one week in 1908. Johnson started three games in four days against the New York Highlanders (now the Yankees, of course), and pitched three straight shutouts – on six, four, and two hits, respectively. By 1910 he was a 25-game winner, and between 1910 and 1919 the guy compiled a record of 265 wins against 143 losses. On a better team, he could have won, well, who knows how many. He had 38 shutout wins where the Senators only scored one run, and 26 losses where the final score was 1-0 the other way.

After Walter retired from the Senators, he and Hazel were making a life on their farm up in Montgomery County, Maryland, just outside Washington, but he was keeping a hand in the game. In '33-'35 he was managing in Cleveland, but that didn't go well. So, last year he hung up his spikes for good. At least it looks that way. He lost Hazel about six years ago. Now he just keeps himself busy on the farm. Mountain View Farm, he calls it.

All JT knew about the farm was that it was near someplace called Sugarloaf Mountain, presumably that of the view. But JT was a city boy through and through, and he had no clue how to find such a place. Could you take a cab from Baltimore? From Washington? Did they have roads out there? Who knew?

But one thing JT did know was that Big Train had a telephone. There were still a lot of rural places around the country that didn't, but if any yokel farmer was important enough that somebody would run him a phone line, he was it. And JT had the number. Dickerson 7. Yeah, 7. So, he got hold of a New York operator who was able to stop laughing and had the ability to patch together a line from the City to Washington to who knows where to Dickinson, Maryland, God love it, and ring number 7. After a few minutes she rang JT back and informed him that someone had answered and was on the long-distance line for him.

"Train, is that you?" he asked, nearly shouting to be sure he was heard.

"Yeah, who's this?"

"It's JT. JT Willett. How are you?"

From there, JT went on to congratulate Johnson on his election to the Hall and to explain his project, how he was traveling around talking to all the first inductees and people who knew them, doing a series of profiles. Could he come down and talk to him? Johnson, of course, was more than willing, but that's when the problem arose.

"So, Train, how do I find you? I don't even have a map that has Dickinson, or Dickerson, on it. Can I take a cab from DC?"

This elicited about the deepest laugh JT had ever heard. "You really are a city boy, aren't you? Know how to drive?"

JT allowed as how no, he did not have that skill. Had never needed it.

"Well, tell you what. I got five kids, you know. And they all been busy themselves, so there's a mess of grandkids. Well, I got a bunch of 'em out here on the farm right now, and they're startin' to drive me crazy. How 'bout this." Johnson proceeded to explain to JT how there was this little place called Glen Echo not too far outside the city. "You won't need no papers, or nothin'" was the way he put it. And there was a fairly easy way JT could get there. "Started out as one of those Chautauqua places, you know, talk, talk, talk. But it didn't last more'n a year. Turned out Washington already had more than enough talk to suit it. Instead, they opened up one of those amusement park places out there, you know, all the tilty-whirls and such. Kids heard about it, and they been askin'" he said. Walter and a couple of his boys would pack up the grandkids and drive down to Glen Echo. JT could come out there and meet them, and they could talk. That was the plan.

Part of it anyway. The rest was work. It was a four-hour train ride down to DC, and most of it was pure boredom. JT packed up his typewriter and his interview notes from Ruth, figuring he could make a good start on that column on the way down. Probably wasn't going to be the kind of column The Babe expected, but at this point JT didn't really give a whit. That was one over-sized pair of cheeks he was never going to have to kiss again.

But he needed a table if he was going to work on the train, so he reserved himself a seat on The Legislator, also known as the Pennsylvania Railroad's train number 111, and made ready to leave at 8:30 the next morning.

Getting on the train that morning, JT could not help but reflect on how far things had come, not only in his life, but for the whole country. Forty years ago, when he set off to seek his fortune in New York, he'd had to go by train to Jersey City, then across the Hudson by ferry. Manhattan really was an island back then, cut off from the rest of the country by the river. But here he was in Penn Station, with its 21 tracks, eleven platforms, and the capacity to handle 144 trains an hour. The station was already a quarter-century old and starting to show it, but to JT it was still a modern marvel. Plus, he was about to embark on a journey under the Hudson in one or the other of a pair of tunnels, the so-called North River Tunnels, that hadn't even been imagined back then. Today, those tunnels were transited by about 400 Pennsylvania Railroad trains every day. And somehow, it all worked.

Of course, he'd made this same journey a hundred times before. Sometimes... most times, he never thought much about it. But for some reason he was in a reflective mood that day. Maybe it was this series on the Hall of Fame. Maybe that got him thinking back to all the things he had seen, done, and written around the game over his career. Or maybe he was just getting old. Who knows? In any event, the 111 was out in the middle of New Jersey and crossing over one or another of FDR's new parkways before he snapped out of his reverie and set to work.

The Legislator pulled into Union Station in Washington only 20 minutes late, a miracle of modern railroading. (There was a reason regular riders referred to this train as the *Legis-Later*.) The station was about the same age as the one he had just left in New York, and truth be told it was a pretty enough place. They had hired a fancy architect, Daniel Burnham out of Chicago, and done the thing up real nice. But walking through, JT always thought of it as a kind of "bloviated" building, a little too full of itself. Perfect for Washington. In fact, that was by design. He'd read a quote somewhere on one of his visits that had stuck with him. It was from a letter Burnham had sent to the commissioners before he was chosen. Something like "The station and its surroundings should be treated in a monumental manner, as they will become the vestibule of the city of Washington, and as they will be in close proximity to the Capitol itself." Well, that's pretty much what they built.

Getting across DC by streetcar had always been confusing. Lines running here, lines running there, and all from different companies. Thank goodness, thought JT, about three years ago the three biggest ones, and three of the few that were still operating after people started to take buses to get around, had consolidated into something called the Capital Transit Company that was switching over to running the fancy new PCC cars. They had a line that got you from Union Station out to Georgetown, and Big Train had told JT that there was another line that ran out from Georgetown to Glen Echo, and how to find it from the Capital car barn on M Street. So, off he went on little more than faith and a general sense of geography, and soon enough

96

PART ~~3~~ 4

THE HALL THAT RUTH BUILT

SPECIAL TO *THE SPORTING NEWS*

BY JT Willett

Baseball without The Babe. Now that's any baseball fan's idea of a Great Depression. And it's a shot that anybody could call.

First as a standout pitcher for the Red Sox, and then, after the worst deal in the history of bad deals, as the cornerstone slugger of the Yankee dynasty, George Herman Ruth, Jr., was the personification of the nation's game for almost twenty years. His records will never be broken, not by any one man. And when he wasn't on the field, his appetites and extravagances entertained that nation through war, peace, prosperity and the current and seemingly endless despair of dust and lost dreams.

The Babe, the Bambino, the Sultan of Swat has retired for good. How will baseball survive? One sure answer is to keep The Babe alive in the imagination and on the field forever.

That, in the view of Your Correspondent, is the genius of the newly ~~created~~ established Baseball Hall of Fame. Can't watch Ruth on the field any longer? Come to Cooperstown. See the memorabilia of his prowess. Read of his achievements cast in bronze forever on a wall. And oh, by the way, stay in my hotel.

Stay in my hotel? Yes, the Hall of Fame was not an idea born of the Baseball Brain Trust, no rival to the one that serves our President in these dark days. There is a word – oxymoron – that captures the essence of the Baseball Brain Trust. Look it up. No, it was a hotel owner, Stephen Carlton Clark, who came up with the idea. Otherwise, what the heck is it doing in Cooperstown, a remote little end-of-the-road village you can't reach on a bet? What is it doing next door to his hotel? Abner Doubleday? He's just an excuse. A myth. But don't tell Clark. The man's a genius. And the only smart thing the Baseball Brain Trust did on this one was to see at once the potential of such an enterprise and throw it's its not inconsiderable weight behind it. In fact, they liked the idea so much they are starting to fill the Hall with players three years before it is set to open its doors.

Because no matter how or why it came about, the Baseball Hall of Fame is a great idea and a real boon to the sport. It assures that The Babe will live forever. But it cannot, and should not, be all about The Babe. There have been other great players, and other large characters in the game. Some were there before Ruth, some played with him, and many more will follow. The game is played by two teams of many, nine to a side. The Hall must be about them. All of them.

For those who have not been following closely, players are to be selected to the Hall by votes of the members of the Baseball Writers' Association of America, a kind of fraternity of we idiots who travel the country for six months every year, eating bad food, drinking bad coffee and sometimes, I must confess, substances that were recently rendered illegal by constitutional amendment, and standing in smelly locker rooms interviewing sweat-drenched athletes about their day's performance. Your Correspondent was privileged recently to be among the voters for this first class of inductees.

While this Column cannot share the intricacies of the voting, you can be assured that the choice was both easy and difficult. It was easy to select five highly deserving men, but difficult to stop there.

We have already spoken of Ruth, so let us consider the others. Christy Mathewson, a true gentleman of the game and by some lights the greatest pitcher who ever lived. Ty Cobb, perhaps the least gentlemanly man ever to set foot on a professional baseball diamond, and yet, also, arguably the best pure hitter ever to swing the lumber and the scariest base runner you'd ever want to put a glove to. Honus Wagner, the best ever in the National League with that glove, though his hands were so big you could never quite be sure he was wearing it, and an amazing pure athlete. Walter "Big Train" Johnson, who, were it not for Mathewson, could himself be judged the best pitcher the game has known.

By the time Mr. Clark opens his doors in Cooperstown there will be ten or fifteen more great names up on his walls. But those five alone are worthy of being honored.

Your Correspondent is on a journey into baseball's past, present, and future. He will be traveling the country for the next several weeks, interviewing all of the new inductees who are still with us (sadly, as you surely know, Mathewson, a genuine national hero, passed away about ten years ago), speaking with those who have known them best, reflecting on the ways the game has changed and how it has become in a true sense our National Pastime. This special series, of which this column is already the ~~third~~ fourth entry, will seek perspective

```
on the game we love, and draw what lessons we can
from it of life in our times.
                                  crisscross
      So, hop on the train as we^ hopscotch the
country, or just buy your weekly issue of The Sport-
ing News, and come along for the ride.


                        # # #
```

found himself clattering along beside the Potomac River on something that was about as far from a modern PCC streetcar as anything he could think of. There were a couple of scary trestles that shook as the car passed over them, but it was a pretty straight shot without too many stops. Before he knew it, JT had arrived at the end of the line. Glen Echo Amusement Park.

After he paid his way in, the first thing that caught his eye was this monstrous 70-foot high roller coaster that looked like it had been jammed into about half the space it needed. Coaster Dips, they called it. This place was just Coney Island on a postage stamp, far as JT could tell. Since they didn't have the ocean, and the river, though nearby, was down at the bottom of a cliff, they just had a big swimming pool. But he was looking for something else. Walter had said there was some new Art Deco building done up Mediterranean style they had opened a couple of years earlier. Spanish Ballroom, he said. JT couldn't miss it, and they could meet out front.

JT smiled when he saw Big Train, and Johnson reciprocated. This was a chance for old acquaintances to do some catching up.

Coming as he was from the Ruth interview, JT had pondered whether he should remind Johnson of the fact Ruth had bested him four out of five back in the early days, when The Babe was still a pitcher, still with the Red Sox. Both were now headed to the Hall of Fame, and Ruth had made a big point of that small fact just a couple of days ago. Typical. But JT thought better of it, unless it just came up in conversation.

It didn't.

Making his way back to civilization from the land of Munchkins, devil drops, and carousels, JT had a choice to make. Head down to Georgia and follow up on Jane's suggestion. Or first head over to Pittsburgh and look up Honus Wagner. He opted for the latter.

That, of course, meant another visit to Union Station, this time for an outbound journey. This was not quite so simple as the last. Three and a half hours to Harrisburg, and another three and a half to Pittsburgh, and that's if you made the connection. Miss it, and you could take the five-hour scenic tour of Western Pennsylvania. Maybe, he considered, *this* was the real reason they had named it the *Pennsylvania* Railroad. And some of the roadbed on lines like that was rough as hell. It was going to be a challenge to do some writing. But JT had been doing that all his life. He was a pro.

The equipment on the Washington to Harrisburg run was considerably older than the stock that rolled between the Nation's Capital and the Big Apple, and to say that it was well worn would be to give credit where none was due. It was just worn; nothing well about it. In fact, it might once upon a time have been used on the mainline run, used until it had fallen at last into a state of near total disrepair. At that point, it was ready for the Harrisburg run.

The surprise of the trip, at least as far as Harrisburg, was that it was uneventful. Uncomfortable, but uneventful. And on time. When did that ever happen? The unsurprise of the trip was that, as expected, his connecting train was running late... an hour, maybe two. No one seemed to be very sure. He was too tired by then to keep working, so he checked his suitcase and grabbed a spot on the station bench, wavering between boredom and a nap that could lead him to miss the second train whenever it deigned to arrive. But he was rescued by hubbub on the far side of the most distant pair of tracks, and by a rush of people through the station in that direction.

Was there a train wreck outside the station? A fire? An escape of twenty dangerous animals from a circus car? His reporter's instinct kicked up enough adrenalin to rouse him from the bench and off he went. And there it was, pulling to a stop in all of its streamlined glory. Here, in Harrisburg on this fine late summer day. The Rexall Train.

As a baseball writer, JT admired balls, and the Rexall Train was about as ballsy as things got in 1936. Louis Liggett, the guy who founded Rexall Drugs, had decided that during the Depression it was unfair to expect the independent druggists who operated his stores to shell out for a trip to the company's national convention, so he decided to take the convention on the road. Well, actually the railroad. Liggett spent about a million dollars and bought himself a train – twelve surplus Pullman cars that he converted to exhibition and meeting spaces, as well as a dining car providing buffet meals and bar service. Everything was refurbished and done up to create a modernistic, streamlined look. And off he went. The train left Boston in March 1936, and zigzagged across the country for the better part of eight months, stopping in well over a hundred cities, until it ended up in Atlanta around Thanksgiving.

The front few cars of the train had been fitted out as public exhibition space, featuring, of course, the products on sale at Rexall Drug Stores. The scheduled appearance of the train in each city was preceded by advertising to promote awareness and build interest. And it seemed to work. It was free entertainment at a time when most folks could not afford amusements, and they came out in large numbers for a look at this rolling wonder of showmanship. Though he had read about the train in *Time* or that new magazine, *Life*, or someplace, JT could not have known that over its 29,000 miles of travel across 47 states and a bit of Canada, the Rexall Train drew 2.3 million visitors.

Well, it certainly drew JT, and for him served its sole purpose – kept him awake until the Pittsburgh train finally rolled in, puffing and screeching to a halt two tracks over. He collected his suitcase and climbed aboard, off at last to see one of the fellows he truly admired: Johannes Peter "Honus" Wagner, known to fans as The Flying Dutchman, and to friends simply as Hans.

Wagner was a big man but not a graceful one, barrel-chested with huge hands, but bow-legged as a wooden Bill Ding. But he was quick and athletic, and in JT's view the greatest shortstop the game had seen. And it did seem he could fly. Wagner led the league in slugging a half dozen times, an indicator that he could stretch a hit for an extra base more than most, and in stolen bases five.

Hans was also a throwback in another way, and one that appealed to JT's sense of style. He was born and grew up in Carnegie, Pennsylvania, a suburb of Pittsburgh. He stayed with the Pirates from the moment he joined the team as a young up-and-comer in 1900 until he retired as a player in 1917, and now, twenty years later, was still with them as a coach and batting instructor. And he was still living in Carnegie to this day. Even ran for county sheriff once a few years ago, though he lost. He was a guy who gave the notion of a "home team" real meaning, thought JT, and it was a shame there were not more like him still in the game.

As JT put the finishing touches on his column about Johnson, he looked forward to sitting down with old Hans. And since he would soon be talking with Cobb, he especially wanted to get Wagner to tell him once again story of the famous old "Krauthead" incident. That should be good for a laugh.

And there it was. Only Cobb was left to interview. Cobb and whatever else it was that awaited JT down in Georgia. If he could even locate this Abner person. And if he was even still alive. And if he would tell JT whatever story it was he had told Jane. And if, and if, and if.

But JT stank of the road, and he knew it. Been smelling his own BO all his working life. Part of the job, and he was not a particularly fastidious fellow in any event. But every so often, he knew, even he needed a change of underwear and a fresh shirt or two. Plus, it was getting harder and harder to read the columns he was turning out. The type was getting lighter and lighter, and he knew he'd catch grief from some editor or mess up some compositor if the typing got much fainter. Needed a new ribbon. Badly. And ever since they'd opened in '32, he knew, the best, longest-lasting ribbons came from Gramercy Typewriter Company on East 23rd.

While the story, if there was one, might be taking him to Georgia, he knew there was no good way to get there from here, or for that matter, of course, from anywhere. Plus, he needed to catch his breath. So, JT decided to grab a fast train back to the City, collect some clean laundry and a couple of new ribbons, and figure out how to make his way south from there.

PART ~~4~~ 5

RIDING THE BIG TRAIN

SPECIAL TO *THE SPORTING NEWS*

BY JT Willett

Whoosh! Fsssst! ~~Buzzzzz!~~ If you have ever had the pure pleasure of sitting in the first row behind the plate when one of the great pitchers is on the mound pumping fastballs, you know that a baseball actually makes a sound as it zips in from 60 feet, 6 inches away. It takes an act of courage for a batter to stand in the box, and exceptional eye and hand coordination to escape in time from an errant throw. Ask the late Ray Chapman. And that was only Carl Mays, a knuckle-scraper with a penchant for unsanitary pitches.

Imagine, then, standing in to face Walter Johnson. Whoosh! Fsssst! Strike One! A couple of years ago, somebody clocked a Milwaukee Road express going 104 miles an hour. Your Correspondent would bet a cold beer that Big Train's fastball could beat that ~~rumbler~~ iron horse to the station. And standing up to that speeding locomotive of a pitch, thrown sidearm yet, why, it would take a hell of a man, a super-man, just to stay in the box.

Don't take this Column's word for it. Here are the words of Ty Cobb, the game's greatest hitter, ~~drerb~~ describing his first encounter with Johnson as a raw rookie hurler: "The first time I faced him, I watched him take that easy windup. And then something went past me that made me flinch. The thing just hissed with danger."

At first glance, Cobb and his Tiger teammates thought that Washington had plucked some "rube out

104

of the cornfields" to face them, a tall, gangly kid whose arms actually hung out of the sleeves of his uniform. But that "hayseed" ended up striking out more than three thousand major league batters.

And yet, when Your Corressspondent had a chance recently to catch up with Big Train, he found a gentle man with a string of grandchild-renkids in tow. We sat on a bench at an amusement park, watching them frolic in a pool, scream on a roll-y coaster, and consume a prodigious amount of ice cream, as we talked about the old days and the new Hall.

In one sense, Cobb's Tigers were right. The Big Swede was a country boy back then, and a country boy he remains in retirement. Johnson lives on a farm in a remote area outside Washington, milking cows, growing corn, and looking at the local mountain from his front porch.

heavy

The baseball record books are ~~loaded~~^ with Walter Johnson's accomplishments. During his career, he notched 417 wins, second only to Cy Young. That pair are the only pitchers ever to pass the 400-win barrier. Two 30-win years, a dozen with 20 or more. The most shutouts in history – 110. Won the pitching equivalent of the Triple Crown when he led the league in wins, K's, and earned run average in the same year… three times. His lifetime ERA? 2.17. Why, once he tossed 55 2/3 consecutive innings of scoreless ball. Nobody's ever going to beat that!

It is no wonder, then, that the Big Train is among the first five inductees to the new Hall of Fame. And to Your Correspondent, speaking as one who has been privileged to know him for many years, it is no surprise that Walter Perry Johnson, gentleman farmer and loving granddad, has not let this go to his head.

Throughout his career, Johnson was known simply as a nice guy. He was even friends with one of his Hall of Fame classmates, The Babe, even though Ruth hit some of his most prodigious blasts off of him. But there was one rumor in particular, pertaining to another classmate, that Your Correspondent wanted to chase down at the source.

The story was that Wahoo Sam Crawford, who played in the Tigers' outfield along with Ty Cobb, was a close buddy of Big Train, and that there were a number of times, when a game was not on the line, that Johnson would ease up just a little and let Crawford hit him. This drove Cobb crazy; he could not understand why Crawford could hit the big right-handed sidewinder and he, the greatest hitter in the game, could not. And that was supposedly the whole point. But when Your Correspondent asked Johnson about that, even all these years later, all he got was a big smile.

Cobb, of course, had his own way of dealing with Johnson. Big Train had told him once that he harbored a fear that he might one day kill some slow or unlucky batter with his heater. So, while most batters were a bit jelly-legged and hugged the back line of the batter's box when facing him, Cobb actually hugged the plate, daring Johnson to come inside with his pitches. After that, Johnson always pitched him away. Advantage Cobb. Still, there was some risk involved. Over the course of his career, Walter Johnson hit more than 200 batters with his pitches. And Your Correspondent can confirm this: he regretted most of them.

> The Big Train is rolling into Cooperstown in 1939. All aboard!
>
> # # #

If he was lucky, he had enough ink left to bang out the Wagner piece on the way.

"What are those guys doing in there?" Elaine asked her sister.

Jenna gave her an I-have-no-idea shrug in response.

"They've been on the computer for hours! If it's not video games, then it seems like they must have found something pretty interesting in all those papers they were telling us about. I mean, he knows this is one of our busier days."

It was unusual, but Jason had called around ten and asked if he and Adam could drop by around noon or so and use the computer. He tried to sound casual, and hoped he was able to keep the tremor of rising excitement out of his voice.

Adam and Jason had spent the last day and a half working their way through the notebooks JT Willett had left behind in his suitcase. It was slow going. The notebooks were falling apart. The pages, many of them, were dry almost to the point of being brittle. The ink was fading, and the pages in pencil were almost illegible. In fact, some were, which left gaps here and there. Then there was the issue of JT's penmanship, which left something to be desired, and his tendency to lapse into some kind of shorthand, or at least a lot of abbreviations, when he got in a hurry. And if that wasn't bad enough, there were all sorts of odd squiggles and shaky letters, suggesting that at least some of the notes had been compiled while he was in motion, either on another of his seemingly innumerable train rides or, in the case of the Georgia notes, apparently, on buses over back roads. As much as they were reading his notes, they were also interpreting them, hoping they were succeeding in ferreting out his meaning.

It was when they got into the notebook labelled "Abner" that interest turned to wonder, wonder to amazement, amazement into a realization

of the significance of what they were reading. If this stuff was true, well....
Couldn't be, could it? Abner, or really what Abner had to say - *that* was JT's
story of a lifetime. And that browned out old pay roster, and that daily diary
thing they'd found in the envelope with the Mathewson letters? That was the
proof. Or if not the proof, and some lawyer would probably argue it proved
nothing, it was the key to proving the tale. And JT was obviously enough of
a journalist to know that. That's why he set off from Georgia to track down
some other members of that Army unit.

Branch Rickey. Christy Mathewson. Ty Cobb. And who knows who
else? They obviously all knew each other. But could it really be that their
paths converged like this? JT was right. This could change *everything*.

"We need to catch our breath and see how much of this we can actually
confirm, or at least find some reason to think it might be true," Adam
volunteered.

"Guess I'd better call the girls and see if we can camp in their back
room again."

And camp they had. They were looking up anything they could think
of. Baseball players in the military in World War I. That one proved especially
interesting, and lined up pretty well with one of JT's draft columns. Army
camps that trained in disposal of ordnance. Didn't add much to what they
already knew about Camp Hancock. All the names they could cull from the
pay roster that they had not already checked out, and much more information
- all they could find - about all those ballplayers on the list.

"I'm sure we could get a lot more information about all this from some
books," Adam said at one point. "These ballplayers - most of them were
pretty famous, I mean being in the Hall of Fame and all. There must be lots of
biographies out there. We could, what's the word... cross-correlate them and
see if they come together at this point. And some baseball nerd has probably
written about baseball during the war or something close. Why don't we shut
this down and go to the..." His voice trailed off in a realization.

"... I know. The local library," Jason finished the sentence with a bit of
a knowing smirk. "I think there must be one in Albany. That's only four or
five hours drive from here. Let's go!"

"Okay, smart ass. I get your point. But I'm not sure how much further we can get here at this point. Best to give your cousins back their office."

It was around four in the afternoon when they left the store, too early for the girls to close, and too late to get any more reading done at home. Doing what came natural, Jason and Adam headed to the local tavern for a couple of brews.

That's when Jenna and Elaine, having learned their lesson, got busy tracking through the "History" listing of the guys' most recent Internet search activity. It was hard to make much sense out of the strange combination of websites they had visited, or the mix of terms they had searched. It was sort of intriguing in a way to think that all of this was somehow related to all of the rest of it, and to some old suitcase that granddad had stuck away seventy or eighty years ago. But you didn't have to read faces like an FBI profiler to figure out that Jason and Adam were excited about *something*, and that something was here in this list somewhere.

How interesting.

PART 5̶ 6

DUTCHMAN'S GOLD

SPECIAL TO *THE SPORTING NEWS*

BY JT Willett

In a sport where, admittedly, the majority of players are boorish and as often as not drunks, the
former at all times and the latter mostly off the
field - with some notable exceptions - how is it
that the majority of men selected for the Hall of
Fame in the first go-round were true gentlemen?
Could this have been a consideration when the baseball writers gathered for the election? It would
certainly comport with the intent of the Hall, at
least on the baseball side of things. One, Ruth,
you built it for, to continue to exploit his popularity. One, Cobb, you couldn't credibly leave out.
And three - Mathewson, Johnson, Wagner - who were
deserving all the way around.

Honus Wagner may have been the most gifted
athlete ever to play this game. He was big and he
was awkward. Nobody would ever mistake him for a
ballet dancer. But he was incredibly quick - fast
hands, fleet afoot. He could stretch a single to a
double, a double to a triple, better than anyone,
and if they put you in jail for stealing bases,
he'd be serving a life sentence. His sobriquet, The
Flying Dutchman, was well earned. He looked more
like a lumpy old umpire than anything else, but he
played shortstop better than anybody ever has. The
man was smooth.

On the diamond, Wagner was not a man you wanted to mess with. Off the field, Wagner was, as Your
Correspondent has already noted, a genuinely nice

person. But he was more, and in a way the game seems to be losing.

Honus Wagner was born in 1874 in tiny Chartiers, Pennsylvania, across the Ohio River and a half-dozen miles or so from Pittsburgh. (About twenty years later, Andrew Carnegie donated one of his libraries to the place, and in gratitude the citizens renamed it after him – Carnegie, the name we know today.) Honus dropped out of school when he was 12 and went to work in the local mines. His brother Albert, who was considered the best ballplayer of the five Wagner boys, started playing professionally at Steubenville, Ohio, about thirty miles and one river bridge away, and when a chance arose, suggested the team add his brother Johannes.

That was in 1895. Within two years, the "less talented" Wagner, Honus, was playing for Louisville, and in 1899 moved, with club owner Barney Dreyfuss, to play for the Pittsburgh Pirates. In 1901, when the upstart American League was trying to buy talent to establish its bona fides, the Chicago White Sox reportedly (by this Column, so it must have been true) offered Wagner the enormous salary of $20,000. What was Charley Comiskey thinking then that he forgot by 1919? Anyway, Wagner turned down the offer, preferring to stay with Pittsburgh. Wagner played the balance of his career for the Pirates, and even coached for them after he retired. His home today? He and wife Bessie still live in good old Carnegie. He was a true Hometown Hero – the sort around whom the game was built in its early days.

Of all the players in the first group of Hall of Famers, Wagner may be the most excited about his selection. But of all of those still with us, his life after baseball may have been the hardest. He did politics for a while – state fish and game commissioner, sergeant-at-arms of the state legislature. He invested in real estate around Carnegie, and he did some coaching – football at Carnegie High, basketball and baseball at Carnegie Tech. And he and some partners had a local sporting goods store with his name on it. But the Depression hit Wagner as it has so many, and he pretty well lost everything. To their credit, the Pirates stepped up a couple of years ago and gave him a job.

It was with a mixture of excitement and wistfulness that Wagner sat for an interview with Your Correspondent. First topic of conversation, especially since it involved a fellow inductee: the famous Krauthead incident. For those too young to remember, this was a set-to that took place during Game One of the 1909 World Series. In the fifth inning, Cobb, playing for Detroit, reached first base, then yelled across to Wagner, the Pirates shortstop, whom he called "Krauthead," that he'd better watch out because he was going to steal second on the first pitch. Not exactly like Ruth calling the location of his home run, but a bit of bravado nonetheless, and typical of Cobb, who once explained to Your Correspondent, "The base paths belonged to me, the runner. The rules gave me that right. I always went into a bag full speed, feet first. I had sharp spikes on my shoes. If the baseman stood where he had no business to be and got hurt, that was his fault."

So, on the first pitch, there goes Cobb into second, here comes the throw from the catcher, and there goes Wagner's glove down for the tag – and straight into Cobb's mouth. Good for some loose teeth and a pretty good split lip. Or so the story goes. Confession. Your Correspondent was at the game, but distracted at the time and missed the play. Cobb has denied this ever happened, and even invited Wagner down to Georgia after the Series to do some hunting. That the invitation was accepted suggests that Wagner wasn't too worried. But when Your Correspondent asked him what really happened – to confirm or deny that he stuck it to the meanest man in baseball – well, old Honus just winked.

In his own way, Cobb himself may have best captured the relationship between the two men. "That god damned Dutchman," he once said, "is the only man in the game I can't scare."

In a couple of years, there'll be a plaque up there in Cooperstown, right next to Mr. Clark's hotel. This Column would not be surprised to see a steady stream of visitors from Pittsburgh filling up that hotel, going up there to see it.

###

Middle Innings

[AUTHOR'S NOTE: *No further typescripts of drafts of the "Down in Front" column's special series are available. Portions of the narrative from this point forward are based on a transcription of the notebooks prepared by JT Willett to preserve a record of his interviews. Direct quotations included below, as well as the descriptions and accounts of persons and events, are believed to be accurate. However, the handwriting in these notebooks is at times difficult to read, the ink has faded in places so much as to be nearly indecipherable, the notes themselves include abbreviations and apparent omissions that require interpretation, and the paper of the notebooks has deteriorated in some places. All efforts have been made to remain true to the story as originally discovered and recorded, but it must be acknowledged that the process of transcription may have introduced certain errors. The reader is cautioned accordingly.*]

Before he knew it, JT was back again at Penn Station, clean clothes and new ribbons packed neatly in his valise. He only hoped that the rigors of the coming trip didn't prove too unpleasant.

It was never as easy traveling south out of Washington, but when your destination wasn't even on most maps - and in particular, on *any* rail map - it was harder still. There was no good way to get to Narrows, Georgia, from New York City or anywhere else. Narrows was this little nothing of a wide spot about halfway between Atlanta and Birmingham, and JT knew Cobb had been born there and had heard somewhere it was the place to find him these days. You could reach it via a pretty spotty bus line - with some luck and good weather. In bad weather, the bus couldn't navigate the roads out there. The only real option was to start out on the *Birmingham Special* and then hope for the best. And even making it that way was harder than it used to be.

The *Special* started out okay on a Pennsylvania train down the main line to DC. But then things started getting quirky. At Union Station, you had to change over to the Southern line train number 29. Until about four years ago, Southern routed that train through Atlanta, and from Atlanta there was a Greyhound that ran close to Narrows on its way to Birmingham, and you could basically bribe the driver to take a short detour. Then, back in 1932, Southern rerouted the *Special*, so instead of Atlanta it ran though

Chattanooga and Knoxville – not exactly urban meccas, even by Atlanta standards. Nowadays, he'd have to ride the train all the way to Birmingham, the closest point now, and then find his way east across the Georgia line.

That's where complication number two came in. Earlier this year Greyhound got some competition from this new bus system called Trailways. Trailways started working more in the rural areas and back roads, places Greyhound didn't usually go. And they were cheaper. So, Greyhound started streamlining its routes, sticking closer to the big highways and ceding the high-cost, low-rent rural riders to the new guys. Between a new city in a state he had always tried to avoid, and a new bus line that might or might not be a help, JT was not sure what to expect. At least he had been able to reserve a Pullman berth out of Washington so he could catch some sleep instead of sitting in coach and watching the tobacco fields blow past the windows.

But first things first. JT hurried through Penn Station once his train was called, down the narrow stairs to track level and onto a carriage, all in time to assure himself a seat at one of the few available tables. That accomplished, he could while away the miles polishing off the most recent column for his forthcoming series, the piece on Wagner. Looking at it, he was pleased that he had finally changed the ribbon on his old Royal. You could actually read this one.

The transfer in Washington was easy. The platforms were mostly covered, but they were basically outdoors, unlike those in Penn Station, or for that matter, Grand Central. Here, you could see – and walk – from one end of the place to the other. That was because, for the most part, Union Station resembled Grand Central more than Penn Station, in that it was a terminus. The tracks ended at bumpers, and led only northward out of the station. There were only a couple that, like all the tracks at Penn Station, actually passed through in both directions. There, off to his left, was where he knew he'd find the Southern Railway trains. The southbound *Special* was waiting, and with the assistance of a porter, JT found his berth, stashed his suitcase after just a moment's hesitation until he realized it really held nothing of value to anyone else, then moved on toward the club car. If he was going to Alabama, JT needed a drink. And from there to visit with Ty Cobb? Maybe two drinks.

By the time Adam and Jason had made their way through the remainder of the notebooks, the weekend was well upon them. Both could use a break, but the puzzle they were slowly piecing together and coming to terms with had a grip on them and would not let go.

"Okay," Adam began to summarize. "These guys all hear from Branch Rickey, or maybe just through word of mouth, that this unit is forming in this corner of Georgia, and they're going to have a great time. Tell some stories, play a little ball, defuse some bombs and chemical weapons. And they all head down there. And it's all just hunky-dory until this thing happens, and then, suddenly everything is different. There's this mad scramble to sort it out, but it's kind of messy."

"Right," Jason kicked in. "Then they take some sort of an oath or something. Like the guys who saw the flying saucer and those space aliens at Roswell in the '40s. They knew what they saw. Obviously, a weather balloon. Case closed."

"Well, that's what's so interesting. Because this guy... Abner... he decides to tell somebody else. Mathewson's widow. But what does that really accomplish? I mean, it's not like she was running off to the tabloids and claiming she had Wilson's love-child while her husband was off fighting the war. She just kept quiet herself, until this guy JT Willett shows up on her doorstep. And even then, she just teases him that there's a story waiting for him down in Georgia if he can track down Abner. I'd say that means she didn't want to be the one to get blamed if people found out."

"True. And even JT, he didn't seem to care all that much either. After all, he didn't just run off on the midnight train to Georgia."

"Woo Woo.

"Sorry. It was there, and I took it. But he didn't do that. First, he stayed in the City and interviewed Ruth. Then, he wandered down to some amusement park near Washington to interview Walter Johnson. And then, he went over to western Pennsylvania to talk to Honus Wagner. And even then, it looks like he went home to change his shorts."

"And he must have finally decided to change the typewriter ribbon. Boy did that make a difference. We could actually still read that last article, about Wagner, without spotlights and reading glasses. And the first one looks like it was written later and added in, too."

"Of course, in fairness, Jane Mathewson had not actually told him what the story was that she supposedly knew. She gave him a couple of letters, from Rickey and Cobb. But that was it. Like, here's some salt and pepper. Go out and see if you can find yourself a nice steak to sprinkle them on. I mean, you can't really blame the guy. And he did eventually head down there, and even went to some considerable trouble to dig up old Abner. And then he started chasing leads like any journalist would. But somewhere along the line, he lost the scent, or got mugged, or just got unlucky. We know from his bio that he died on some train. Of course, the way he traveled around so much, there was probably a fifty percent chance of that anyway. And we know, or we can guess, that he didn't have his notes with him when he passed. Or else the authorities, whoever they were, overlooked them in the commotion and they ended up in some lost and found at some train station."

"All of which brings us," interjected Adam, "to the one big piece we have not been able to fit into this puzzle. How the hell did your grandfather get into the middle of this story?"

"Ah, yes. Grandpa Jocko. I'd almost forgotten about Grandpa Jocko."

"You said he died back in the '50s. Was there some sort of accident or something? Was he ill? What happened to him?'"

"I'm not completely sure. I don't think it was an accident, so he must have been sick. No idea what his problem was. But he was pretty old by then, and like I think I told you, he had led an "interesting" life."

"Did he leave a will?"

"Yeah. I actually came across it once a few years ago when I was looking through my parents' old papers. I never really did that back when their accident happened. But I came across that old will. Nothing unusual. There was a trust for my grandmother. Then they basically divided the farm in two, with the road in the middle. My dad got this side. Uncle Paul got the other. So, when I bought out Elaine and Jenna a few years ago, I was basically putting the original old farm back together. Let them stay on rent free, since I wasn't going to do anything with the other house anyway."

"Nothing about the suitcase or any special personal property or anything?"

"Nah. Course, the way it was buried, I don't know that he would have wanted grandma to know about it. Or maybe he just forgot about it.

"Only odd thing I remember, now that I'm thinking about it, was something my dad told me that Jocko had said to him. Something like, 'Look in the book. Keep your mouth shut.' Some shit like that."

"What book?"

"I haven't the slightest idea."

The hundred-mile run down to Richmond passed uneventfully and fairly quickly. From the number of freights they passed on sidings, it was clear that the *Birmingham Special* had priority status.

JT had been to Richmond once or twice over the years, though at the moment he could not remember why. Probably chasing some prospect for a profile piece. Each time, it struck him just how close the Old South was to Washington. Basically, when you crossed the Potomac on that fancy new stone bridge, you were there. Arlington Cemetery? That's the old Lee property, as in Robert E. And by the time you got to Richmond, the spirit of the old days was nothing less than pervasive. They even had a main road there – what was it, Monument Avenue? – that had great big statues of all the Confederate heroes in the medians at every major intersection. But at least, he thought, it was the capital, and it was sort of genteel looking. Once you got further south, into the Deep South, the theme carried on, but to JT it seemed that the gentility disappeared. But maybe that was just him. There were still a lot of those veterans around, and they surely had some expectations.

Not too far south of Richmond, the train turned west, away from the coast. Almost immediately, the track got rougher. Obviously, there were a lot more freight trains that ran this way. Their greater weight, plus the fact that the only people on them – at least legally – were the engineers, the brakemen and such, meant the railroad was less concerned about how smooth the ride was. As for the hobos and other free riders, the railroad could care less; if a rough ride bounced them around real good, and maybe even bounced a few off the train, then so much the better. Running a train over the line once or twice a week for paying passengers was a nonfactor.

The miles clicked by, one rail seam after another. And it was slow going – much slower than the schedule called for. Better safe than sorry, he guessed, on the chance that safety concerns were causing the slowdown. But by the time the train chugged into Chattanooga the following day, JT did not know how much more of it he could stand.

Fortunately for him, Chattanooga was the last major stop before Birmingham, where they arrived around mid-morning. But that was when the real adventure began. Greyhound did still serve Birmingham, and the bus station was near the train station there as in most towns. But as he had expected, Greyhound did not go anywhere close to Narrows. Their only route to the east made a beeline for Atlanta.

Unlike well-established Greyhound, the interloper, Trailways, put their stations out near the edge of the towns they served. Lower rents? Less time-consuming city driving? Or pure passenger inconvenience? Who could say. In any event, JT had to chase down a taxi in Birmingham, a place that didn't have but a half dozen or so since there was limited demand, and then overpay for a ride to the outskirts of town. There, in an old abandoned gasoline and service station, he found the Trailways counter, where he was able to negotiate with the clerk to find a route that would pass near enough to Narrows that the driver would accommodate him. That particular bus would be coming through in about five and a half hours. Assuming it was on time. That would put JT in Narrows after nightfall. But at least it would put him in Narrows.

In the event, the bus arrived forty minutes early, great for JT, but a potential problem if you were a passenger trying to meet it somewhere along the route and were going by the schedule. Then the reality of the situation hit him. This was *yesterday's* bus. Looking at it, listening to it, and smelling it, he immediately understood.

It was, then, in an advanced state of bedraggled that JT stepped down from the vehicle in the beating heart of Narrows, Georgia, early that evening. In the rain. And the mud. It was a much smaller place than even he had imagined, and one that had clearly suffered from the ravages of the Depression. But he asked the way to the one rooming-house in town, and that's where he headed. The proprietress, a Mrs. Butler, took one look at him and started closing the door. But when he identified himself and indicated he would pay in advance and was in town to interview Mr. Cobb, she relented. Cobb's name was still magical in these parts. Clean sheets, some hot water to wash with, and even some hastily reheated leftovers from dinner, and JT almost felt human once again.

He thought he knew where he could find Cobb. First thing in the morning, after eggs and grits and some coffee that was, he thought, two parts coffee and six parts chicory, that's where he was headed. But Mrs. Butler stopped him short.

"Mr. Cobb, he still comes here once in a great while. But he don't live here. Really never did since way back. He lives over in Royston I think. Other side t' Atlanta maybe forty mile or so."

It took a moment for the full impact of that statement to register on JT. He had just bumped his way across Southside Virginia, half of North Carolina, and the better part of Tennessee, and humbled himself before a Trailways clerk, only to find by the light of day that he was in the wrong place. Plus, he could have gone straight to Atlanta in the first place. Shit!

But on the outside, he only smiled. "Mrs. B., how would one get from here to... Royston was it?"

"Oh," she replied. "That's real easy. You go over thar to the feed-n-seed and you wait for somebody who's driving toward the south of town. You catch a ride down to the highway, and you can either hitch to Atlanta - mos' folks'll stop for y'all these days, especially dressed all nice like you are - or there's a new Trailways bus that runs right through there and you can flag 'em down. They go right to Atlanta. Royston's a little town on the main rail line east of Atlanta, so you can surely catch a train to get out there. Though I have to say I never done it mysef."

Go ahead, thought JT. Twist the dagger just a little bit more. "Thank you, ma'am. I'll give that a try," was all he said.

Warm Springs isn't that far from here, JT thought. What on earth does FDR see in these people?

"I don't even remember seeing any books in the house," Adam observed.

"Nah. I'm not much of a reader. By the time I get done with the daily farming stuff, and knowing it's going to start again bright and early - or actually dark and early - I just don't have the energy.

"Besides, we've never really been a family of readers. My mom liked books, and I think there were some old ones that grandma must have read some time. From what I've heard about Jocko, they wouldn't have been his."

"Okay. But he must have been thinking about some kind of book.... Was there an old family Bible? Something like that?"

"I don't know," Jason replied. "A couple of years after the accident, I packed up all my folks' stuff and tossed it in the attic. Well, I gave away the clothes, and put the rest up there. Now that I think about it, I remember there were some boxes of my mom's books. They're probably still up there. If we had a family Bible, it would most likely be in one of those boxes."

"How do we get up there?"

"I'll grab a ladder. Follow me."

Adam and Jason opened and secured the ladder. Jason climbed up a couple of rungs and pushed open a hallway trap door leading to the attic. A cloud of dust descended on the pair, with Jason getting far the worst of it. They rubbed dust from their eyes and waited a few moments for the air to clear. Then they proceeded up the ladder and into the half-height darkness. Jason flicked on an LED flashlight, and in the unexpected brilliance something scampered away toward one corner."

"You have lodgers," quipped Adam.

"Got to make a living somehow," came the rejoinder.

"Over there," Jason indicated as he swung the light toward what Adam thought must be the front of the house. The light revealed several stacks of boxes, each four or five high. "Some of those over there. Probably the ones on the bottom, since they were heavy as hell. I'm starting to remember the time I had getting them up here. Melvin is a good guy and all, but he's afraid of heights, if you can believe it. Came up here once, made the mistake of looking down at how he got here. Never would come up here again. Now I have to say, I've seen Melvin up on ladders, on roofs even, a hundred times. So, I know it was all bullshit. He just didn't want to be carrying boxes full of dead people's belongings. Can't say I blame him, but I didn't have a choice."

A quick inventory found that there were about forty boxes in all, and that Jason, no doubt figuring that he was unlikely to ever see them again, had not bothered with labels. But they were folded closed and not taped, so opening each to check the contents wasn't too big of a challenge. If they'd been looking for one particular thing or another, it might have been a problem. But simply identifying the boxes that held books? That was a piece of cake. That was the good news.

The bad news was, there were at least two dozen boxes full of books, and every one of them was full to the limits of liftability. The worse news was that it was far too cramped, dark, and dusty to sort through them up there in the attic. They would have to haul them down the ladder, dust them off, and sort through them down in the daylight. Then, of course, they'd all have to be repacked and hauled back up the ladder to be stored as before. And, since neither Adam nor Jason had any real idea of what book, or even what kind of book, they were looking for, they couldn't be picky. All of the boxes had to be examined.

By the time the pair had manhandled all of the relevant boxes over to the trapdoor and down the ladder and dusted them off, they had lost the daylight. Plus, both were exhausted from the effort. Jason pulled the trapdoor back into place while Adam stowed the ladder.

"I've got about one more day here before I really need to get back to the City. It's been nearly a week, and I need to feed my cat."

"You have a cat?" Jason exclaimed in horror, picturing a starving feline writhing in hunger.

"Gotcha," Adam smiled. "But I do have to get back. I left some things in the middle. Never expected to be up here this long."

It turned out that Mrs. Butler's information, too, was out of date. Cobb's family had lived in Royston, but when he retired, Cobb himself split his time between the West Coast and another corner of Georgia, Augusta, where he had played his first professional games with the Augusta Tourists. That turned out to be an easy bus ride from Royston, and there JT's luck finally turned. The whole town knew where the local hero lived, right over there on Williams Street, and there was a consensus, proved correct this time, that he was in town on some business.

Ty Cobb was one of those fellows who could blow hot or cold, as the mood struck him. He was a pure terror on the diamond, but he could be pleasant enough off it. Or simply mercurial. JT mentally flipped a coin, betting with himself over which he would find.

JT got lucky again. Cobb was on his very best behavior. More than that, he seemed to be in a reflective mood. This visit, and JT's plan to profile him among the greatest of the great in *The Sporting News*, may have been the thing that brought home what a sweet honor he was about to receive, and the brush with immortality that came with it.

"You know, baseball was a hundred percent of my life," he opined. "There's not a day goes by I don't thank the Lord for sending down that Grantland Rice fellow. Wrote for the Atlanta paper, he did. Wasn't for him, I'd o' never got outta this town and into the bigs."

"Well that may be," offered JT. "But you have to admit you had something of a reputation." That elicited a toothy smile. "When was it, '09 when you spiked Home Run Baker? Wasn't it Connie Mack after that who called you the dirtiest player in the game?"

"He did, that sonovabitch. But you know what? That just opened my eyes. That's when I realized that, if I played really hard, I could intimidate those guys like Baker. I stuck to the rules, but I pushed 'em as far as I could, I will say that. Just ask old Clyde Engel."

"Well, let's talk about that. How about that time a couple of years later when the Tigers were playing at the Highlanders, and that fan — what was his name, Claude Lueker, I think, or something like that – he was really giving it to you."

"Yeah, and I was givin' it right back to that guy."

"Yes, you were. Right up until the point where you ran up into the stands and beat the living tar out of him."

"He was going on about my mother! The Goddamn nerve. I warned him to pipe down but he wouldn't! If it'd been you, you'da done the same, I'd wager."

"Ty, the guy only had one hand!"

"Well hell, JT, I only *used* one hand! My guys knew. They all backed me up against Ban, said they wouldn't play if he kept me suspended."

"I promise I'll move on, but one more question. About ten years ago, when Dutch Leonard wrote to Ban Johnson accusing you and Tris Speaker and Smoky Joe Wood of gambling on the game, and you all had a sit-down with Judge Landis about that... was there anything to that? I know Landis cleared you. Were you clean?"

"Is this the kind of shit you plan to write about? Because if it is, you can do that without me helpin' you." Cobb started to get up from his chair.

JT backed off and made nice, and the conversation continued, asking mainly questions about Cobb's interactions with the other members of the first class, getting the other side of some tales he had pursued, for example, with Johnson and Wagner. It was Cobb who brought up the subject of the war.

"JT, did you know that Matty and me served together over in France? We were both captains in this cockamamie gas and flame division some general dreamed up. Said he thought a bunch of hard-case Army trainees would listen to famous ballplayers. But we all knew it was nothin' but some publicity thing. Can you believe that? I think that cocksucker just wanted to rub some elbows with us or some such."

Then he continued, "JT, I saw Matty doomed to die. None of us who was with him at the time realized that rider on the pale horse had rode by, and he didn't neither. But we were workin' with that poison gas. Truly nasty shit. And somethin' went wrong, and we all got a whiff. I was hackin' for weeks. But Matty, he got it worse. That's what killed him."

"Okay, let's dig in," Jason said as he rose from breakfast. "If you are really going to head back later on, I want to get going. I could use the help with these damn book boxes."

"You just mean you want to get through them so there's time for me to help lift them back up into the attic before I go, right?" poked Adam.

"Of course! It's not like I value your opinion as a writer, or the fact you might have actually heard of some of these books. I mean, they are ancient. Like from the '60s or '80s or whenever. I don't honestly know. So, let's find out. And let's see if any of them look special, like the title, or writing in the margins, or a Bible, don't forget."

It was slower going than they had anticipated. Jason had forgotten just how many books he had packed up back then.

"Where did she keep them all?" queried Adam. "You'd need walls and walls of shelves to hold all these, wouldn't you?"

"Yeah. The room where I have my office now? That was my mom's sitting room, and she had built-in bookcases on two or three of the walls. I took all that out when I started using the room for work. Plus, the books being there were just a reminder, and I didn't need that."

After pawing through the contents of three or four boxes, they were already dusty and bleary-eyed. But the work continued. The papers from Willett's suitcase were so interesting that both knew they simply *had* to find the link between Willett and Jason's grandfather, Jocko. Neither was sure they would find it in these boxes, but both were motivated to continue the search as long as they could.

"Wow, here's something," said Adam somewhere in the fifth box. "A hard-cover first edition of *To Kill a Mockingbird*! You could probably get some serious coin for that." And in box seven or eight, "Jason, did you know your mom was into romance novels? I didn't even know they had them back then."

"Bingo!" shouted Jason, working his way through box twelve. "We have a winner!"

"What'd you find?" asked Adam, his voice rising in anticipation.

"Family Bible!"

"Well, alright! Let's check it out."

They pulled two chairs together at the corner of the table and began to page through the Bible. "Not sure what we're looking for, but I guess we'll know it when we see it," Jason proffered.

"We should read every notation at the front or back," Adam suggested. "And if that doesn't get us anywhere, we'll need to page through every page and look for margin notes, or pieces of paper that are dropped in between pages, or any kind of anomaly like that."

And that is precisely what they did. There were a lot of notations. Births, deaths, marriages, little biographical notes, that sort of thing. All mainly from his grandmother's side. But nothing that seemed to cast any light on the matter at hand. Then they went through the pages looking for marginalia. Neither being regular churchgoers, they were surprised at just how many pages there were in the Bible. A lot. And in the end?

Nada. Zip zero. Bupkis. Back to the boxes.

The prize, as it turned out – and there most assuredly *was* a prize – was buried in box twenty-seven, sandwiched between an Updike novel and a book on crewelwork stitchery, whatever the hell that was. Neither Adam nor Jason proved to be curious about that.

But nestled between them, and easy to miss back when Jason was packing up the library, was a thin leather covered book – not anything printed or published, but a small journal of sorts. This just had to be the book that Jocko had mentioned to Robbie, his son and Jason's father. Jocko did not sound like the kind of man who would have kept a diary or done much writing. If he thought this book important enough to call to his son's attention, and they both had implicitly leaped to the conclusion that this thin volume in Jason's hand was "the" book in question, then surely it must hold the keys to the kingdom, so to speak. At last their questions might be answered.

Tentatively, Jason opened the cover of the journal. On the first page was simply a signature that read: Jocko Drumm. "We have it!" they both thought in unison. Carefully, Jason turned the page.

"What the heck is this?"

Well, thought JT, that was interesting. Especially there toward the end. I guess we have Cobb's version. But now the hunt for the real story begins, if there is one. I hope Jane didn't send me down here for nothing. Now, where the hell is Waycross, Georgia? How the hell can I get there from here? And who the hell is Abner? The answers, at least some of those questions, were soon forthcoming.

Waycross, it turned out, was down in southeastern Georgia, maybe fifty miles from the Florida border, and closer still to the Okefenokee Swamp. Great. *And* Waycross had rail service out of Atlanta. Actually, Jacksonville, Florida, over on the coast at the state line, had rail service that happened to run through the place on its way to Atlanta. And the train would stop briefly in Waycross when it ran, which was every third day. Nobody he asked in Augusta was sure which days, but they all knew it ran. And there were enough locals making the trek over to Atlanta for supplies or visits or such that everyone was just as confident that JT could find a ride to the city.

They were right. He did find a ride. With a hog farmer making his weekly delivery to some lucky Atlanta butcher. They had a long and particularly stimulating discussion of hog prices and how lucky JT was not to be a farmer the way things were in the country. And did he really know Babe Ruth? Wow! Lucky Man!

And they were right. There was a Jacksonville train on the Southern out of Atlanta, but only because the massive consolidation that created the Southern had included three Georgia railroads, and the company seemed to be stuck with them. Or at least that was the message that the hit-or-miss schedule and, as he was soon enough to discover, the quality of the rolling stock conveyed. He was lucky in one respect, though. The next scheduled departure was at six the next morning. Not wishing to spend the night on a bench, JT found a hotel near the depot, checked himself in, took a quick shower in the communal room devoted to such purposes, dropped onto the lumpy bed, heard a groan that he was unable to assign to either the bed or himself, and fell asleep. After so many years, he had to concede, this kind of thing was starting to grind him down. Still....

As he had requested, a clerk knocked loudly on his door at five the next morning, and JT roused himself, quickly dressed, and walked back to the station lest the damn train leave early without him. You just never knew.

The seat he found on one of the two available passenger carriages had once, he was sure, been padded and upholstered. There seemed to be evidence of both, along with a lingering essence of prior occupant. Make that occupants. And the car itself had that certain musty character that anyone who has lived in a fifty-year-old house would instantly recognize. It may have been a long way to Tipperary for the doughboys, but he was confident it was a much longer way to the aptly named Waycross, Georgia—or that it would at the very least feel that way.

Then there was the matter of locating Abner. Which wasn't actually his real name. Jane had shared that much with him. The man he was looking for was one Hobart Franklin Barnum. Barnum had been the company clerk for one of the units that reported to Matty at that Army camp up near Augusta. It was his letter to Jane that had started this whole thing.

In the time-honored manner of journalists everywhere, when he arrived in Waycross around midday, JT looked for any bars near the train stop. Then his heart sank as he realized just where he was. They may have repealed Prohibition in the rest of the country, but in places like Waycross that made no difference at all. Dry before, dry during, and just plain dry. Next bet? The banks, of which there were two. Not that may people had savings accounts any more. But there were a lot who had debts they owed to the bank or to local merchants. So, if old Hobart Franklin Barnum was a success, or if he was a failure, chances were some banker would know him. Turned out he was a little of both.

"Good afternoon," JT said as he introduced himself and sat down at the desk of some officer at his first stop, the Waycross Safety and Security Trust, clearly named to give depositors a sense of, well, safety. And security. And, of course, trust. The institutional version of 'I'm just an old country boy.' "I was hoping you could help me. I'm looking for a local man who I think has lived here a long time. Name's Barnum, Hobart Franklin Barnum. Any chance you know him?"

"No. No, cain't say as I do," replied the banker, portly in the way of stereotypes, but friendly in the way of the South.

"He might also go by the name Abner Barnum."

"Oh, hell yeah. Everybody knows Abner. Did you say his real given name was *Hobart*? Ain't that a trip."

"Can you tell me where to find him? He's not in any trouble or anything. A mutual friend asked me to look him up is all," JT prompted once it had become clear that the information was not going to be volunteered.

"Oh, sure. Abner runs a fillin' station on the highway up toward the north end of town. It's up there on the right, maybe 'bout a mile from the city limits. That's 84, I mean. You just go out Plant Avenue for a ways and you cain't miss it. No cross-streets to give ya, 'cause the train tracks run on that side the whole way, and there's nothin' on t'other side at all. Abner's just got him kind of a wide spot 'tween the road and the rails. But if y'all get to the old cemetery on your right, Red Hill it is, but I don't recall if there's a pointer out there on the road, you'll know you've gone too far. Abner's place's seen better days, like just 'bout everything 'round heah. But you cain't miss it. Old Abner got his name in lights right up there on the sign."

"This is supposed to help?" Adam continued. "It looks like so much gibberish. I mean, you can see words in here. At least they look like words. But they all run together and they make no sense at all. And then there's these weird drawings. It must be some kind of code, if it's anything. We've leapt to a conclusion about finding the key to a minor mystery in some book your grandfather once mentioned to your dad. We don't even know if this is the book. This could be anything."

Jason continued to flip through the journal, if that's what it was. "Hold on, bro. Look at the top of the third page."

There it was. They might not be able to decipher what the message in this little book was, but they now had to believe it was somehow what they had been looking for. Part of the line at the top of the page read "WILLETT."

They both thought about that for a moment.

"Okay. Obviously, we now have to figure out what the hell this all means. Jocko obviously knew who Willett was, or at least his name. And we can assume from that that he knew the suitcase he wrapped in the oilcloth was Willett's." This from Adam.

"And I guess from the way he hid the thing away, we can assume he knew he wasn't supposed to have it. And maybe that he also thought he couldn't afford to let it go. This just gets more and more complicated."

But Adam thought otherwise. "You might be right. But that depends on what this thing says. It very well might have just gotten simpler, if only we can figure out what he was saying. I mean, you can see the words. It doesn't look that hard. But he's obviously writing in some kind of a code that we don't have. Did you look at the end papers and riffle through the pages in case there's a key of some sort?"

"No," Jason said. "But let's do that. Maybe we'll get lucky."

They did, and they did not.

"Look," said Adam, glancing at his watch, and not for the first time. "This is fascinating, and chances are that one thing or another in those papers might have some real value. From the Internet, it looked like maybe the letters or the signatures might be worth something, if nothing else. But I really have to get back to the City."

"Truth is, I have to set this aside for a while myself," Jason replied. "I've spent so much time pawing through this old suitcase and reading and researching and all, I forgot that I have a farm to run. Melvin's getting along in years, you know, and there's only so much I can push off on him. I'm going to pack this stuff back into the case and try to put it out of my mind for a while."

"Tell you what. I got a buddy back at home. Works for some big corporation. But he's an okay guy. And his wife teaches English over at Columbia. Writes articles about the history of the English language or some such crap. I tried to read one once and it might as well have been Greek as English. Can you believe people can make a living doing that? Anyway, she's a smart lady, and she just might have some way of figuring out what this journal-looking thing says. Let me take that back with me. I'll make a copy, and then I'll show it to her. See what she says. What do you think?"

So it was that Adam found himself with a precious cargo, driving back through the Lost Quarter of Upstate, past the cement kingdom that was the state capital at Albany, and down the Hudson Valley into the bowels of the city he loved. Had it been only a week since he'd left?

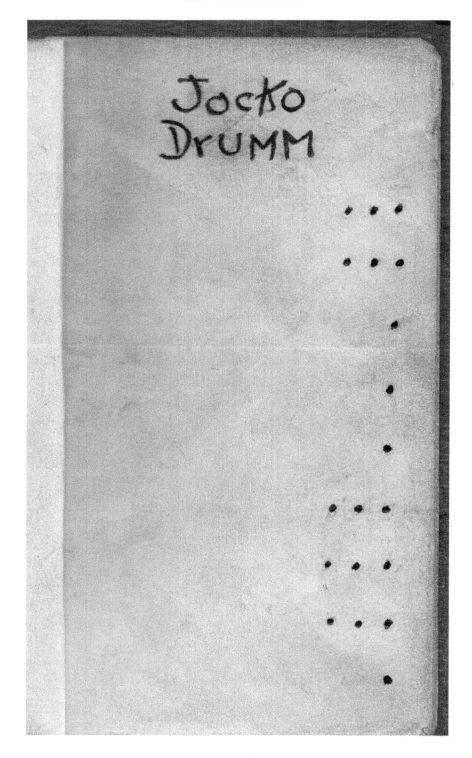

ROADWISES
NAPPERRI
G $\frac{2}{10}$
⟶△⟵ ⌢ ⊘⟶
CHASEFORT
HEVARNISHN
AILEDSTRE
AMLININGB
LINDBAGG
AGETOURIS
TMISSEDTH
ESKIPPERG
RABDUCKET
FROMSLEEP
ER ⌂
RIDINGTHE
CUSHIONSSI
TBYBOSTON

BUMWILLET
TWHITECOL
LARWITHCA
NDYJOBCAL
IFORNIABL
ANKETSGLA
DRAGSSTO
GIESBIGW
HIFFLE
WHITECOLL
ARCAUGHT
THEWESTBO
UNDJACKRO
LLEDPOKE
TOADSKINS/
//// LE

FT4NICKEL
NOTESTOOK
KEISTER
CAPTAIN

DITCHEDA
DRIFTING
TRAIN
CHEKROLL
ANDKEISTE
RGLABRAG
SSHEETSSTA
KEINKICK
PADDINGTH
EHOOF
YONDERWAL

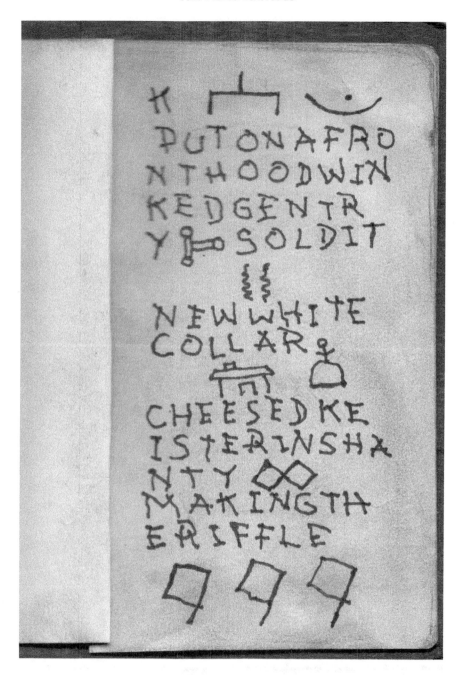

"GET GAS FROM ABNER"

Sure enough, there it was. Directions were best when they basically said "go in a straight line," and JT had followed them to a "T." Well, more accurately, to an "I."

It's a good thing, though, that the station had the sign, because otherwise there was nothing particularly remarkable about the place. Ramshackle little building with a couple of old visible pumps on an island out front. Both just said "GAS" in a globe on top, suggesting that no known oil company wished to take credit for the product inside, and the measuring glass on each one was dirty, though you could still see how much they held. The hand pumps were the littlest bit rusty, but obviously still functional. It looked like a thousand other filling stations JT had passed by on his travels around the country.

There was a beat-up farm truck at one of the pumps, and JT waited until the attendant had finished his work and the truck had departed before approaching the building.

"Good afternoon," he said in what he thought of as his "pleasant professional" voice. "I wonder if you could help me. I'm looking for Abner."

"That'd be me," replied the attendant, who also turned out to be the mechanic, manager, owner of the establishment and its sole employee.

Abner looked to be in his mid-thirties, maybe five-foot-eight, and thin in the way that so many men were thin after half a decade of troubles.

"Abner, my name is JT Willett. I'm a writer for a national newspaper, *The Sporting News*. Don't know if you're familiar with it."

"No, sir," Abner replied with a hint of curiosity in his voice. "Cain't say as I am."

"Well, we cover sports news all over the country. Myself, I write about baseball. And that's what brings me here. I've traveled for several days to come down here and talk with you."

"Well, mister, it sounds to me like y'all went to a lot of trouble to get to the wrong place. I don't play baseball. Never have. Hardly ever watch it any more, what with the price of tickets. We don't even have no local team here in Waycross.

"Now, there is a team over t' Moultrie. Steers. Packers. Sump'n like that. And Thomasville and Tallahassee got 'em, too, I think. There's this

Georgia-Florida League they all play in. Not very good, I 'spect. But that's 'bout what's 'round heah. So, maybe y'all want to go to one o' them places 'stead of standin' here talkin' to me."

"Actually, Abner, I didn't come down here to catch a game or write about the local teams. I came down especially to talk to you. Is there a place we can sit down?"

JT regretted the question almost as soon as it passed his lips. Because Abner was an accommodating fellow with strangers, and led him into his "office," which was how he referred to the nearby building. The dust was thick, papers were strewn about seemingly haphazardly, and there were stacked cans of oil and other lubricants in three of the corners, and what appeared to be beans in the fourth. But there were two chairs, and Abner offered the sturdier-looking of the pair to his guest.

"Alright, mister JT. How can I help ya? Can I offer y'all a CoCola?" That was Georgian for the local soft drink of choice and point of industrial pride. His hand swept to the right, indicating a dust-covered case of bottles with an unmistakable shape.

"No thanks, Abner. I'm good. Let me tell you why I'm here. There are some folks up in New York who are building what they're calling the Baseball Hall of Fame, where they're going to put up plaques and things to honor the very best players in the history of the game. Kind of keep their memories alive for the future."

"Yeah, I did hear tell of that. Up in Copperville or sump'n."

"Right, Cooperstown. It's a little town up north of New York City. Well anyway, the Hall won't actually open for a couple of years yet, but they've already started electing the first members. Pretty famous players. You might have heard of some of them. Babe Ruth, of course. Everybody knows The Babe. But also Walter Johnson, Honus Wagner, Christy Mathewson, and Ty Cobb." As he mentioned the last two, JT watched for any flicker of recognition in Abner's eyes. He saw none, which made him wonder if this really *was* a wild goose chase that Jane had set him on.

"In the world of baseball, this is a pretty big thing. So, what I'm doing is writing profiles of all these players for my column in the paper. And I'm traveling around interviewing the players and their families, really anyone who has known them well." Still nothing.

"I decided to start with Christy Mathewson because he's the only one of these players who, unfortunately, has already passed away. Matty was actually a friend of mine back when he was still playing, and I knew his wife, well now his widow, Jane. So, I went to see her." A flicker of something JT could not interpret; perhaps a glimmer of hope.

"Turned out that Jane knew about the new Hall and that Matty was going to be in the first group of players to get in. But she didn't know who the others were until I told her. And when I did, she stopped me and told me that, if I wanted to write the real story of some of these players – two in particular, of which Matty was one – I needed to come down to Georgia and talk to Abner. And that's why I'm here. To get the real story."

"Well, now, mister JT, I truly am sorry, but it does seem you have come all the way down here for nothin'. 'Cause I don't know all these famous people y'all're talkin' 'bout, an' I don't have no story to tell ya."

"Abner, Jane said you might be reluctant to talk to me. Maybe even unwilling. I mean, you don't know me from Adam. I could be anybody in off the road, or even somebody trying to get you in trouble. So, she gave me this to pass along to you."

At that, JT handed Abner a hand-written note from Jane.

"Just so we are clear, let me make sure I understand what you're telling me. You found these papers and this little typewriter in an old suitcase that your grandfather, or somebody, had apparently left in a rundown old barn on your property. And you didn't think much of it until you started reading what seemed to be notes of interviews with a lot of famous ballplayers, in fact, all Hall of Famers. And I can tell you as well, three from the very first cohort of players elected to the Hall. And I can also tell you that the man who took the notes and wrote these short articles, this JT Willett, was a famous sportswriter back in the early years of the last century, right up until the time when the Hall was getting started.

"There was a story going around when he died that he had been working on some big 'scoop,' as they used to call it, but nobody seemed to know what that was, and no record of it was ever found.

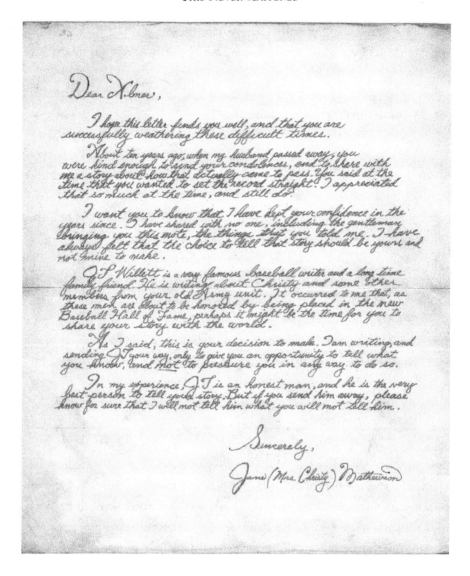

Dear Abner,

I hope this letter finds you well, and that you are successfully weathering these difficult times.

About ten years ago, when my husband passed away, you were kind enough to send your condolences, and to share with me a story about how that actually came to pass. You said at the time that you wanted to set the record straight. I appreciated that so much at the time, and still do.

I want you to know that I have kept your confidence in the years since. I have shared with no one, including the gentleman bringing you this note, the things that you told me. I have always felt that the choice to tell that story should be yours and not mine to make.

J. T. Willett is a very famous baseball writer and a long time family friend. He is writing about Christy and some other members from your old Army unit. It occurred to me that, as these men are about to be honored by being placed in the new Baseball Hall of Fame, perhaps it might be the time for you to share your story with the world.

As I said, this is your decision to make. I am writing, and sending J. T. your way, only to give you an opportunity to tell what you know, and not to pressure you in any way to do so.

In my experience, J. T. is an honest man, and he is the very best person to tell your story. But if you send him away, please know for sure that I will not tell him what you will not tell him.

Sincerely,

Jane (Mrs. Christy) Mathewson

"From what you've told me, and from what I see in these papers – assuming they are authentic – you may have just found it. And if the papers actually show what you have just described to me as being their content – well, this might be a story that could still elicit a great deal of interest. It would appeal to baseball collectors, World War I collectors, and perhaps even to one or two people who simply collect the most interesting things in the world.

"I could see a great deal of excitement if we were to put these items on the block. The auction value could easily be close to ten million dollars."

This last elicited an expression from his visitor that might best be described as a combination of an eye pop, a gasp, and a nod.

"We sort of thought there would be some value here. But we had no idea it would be that much!"

"Now you understand... we at Marbury House will have to do our due diligence. We put our reputation on the line with every item we sell. We simply must be convinced of its authenticity before we can certify it. In this instance, there are signatures to be verified, events to be confirmed as historically accurate, documents to be tested for things like the papers and inks that were used to make sure they are period appropriate. You get the idea. You understand that people do go to some surprisingly great lengths to fake documents or forge signatures or make things up out of whole cloth. We'll also want to confirm that you are, as you claim to be, descended from this fellow Jocko Drumm, and that you live on this farm in Upstate that you inherited from him through your father. Have a look at the will, make sure you were entitled to your father's personal property, which this would be... that sort of thing. Now I am not suggesting for a moment that you have done anything nefarious or that you are trying to put one over on us. But with that kind of money at stake, we cannot take any chances."

"Of course. That was to be expected. Especially since it's just something that turned up in an old barn. In fact, the results would be interesting on this side of the desk as well. I mean, it's not the kind of thing you expect to come across in your barn."

"Precisely. I'm glad you understand. Now, we have all the contacts that would be needed to conduct all of the tests and verifications – handwriting experts, document specialists, historians, baseball experts, and the like. We would be happy to make all of those arrangements. In fact, we would insist on that since we will be the ones to certify this treasure trove, if that's what it is. And for a collection of this potential value, we would agree to cover the cost of all that work out of our commission, which is, as you know considerable, but nonetheless is standard for the industry. Realize that in addition to the detective work, if you want to call it that, we'll incur expenses for photography and a writeup, for displaying the items, and for the actual auction sale itself. And everything will have to be insured against damage or theft."

"Yes, completely understood. Fair is fair. And if this stuff is as valuable as you seem to think, there will be plenty of money to go around."

"So," he pressed, ever so gently, "do we have a deal?"

"Absolutely! "

"Excellent. Then give me just a few moments to have my staff assistant prepare the consignment papers, and we can go from there. We will, of course, require that you leave all of this material with us so that we can undertake the authentication process. We ought to be able to complete that in six weeks or so, which would put us on schedule for our first feature auction of the new year. Will that work for you?"

"It certainly will."

Seventh Inning Stretch

Abner read the letter from Jane and fell into a pensive mood. He was quiet for a long time, long enough that JT feared he had pushed too hard and too fast, over-played his hand. Then Abner broke the silence.

"Mister JT, I have ben sittin' on this for a long, long time now. Followin' orders, as it were, for like onto twenty years. But that there Cobb fella, I seen him do a really bad thing, and to see him gettin' honored and all puffed up like he can be, well, that just sticks in my craw. It's one thing to do like you're told, and another to see sump'n like that.

"So, yeah. I'll tell y'all some things'll make yer hair curl. What do ya want to know?"

"Let's start at the beginning, and just go where that takes us. How did you end up meeting Christy Mathewson and Ty Cobb in the first place?"

"Well, there was the War. I'm sure you remember. Must have been in the news even up there in New York City." Abner offered a little bit of a wink there to let JT know his leg was being pulled ever so slightly. JT flashed a small grin of recognition.

"Now everybody 'round here was joinin' up. The patriotic thing to do, don't ya know. And I wasn't goin' to be left behind. A lot of these old boys back then, they didn't have no schoolin'. Lived out on the farms and all, workin' all day like farmers do. Ain't never been much money in peanuts, which is most of what they was growin' in these parts. Not much of what ya'd call spare time, like for goin' to school.

"But me, I was lucky. My daddy had a store in town, right in the middle of Waycross. I know Waycross don't look like much to the likes of you, but it's the biggest thing around here. Was then, too. An' when the farmers said they was goin' to town for supplies, like as not they meant they was goin' to my daddy's store.

"We wasn't what ya'd call rich, but we was comfortable. And that meant I got to go to school, straight through high school even. They was just buildin' high schools all over back then, and we got one just in time for me.

"So when I got over there t' the Army recruiter, they must a' thought 'we got a smart one here.' So, after I did boot camp like ever'body else, they pulled me aside and they sent me off to learn clerkin'."

"Clerkin'?"

"Yeah, you know. How to fill out all them forms the Army has. How to figure out the rules for stuff. How to keep records. Even taught me how to do accountin', which we never had at our school, and which my daddy'd never had me doin' at the store. Don't know if he really knew that hisself. Anyways, I was okay with my numbers, but I'd never learned to do that with money in and money out and all. So, they taught me that. Then they told me I was trained to be a company clerk, yes sir, and that's what I did."

"So, they 'signed me over t' this big Army base outside Augusta. That was fairly close t' home heah, so I thought that was plush. And they started me in on clerkin'. Camp Hancock, it was. Really just thousands o' tents all lined up in rows like the Army does. It was a big trainin' camp, and they had soldiers comin' there from all over the country. Bunch o' Yankees such as yersef, whole lot of Crackers an' such, an' even some boys from out west. And they was trainin' for all kinds of things. You'd hear machine guns 'n booms goin' off at all hours of the day and night, 'til ya jes didn't notice no more. You serve?"

"No, afraid not. I was too old by the time we got into that war."

"Well, if ya had, y'all'd understand. Them boys, they was fixin' to ship out and do some real dirty work. And the job at Hancock was to get 'em ready as could be.

"So there I was, clerkin' for this company and then for that, 'cause they wasn't there more than a month or so, each of 'em, then they'd ship out and a new bunch'd show up in the same tents.

"And then one day, the Lieutenant, he says to me, Barnum – that's my family name, ya know – Barnum, he says. You are excellent at your work. That's what he says. I'm promoting you to Corporal, Barnum. And 'course I got all puffed out. I mean, *Corporal* Hobart Franklin Barnum – now that was somethin' to write home about. And doncha know I did."

"That's actually something I wanted to ask you about. Jane had told me your full name, but she also told me everybody calls you Abner. And when I got down here to Waycross, I found out right away that's true. But I have to ask, how did you get from Hobart to Abner? Is that an old family name, or something?"

"Now, mister JT, I'm comin' to that. Do you want me to tell this all my own way? Or do you want to jump on in any time and spoil my train o' thought? Tell ya what. Let's just have a sip o' this and all calm down. I'll get to my name in good time."

And with that, Hobart Franklin "Abner" Barnum reached into a desk drawer, pulled out a bottle that was about half full with a clear liquid, and a pair of once-clean glasses. Glancing at the bottle, JT decided that whatever was in there would kill whatever on the glass he was handed needed killing.

"Matty. Thanks for coming out here to St. Louis to help me out with this. And especially, thanks for agreeing to take the commission. When General Sibert and Perry Haughton from the Braves asked me to take this on, I told them I would, but I couldn't do it without you."

"Branch, how could I say no? But it's not for you that I'm doing it. You know, don't take it personally. But this war is the real thing. I know it's important for Baseball to look better than we've been looking. But it's more important for our country. If we're going to mix it up over there in Europe, then it's not really for you or me to decide whether to serve. It's a yes sir, how high thing. So, yes sir, Major. How can I be of assistance?"

"Well, I'm right there with you on all of that. And I couldn't want for a better number two. So, Lieutenant, let's get to work. We need to fill out this unit before it's time to report down to Camp Hancock."

"That shouldn't be any problem, should it? I mean, there's lots of ball players who feel like we do, want to do their part."

"Matty, this is a little embarrassing, but there is a small thing I neglected to tell you before. Maybe not such a small thing. This General, Sibert, he's in charge of the First Gas Regiment of the Chemical Warfare Service. We're going to be training on how to disarm those damn things.

"Now Sibert, he has a nose for publicity, and he wants us to fill the unit with well-known players – kind of a show unit if you will. 'If these top ballplayers will serve their country, why don't you join up, too' kind of thing. But there's going to be some serious danger involved, although I must say I don't think the Army would want to put us right in harm's way. Sort of defeat their purpose, don't you think?

"Problem is, when we tell our guys what we want them to do, there's going to be a bunch who don't want anything to do with it. Or at least think twice or more about it."

"Like me, you thought?"

"That's fair. I knew if there was one man who wouldn't back away from danger in this circumstance, you'd be that man. And there's still time to back out. But yes, I have to confess to you I was concerned about it. But I do believe we'll all come out of it just fine."

"Well, it's something to think about. But, of course I'll do it. I wasn't blowing smoke at you before. Hard to think of anybody this country's been better to than me. So, where do we start?

"I've been thinking about that. We need some pretty well-known players, either still in the game or retired but still young and tough enough to do this. And patriotic, because this is a hard thing to agree to. But like you say, it's good for the country *and* given the way we've been painted lately by the government and some of the fans, important for the game.

"I think we've got to have Cobb. He's known far and wide as a tough guy, and he's smart as a whip. We need smart guys to do this work. That's the only way we can all stay safe. I want Cobb bad enough that I'd be willing to make him an officer, too, like you. But you'd outrank him by seniority. One reason I asked you first. You okay with Cobb?"

"Yeah. Lot of people have a problem with that guy, and he thinks the whole world is out to get him. He can be a handful, but I was always okay with Cobb. I think that can work. But can I offer a suggestion?"

"Of course."

"If we get Cobb, we need to get Davy Jones, too. You know, Davy played in the outfield with Cobb for a few years, and he just seemed to have a way of saying or doing the right thing to calm the guy down when he got all heated up. I don't know Davy real well, but might be a good idea to bring him in too, to keep Ty company, so to speak."

"Good idea. I'll get started on that right after I hear that Cobb is on board. I also want Ed Walsh. Solid fellow. Can you take care of asking him, sort of pitcher to pitcher?"

"Sure. His arm may be dead now, but his brain still works, and he was one of the cleverest guys I ever watched throw a baseball. What about this phenom, Ruth? Should we ask him?"

"I think he might be too young, and I don't know much about what kind of fellow he is. Maybe let that one go for now."

"Okay, now who else?...."

"So, this Lieutenant says I'm a corporal now, and that means a lot more responsibility. And he says, Barnum, there's this new company we're formin' and it's gonna be yer next assignment. But this is kind of a special company, doncha know, because it has a lot of famous baseball players in it. So, there's people gonna be watchin' this bunch real closely, and we want t' train 'em up right. And you're gonna be the clerk. And they ain't none of 'em regular Army, so you need to help 'splain to 'em how things work 'round here. Do I make myself clear, he says. And I go yes sir.

"So sure enough, a few days later these guys all show up. And they not all spring chickens if y'all know what I mean. They was about three old boys pret much like everybody else been comin' through there. But all the rest was these baseball players. And I'll tell ya. I never really followed the game very much back then, but even I heard of a bunch of these guys. They was a Major Rickert or Rickey, seemed to be one of 'em, but I never heard of 'im and bein' as he was a Major 'n all, I never had much to do with 'im. But the Lieutenant, he was Christy Mathewson. *The* Christy Mathewson. Weren't no red-blooded boy alive di'nt know who he was. And there was another one I heard of, and it was Ty Cobb. Ty Cobb. Can you believe it? And they was this big old bow-legged cuss, turned out to be Honus Wagner. He was a sergeant as I recall. And I'm thinkin' Holy Sweet Jesus, what am I doin' bein' around famous guys like them. And they was more. There was this JF fella, an' they kep' callin' him Homer, which t'weren't his name. Why that was Home Run Baker. They was eight or nine of these players, and they was from all over. Mr. Cobb, he was a local boy from somewhere up in North Georgia, so he felt right t'home, I 'magine. Said he'd ben 'round Augusta a few times playin' an' trainin' for baseball an' even decided to move there. But the rest of 'em was mostly from up north, or even California if I recall correct.

"Now there I was, this young kid from Waycross Georgia, and I'm the clerk for this company of major league baseball players. Now I won't say they was unruly. No sir. But I will say they was fun-lovin'. Real fun-lovin'. An' they was always tellin' stories and pullin' pranks, and they wasn't always takin' things like the rules real serious. And I keep hearin' the voice o' that Lieutenant sayin' I need to show 'em the Army way. And the officers, they not real Army neither, so it was all kinda on me. Or so I was thinkin', anyway. I *was* a Corporal, after all.

"So real quick I kinda got me a reputation of an old stick in the mud, if y'all know what I mean. I was always tellin' them boys how the Army did this and how the Army did that, and what the rule for this was and what the rule for that was and so forth. And finally, I think it was Sergeant Wagner, he says, 'Corporal Barnum.' That's what they called me all the time, by my name and rank, even though we was all in the same company, so t' speak. He says, 'Corporal Barnum, you seem to know every rule in the book. And if the rule you want ain't in the book, well, you seem to just make it up on the fly.'

"Now that weren't true. I never done that. But that's what he said, and they was all kinda noddin' like they 'greed. And he says, 'You know, we had a man like that in baseball years ago, thought there ought to be rules for this an' that when people was jes' playin' for the fun of it. So, he went an' wrote 'em all down. Made him a rule book. His name was Abner Doubleday. An' you jes' like him. I think we gotta start callin' you Abner.' An' they all of 'em got a good laugh outta that, and that's what they started callin' me. I weren't Corporal Barnum no more. I was Abner. An' of a sudden, I was jes' one o' the boys. An' they was pert nice fellas when ya got to know 'em. Most of 'em anyways.

"An' the name kinda stuck with me. So, that's the answer to your question. I been Abner Barnum ever since. Been what, twenty years now? Ain't hardly anybody even knows or 'members my real given name."

JT was entranced by this tale, but he had learned long ago that being entranced was not always the best way to find the truth of a story. As a test, he had to find a way to pose a sort of proof-of-life question.

"Abner, if I may call you that. That is a fascinating story. I've never heard anything quite like it. But I have to say, I have also never heard of this

Army company of great ballplayers, and I've been around baseball for about forty years now. I know Mathewson was gassed over in France – everybody knows that – and I know Cobb was over there, too. Went over there in October or November of 2018 seems to be the way the story goes. Then there was some accident while they were training. But this? I've interviewed pretty much everybody you've named. And I never heard about this. Of course, I also never thought to ask about it. But if I'm going to write it all up for my paper, I'm afraid I need more than just your word that it happened. Do you have any sort of proof, like say, a photo that you took with all of these guys? Anything like that? If you've got something like that to make my editors happy, then Jane was right. This *will* be a great story."

"Tell you what, mister JT. I got sump'n that'll prove what I'm sayin'. Maybe better'n a picture. It's late now, an' I gotta close up and get home t' feed my dogs. But you come on back out here in the mornin' and I'll show ya that I'm not spinnin' no yarn here.

"But let me tell y'all this, too. You ain't heard the story yet. An' it's a doozy."

It didn't take very long for the returns to come in.

The typewriter? It was a 1928 Royal portable, and one of the smallest mechanical typewriters ever made. Period correct, and matched to the apparent function as well.

The handwriting? The consultant had been able to locate some notes that JT Willett had taken on other stories he'd written. Everything looked the same, not only the technicalities of the writing itself, but also some of the abbreviations and short-hand symbols. And he had favored the same kind of small notebooks. Spot on. The notes had been written by Willett. In addition, the Branch Rickey signature on his letter to Mathewson was a dead match for known exemplars, and the paper was period correct. As for the Cobb letter, a centerpiece of the collection, it was correct in all ways and destined to become the second go-to exemplar of the player's handwriting. The first was a letter he wrote late in life to another player, Bobby Doerr. That one was on display in Cooperstown.

The chemistry? The onionskin paper was of a type that had been manufactured from about 1910 through 1946. But there was a watermark that dated these sheets between 1927 and 1939. Another match. The composition of the ink on the typewriter ribbon and the typed pages matched, and was of a type Royal had sold under its own label in the 1920s. Another match. In addition, the US Army pay roster exemplar was period appropriate, and the paper and ink were both correct. The writing in pencil couldn't be dated.

Provenance? An investigator had located a copy of the will filed when the seller's father passed away. Everything looked consistent, including the transfer of all personal property in the estate. No surprise heirs. Even the home address they'd been given checked out.

The contents? Here the House had contacted several historians covering a diverse set of fields from baseball to the military to weapons and technology. All of the core elements of the story checked out - the Army training unit, Mathewson's early death, the chain of command - all of it. There were notable variations from the known historical record, but they were precisely the ones that gave this collection the high ceiling on its potential value at auction.

Everything about this material looked like the real deal.

Acquisitions flashed the green light. The writers and photographers in Marketing got to work. Testimonials were solicited from the experts and consultants. A suitable display case was constructed. A sale date was set. Catalog copy was printed and distributed. A special interactive web page was created. Prospective buyers were identified and alerted. And at the end of the process, the special lighting was arranged just so, the chairs were set up and placed in rows, the numbered paddles were readied, the phone bank was switched on and staffed, and the doors were opened. Two hours of inspection time, then down to business.

Take it away, Max.

"Good mornin', mister JT. I see you made it back over here."

"Are you kidding me? I don't know how good you are at selling gas, but I can tell you I haven't seen many better at getting a fellow's interest all stirred up." At that, JT's smile was returned twice over by Abner.

"Looka here at what I brung over from home. Some of this is a little hard to read, but you'll get the idea pret quick."

Abner handed JT a small stack of browned out papers. On the top was a payroll roster from something called Ordnance Depot Company Number 44 at Camp Hancock. It was dated June 1918. Another appeared to be the Company's day book, or a daily journal, from early June of 1918. Taking a quick glance at the documents, JT noticed two things right away. The list of members of the company included all of the men whose names Abner had thrown around yesterday, plus a few more. And down there at the bottom was the signature of one H.F. Barnum, company clerk. Several other papers of a similar nature reinforced the point.

"Abner," said JT. "I've got to hand it to you. This is pretty darn convincing. But these look like they're official Army papers, I mean basic records that the Army would have held onto. What are you doing with them?"

"Well, mister JT. You can see there I was the company clerk for this unit, so I had all the paperwork. But after what happened and in all the confusion, well, there was officers all over the place, goin' through stuff, and papers was gettin' lost, if y'all know what I mean. An' the Major was there, askin' all sorts of questions, an' people was gettin' in the stink, doncha know. An' well, I just thought maybe I best hold onto one or two little things that nobody'd miss in all that, 'cause if they was blame goin' 'round or somebody got nosey or sump'n, then someday I might jes' be glad I had 'em. It was easy for me. I was the one keepin' all the records. And now, what is it, twenty years later, well here you are."

Remarks.

Day of Month	Remarks.
June 1	Forty fourth Ord. Depot Organized with two officers — nine enlisted men
June 2	Corp. Frank Baker from Camp Sevier S.C. S.O. 5/21/18 16 —
June 4	Pvt. J.A. Armstrong from Camp Fremont Calif. S.O. 5/30/18 63 —
June 4	Pvt. D. Jones promoted to Corporal. Warrant Chief of Ord
June 5	2nd Lieut Matthewson Hosp. Pvt. Chance Hosp. Pvt. Stone quarantined
June 3	No Change
June 6th	Pvt Armstrong transferred to Camp Merritt Pa. 7 S.O. 118 6/6/18
June 16th	Corp Barry Jones on furlough.
June 7th	Pvt. Stone returned to duty
June 8th	Pvt. Chance from Hosp. to duty.
June 9th	2nd Lieut C. Matthewson Hosp. to duty. Corp Jones F. to Duty
June 10th	No Change.

"You've got me on a hook now, Abner. I do believe you were there just like you said. And I'm sure I can convince the people at the newspaper of that. But apparently, I don't have the story yet. You said there was something that happened, and then there was a lot of confusion and people poking around. What happened, man? Was that what you wrote to Jane Mathewson about?"

"Well, ain't you got the nose for the news?" Abner joshed. "And to answer your one question, yes it was what I wrote missus Mathewson about. But I ain't there yet. And you got to hear the story from the beginnin' or you won't hear it t'all."

Given no real option, JT shut his mouth and sat back in his chair. It appeared this was going to be a long morning.

"So there we was, buildin' up what the Major he called unit cohesiveness or sump'n like that. Meant we was all learnin' to get along, which is a good thing when ya spend ever' day and ever' night with the same people. Kinda like bein' married, I guess, though I never did try that. But you know, when people are married or such, they kid around a lot, but they fight some, too. Get on each the others' nerves, doncha know. And that was happenin' to us jes' the same, the more so as we went longer 'n longer.

"Now mos' those baseball fellas, well they was alright. But that mister Cobb, he was the most difficult man I ever did meet. Jes' di'nt take much to set that fella off. And Lord he had a temper. Somebody'd say somethin' to 'im, jes' a joke or a poke or sump'n, and next thing ya knowed, mister Cobb, he'd be steamin'. Jes' weren't no letup in that man. Why they made him a Corporal like me I do not know. But they did.

"Anyways, there was this thing happened. Now, mos' the time in the Army, as I'm sure y'all know, it's ever' man takin' care of hisself ~ cleanin' up, makin' his bunk, and so forth. But some officer got the bright idea that these ballplayers, why, they was sumpin' special, and they shouldn't oughta need to be doin' that. So after they was there for a day or so, they sent Petey over to take care of that kinda thing.

"Ever'body in the camp know'd Petey. Well, ever'body that was there long enough, like me. Petey was this kid ~ well, I say kid, but he was pret' close to my age back then ~ and he had volunteered back when we first got into that war, and he shipped out to France, and not long after he was shipped back. Nobody was sure jes' what happened to 'im, but he come back with a gimpy leg and he wasn't quite right in the head. But he was a good kid and ever'body liked 'im.

"Now back then, somebody come home from a war like that, and people in Augusta, they was real good to 'em. Tried to find 'em some work and all. But fact is, a year or so before the war started, they had themselves a great big fire up there. Took out the whole downtown, it did, all the way along the river. An' it took out the warehouses where they shipped out all the cotton an' such. An' those were the jobs that would have been there, 'cept they wasn't.

"So, Petey bein' a veteran and all, somebody at the Camp took to lookin' out for him, and they put him to work doin' odd jobs around the place as he was able. Worked a lot in the hospital, he did. We had us a great big hospital on that base, 'cause that trainin' could be dangerous. So Petey worked there, or in the mess cleanin' up, or wherever. He wasn't much for thinkin', but he was pretty good at doin', an' I think it made 'im feel like he was still a soldier, even if he didn't have no uniform. An' on this one day, like I said, some officer sent 'im over to clean up after these ballplayers. But nobody bothered to tell them 'bout it. Course, I knowed who he was, but I was busy clerkin' when the ruckus started.

From what I heard, Petey was jes' a-mindin' his business and goin' 'bout his work. And he was in mister Cobb's tent middle o' the day when mister Cobb, he come back t' the tent to git sump'n or other. An' he sees Petey, who he don't know from nobody, movin' papers aroun' on his table there, ya know, like to straighten up or such. An' he started in on that boy sump'n fierce. I was doin' my clerkin' over t' the next tent, an' I heard it real good.

"So now Petey, he sound like he's backin' away an 'pologizin' and 'splainin' to mister Cobb, and mister Cobb ain't havin' none of it. An' course, Petey, he don't talk too plain anyway, let alone when he thinks he done somethin' wrong. An' I can hear 'em and Mr. Cobb he starts whalin' away. An' he's yellin' at Petey. I think he had a belt or sump'n. By this time, I come over there and so did a bunch o' others. An' there's Petey jes' kinda curlin' up and not fightin' back or nothin'. And mister Cobb, he sees them other men there - Armstrong I 'member was there, and maybe Stone or Simpson, one or t'other, and a couple of them ballplayers, I think maybe Jones, Chance, one other. They all come rushin' to the noise like me. An' Davy Jones, he starts talkin' to Cobb an' about a minute later he just sort of wound on down and walked on outta there. An' somebody - one o' them other fellas - helped ol' Petey get up an' talked to him a bit. An' he was alright, doncha know. But he was shakin' somethin' fierce.

"So everythin' quietens down for a while. But then it gets real crazy-like. Ya see, somebody had gone ahead and made mention o' this little fracas to the Lieutenant - that'd be Mathewson - and he 'pparently got really pissed off - sorry, angered - at Corporal Cobb. An' I don' know if he said sump'n to mister Cobb hisself, or if he went off and discussed it first with the major - that be Major Rickey or Ricketts or whatever. But pret' soon the two o' them come over in they full uniforms - sump'n ya di'nt usually see in that Camp - flashin' more brass than a candelabra and they huddle down wi' mister Cobb in a quiet, private way. And that Major, ya could jes' tell that he was madder'n a mess o' hornets. Lookin' at mister Cobb, I think they mussa tole 'im he needs to find Petey an' 'pologize or sumpn, 'cause they was givin' it back an' forth for a goodly while. Las' I heard 'im say, kinda loud was "thassa order!" An' off he went, with Lieutenant Mathewson trailin' behind 'im.

"Now you'd think, sump'n like that happened, that mister Cobb'd come outta there in a tail tuck. But not him. He bowed and scraped until the two o' them was gone, and I think he did feel pretty bad once he found out who Petey was and all. But that weren't the end, and you never seen such a fury. I grow'd up country an' I thought I'd heard 'bout every cuss word there is, but I learned fourteen or twenty new ones that day. That man was madder'n anythin'. An' ya jes' knew no good was gon' come of it.

"Now as it happened, ain't nobody ever seen Petey again 'round there. So, unless mister Cobb go off and find 'im somewhere's, well, they wasn't no 'pology given. An' truth be tole, I 'spect that was jes' fine with that boy. I jes' hoped he made out alright, maybe in town or somewhere else on the base."

Once he got back to the City, Adam could not get the suitcase and its contents out of his mind. There had to be some way of making sense of what he and Jason had found. And then he came to a head-smacking realization. There might not be a library within a hundred miles of the Falls, but in New York City? And at his own desk? Between the New York Public Library, unrestricted access to the Internet, and all of the other resources the City put at a writer's disposal, he could begin to get some answers. After all, what else did he have to do?

With a little digging and some heavy reading, he was able to piece together quite a bit of the puzzle. In 1917, it seemed, with the nation on the brink of entering the Great War, the War Department was a bureaucratic morass of competing interests. Only twenty years earlier, the standing Army of the United States of America had numbered all of 39,000 men – the smallest by far of any world power of the era. So, weak was the force, in fact, that when the nation entered the Spanish-American War in 1898, that effort had to be fought primarily by volunteers and militia units. Teddy Roosevelt and his Rough Riders were a perfect example. Part of the problem was simply that Americans had no experience of standing armies for foreign ventures, and no interest in world affairs that would require one.

The other part, this being Washington, DC, was the product of seemingly endless turf wars between the generals and a range of military-related civilian bureaus, and then among the bureaus themselves. If there was to be such an army, how would it be organized, and who would control it? Elihu Root, who was Secretary of War from 1899-1904, tried to impose order on the situation by creating a structured management system with a chief of staff and a general staff to conduct the affairs of the Department. His successor in the post, William Howard Taft, then reversed all of Root's reforms. In 1911, Taft's successor, Henry L. Stimson, reinstated the Root reforms and named Major General Leonard Wood as his chief of staff. Then Congress got into the act, literally, by passing the National Security Act of 1916, which restored power to the bureaus and cut back the general staff to a skeleton-crew level. And on it went, with lots of noise, but little progress. The ferment carried over into the war years of 1917-1918 under the stewardship of Wilson's Secretary of War, Newton D. Baker, who, depending on the time and circumstance, took both sides in the dispute.

And the physical arrangements, Adam came to understand, were fully indicative of the state of play. The Department itself was housed in something called the Munitions Building, a temporary structure that was not even built until the war had begun. But saying that it was "housed" anywhere was a misnomer. The civilian staff that oversaw the Army was spread through many other buildings, temporary and permanent, all across the city.

Adam had never really thought about it much before, but clearly the United States was unprepared for any significant role in the Great War. And yet, that role proved unavoidable.

Then there was the need to sign up huge numbers of soldiers to do the actual fighting. Selling the war to the population of military-eligible men, let alone the rest of the population, whose support was critical, was every bit as big a challenge, and the ways the government went about it were apparently not always in keeping with traditional American expectations. Perhaps the most public and comprehensive of these was the effort managed by George Creel and the Committee on Public Information, a group of experts charged with teaching Americans how to resist the newly sophisticated art of enemy propaganda while, at the same time, practicing that same art on the nation's enemies in turn. Among its better-known domestic initiatives was one that Adam had actually heard of, the so-called "Four Minute Men," a cadre of trained speakers who delivered four-minute patriotic speeches in movie theaters while the film reels were being changed.

Creel actually wrote a whole book about it right after the war. Called it *How We Advertised America*, and he was pretty candid. One passage really got Adam's attention. "There was no part of the great war machinery that we did not touch," Creel wrote, "no medium of appeal that we did not employ. The printed word, the spoken word, the motion picture, the telegraph, the cable, the wireless, the poster, the sign-board – all these were used in our campaign to make our own people and all other peoples understand the causes that compelled America to take arms. All that was fine and ardent in the civilian population came at our call...." All that was fine and ardent. That certainly described Mathewson, he thought to himself. And maybe even Cobb and the rest.

But it was when Adam started reading up on the Chemical Warfare Service that he hit real pay dirt. That's when he discovered Major General

William Sibert. Sibert, he learned, was for much of his military career something of a fish out of water. Trained as an engineer, because of the inefficiencies and simple oddities in the Army's system of promoting officers, he found himself early in the war leading the 1st Infantry Division, a job for which he was, by his own admission, entirely unqualified. Eventually he was moved around until he found the posting for which he was uniquely prepared when, in 1918, he was appointed to organize the Chemical Warfare Service, known to some as the Gas and Flame Division.

Sibert knew instinctively that recruiting men for such a function would present a special challenge, and he hit upon a solution of which Creel and his fellow propagandists would certainly have approved. He needed a cadre of athletic young men to point the way ~ a "show" unit comprised of prominent role models that other young men would seek to emulate. So, he and others on the staff staged what Adam, a hundred years later, would have called a press conference, gathering together reporters from several influential newspapers, to announce the new unit and position it as an elite fighting force. In his own words, "We do not just want good young athletes. We are searching for good strong men, endowed with extraordinary capabilities to lead others during gas attacks." Where to find such men? Sibert had an answer. He knew that Baseball was under pressure from Secretary Baker to send its players into the military. And Baseball was a repository of many suitable candidates. Would it not make sense, not only for the Army and the nation, but for Baseball itself, to place the best of the best in this new elite unit?

How he settled on contacting Branch Rickey is one of those things that is simply lost to history, or at least to the history Adam was able to uncover, though it seemed to have involved Percy Haughton, co-owner of the Boston Braves baseball team, who would have known Rickey and probably also known that he had just been fired as manager of the St. Louis Browns. But through that or some other channel, contact him he did, and Rickey was game. He used his baseball contacts and his flair for promotion to recruit the kind of high-profile volunteers he knew Sibert needed. He began with Christy Mathewson, then moved on to Cobb and several others, each a prominent potential symbol of self-sacrifice in the name of service to country. He and

Mathewson put together one elite company to train and be trained. It was this group, or at least some parts of it, Adam realized, that must have formed the core of Ordnance Depot Company Number 44 at Camp Hancock.

"So mister Cobb, he went on stewin' an' boilin' an' grousin' for a day or so, an' then all of a sudden he jes' got kinda quiet. Like he'd figured out sump'n in his haid, or else he'd finally jes' decided to move on with it. We all shoulda jes' know'd that sump'n was comin', but truth is, nobody else even remembered the thing, and mister Cobb, well he was jes' like that anyway, near's I could tell. So, nobody was payin' him any too much mind.

"Now I cain't swear that it was him done it, or even really what t'was he done exactly. So I'm jes' sayin' what I think. But I can tell you this.

"These home run heroes as some down there was callin' 'em, they was workin' with some serious stuff. I mean this was a real Army outfit, and they was learnin' how t' handle and dispose o' chemical weapons, poison gas an' such. So, you needed your haid on straight pret' much all the time. An' that mister Cobb, he was a smart man, and he knowed what he was doin' all the time.

"Now, we had this duty roster. One o' my jobs as the clerk was to post it the night before so ever'body'd know what they was supposed to do the next day. An' this one day – this would o' ben June 5th, ya'll can see from this here paper – ol' Armstrong – Three we called 'im cause his granddaddy and his daddy had the same given name, so he was a third, or whatever – anyway ol' Three Armstrong was assigned to learn some new ways to dismantle a gas cannister. Guess the Germans had some new system or sump'n, and he needed to learn how to work with it.

"Now that wasn't unusual. And when they was learnin' like that, well they always worked with duds. I mean with empty shells and cannisters and such, so's they could learn without killin' no one, leastwise theyselves. Ya' jes' had to be real careful when ya' went over to the ordnance shed that you got a dud to work on, cause if they somehow got switched aroun', well, there weren't no good gonna come from that. Had to make sure there weren't a piece o' red tape on the thing, cause that was how they marked the real ones.

"So Three, he was in this little chamber they used for workin' with this kinda thing, and they was some others in there with 'im. They was mostly from some other unit, and I don' rightly know who they was. I think Private Chance might o' been in there. So, anyway, Three goes to work practicin' how to open or disarm this thing, or whatever they was supposed to be doin' with it. And while he's at it, here comes ol' Lieutenant Mathewson 'round the corner. Y'see, he was a pretty hands-on kinda fella. Ya could see why ever'body seemed to respect the man. So, he comes 'round the corner like for an inspection or sump'n, I guess cause they's tryin' to figure out this newfangled device an' he wants a look.

"Well, mister Cobb, he was standin' 'round outside that place and I swear to God above and the Lord Jesus, that man turned a shade o' pale I ain't never seen before or since. And it looked like he started to say sump'n, but before he got it out, the Lieutenant well he opens that door and starts into the place. And jes' then, there's this 'pop' kinda sound an' this scream from inside, an' the Lieutenant, well he staggers back and kinda spins down onto the ground, an' this smoke – well actually, it was chlorine or some kinda gas – comes spillin' outta that room and ever'body goes a-runnin' t'other way. But mister Cobb, well he runs over that way and he drags the Lieutenant away from the door. Pretty brave, I'm thinkin'. Probally saved his life, at least a bit. But the Lieutenant, he ain't lookin' too good, coughin' an' eyes waterin' and all. Not good a'tall.

"An' then before ya know it, they's ambulances and doctors and medics and I think a big ol' water truck an' all kinds o' goin's on. An' they took the Lieutenant an' some others over to the hospital – like I said, they had a big ol' hospital on that base – and then after a while, they put on some gas masks and went inside. And from what I hear, 'cause I di'nt see this part myself, there was ol' Three jes' a layin' there on the floor coughin' and moanin' somethin' fierce – now all of us could hear that – and fadin' out pret' quick. I saw them bring 'im out on one o' them stretchers, and he weren't movin' much. An' off they took 'im.

"Now, if you'll forgive my language, 'cause I jes' don't know no other way to say it, this started a real shit storm down there in that unit. The ballplayers, well they was all cryin'. Growed men all, and famous y'know, but they was bawlin' away like babies. I think they really had a great likin' for Lieutenant Mathewson, even though he was a officer an' such. An' the work chamber, well, that was all roped off and guarded. They had these big MPs standing around with rifles at the ready for I don' know what. I mean, who would ever want to force their way into a place like that?

"An' then the strangest thing happened. Some men come in trucks, an' they got the whole Company loaded up into one truck, and then they packed ever'thing up from inside all our tents and they took down the tents, and they loaded all of that stuff into the other trucks, an' then they drove us lock, stock, and barrel out to a corner of the encampment there, an' they tole us to stay put. Ever'body stay put. An' they kep' us out there for two or three days, and brought out food and such. An' then, well, they moved us all right back again, an' things got back to normal, or sort of. 'Cept people started gettin' reassigned lef' and right.

I never did see Lieutenant Mathewson again after that. But that weren't the end of it. No sirree, not by a long shot.

Pitching Change

"Adam, hey it's Jason. It's been about a month or so. How are you?"

"I'm good. I got caught up on a bunch of stuff. Did a little writing. Oh, hey. I meant to tell you. I did try to take that notebook or journal thing over to my friend's wife at Columbia right when I got back to town, but she was off on some academic boondoggle of some sort. I think he said she was in Bologna, of all places, or maybe it was Basel. All I remember is that it was someplace that sounded like it was named for food. Funny place for an English professor, but I guess it's one of the perks. Anyway, she supposedly just got back this week, and I have an appointment to drop it by tomorrow morning. So, maybe we'll get lucky and she can figure out that code, or whatever it is."

"Actually, that's why I called you. I don't know how to say this, so I'll just say it. It's gone."

"What do you mean, it's gone? What's gone?"

"The papers, the notebooks, the records, the typewriter, the suitcase. It's just all gone. As in not here anymore."

"I don't understand. What the hell happened?"

"Well, about the time you left I was starting to fall way behind on my work around here. I mean it's not all just feeding chickens and gathering eggs. There's a lot of work to farming, and I was neglecting it. We spent a whole week or so just picking over those papers and researching on the Internet and all that. Melvin was taking on more than his share of the load, and even he couldn't keep up. Well, I just had to set the whole thing aside in a corner and try to forget about it until I got caught up. And that's a slippery slope, because you've got to do your full day's work and then more on top to catch back up. I just got to that point a couple of days ago. Then I tried to catch a little rest for a day or so. And I just went back to take another look at the documents and, well, they weren't where I left them. Vanished."

"Maybe Melvin just moved them somewhere to get them out of the way. Did you ask him?"

"Well, that's the other thing. Melvin's gone, too."

"Gone as in dead, or gone as in gone somewhere else? I mean, he was getting on in years, old Melvin."

"Yeah, he was, and that was part of the problem. While I was playing research detective, the bulk of keeping up fell on old Melvin. And about two weeks ago, he pulled me aside and said he just couldn't do it anymore. Getting too old. Said he just had to leave off and go retire and collect his Social Security before he killed himself.

"Of course, I understood. And I've started looking around up here for somebody to take his place. Not that easy to find someone today who wants to help work another man's farm – and who's qualified and who you'd trust to do it."

"Well, Jason, that does point to one obvious question. Do you think Melvin took the suitcase?"

"I've been thinking about that, as you might expect. And I have to say I just don't see it. Melvin has been a loyal helper and a good friend for decades. He's like a member of the family, and, with no disrespect to the girls, in a way my only family. Plus, unless he was eavesdropping pretty often, I don't think he actually knows very much about what's in that suitcase or why it might be worth taking.

"No, I don't have any suspects at all. You know, we're still country out here. I never lock the house. Never had a reason to. Not a lot of axe murderers in DeKalb Falls. But to the point, it could have been just about anybody. Most likely it was some itinerant guy who came through looking for work or a handout, came into the open house, and saw a suitcase he liked. I was just thinking... Wouldn't *that* be ironic?"

"Hah! A modern Jocko Drumm playing to the fates. It does have a nice dramatic arc to it, but I have to say that seems a stretch. You, or Melvin before he left, probably just moved the thing and can't remember where to. My advice is just keep looking."

"Yeah, maybe you're right."

"I'll give you a call as soon as I have something back from the professor."

JT had not moved more than an inch in an hour or more, except for taking notes as fast as his hand would go. Jane was right. This was a story worthy of the trip to Georgia. And by now, Abner was really into telling it.

"So the next thing I know, the place is crawlin' with officers of every stripe there is. The Major, he was there o' course. But that was just the start. The camp commander was always hangin' 'round now, too. Used to be

Gen'ral Clement, who I'd seen aroun', but this was the new guy. Don' rightly recall his name. But it was him, and he was there a lot. Then there was this big Gen'ral down from Washington, DC, someone said. Gen'ral Sibert. I remember that, b'cause that man was in charge of the whole shebang – all the chemical weapons work at Hancock and ever'where else, wherever that was. Well, he was there in Georgia, and that man was pissed. Lord, he was pissed. He was cussin' out Majors and Captains left and right, and probally the other Gen'ral when they went off on their own. They were pret' careful not to show each other up in front o' all the men, ya know.

"Now this is the part that I cain't tell y'all first hand, b'cause I was not there for it. But ya remember that I was more or less permanent assigned to clerkin' at Camp Hancock, and that was the way they done it then. So, there was actually a bunch of us that more or less was there all the time. An' we got to know each other and got to hangin' 'round when we wasn't supposed to be doin' some other thing. An' I will confess to ya, mister JT, we did gossip. I mean, one or t'other of us was almost sure to be where sump'n worth knowin' was happenin'. An' that was the case here.

"This other Corporal, Johnny Reed, his name was, he was assigned to the headquarters there at the camp, takin' notes and doin' letters and such for the top Gen'ral. An' he was a goooood lis'ner, if you know what I mean. Now Johnny heard and saw some things, an' he tole me 'bout 'em. Jes' me, I think, 'cause he knowed this was my unit they was talkin' about.

"I'll tell y'all those things, mister JT. But y'll have to take my word for 'em. Ya see, old Johnny, well not too long after this, well he got shipped off to France, an' he di'nt come back. Least not in one piece. So, he ain't aroun' to whattaya call it, verify what I'm fixin' to tell ya. You want me to go ahead anyways?"

"Abner," answered JT, "there is not a thing in the world I want to do more at this moment in time than to have you continue. Well, there's just one thing. I have got to pee something fierce. How about a five-minute break?"

"You got it. Privy's out back. We can have a nice CoCola when you get back."

The brass descended on Augusta, Georgia, like flies on a carcass. This was no great military disaster, to be sure, but it was an emergency situation nevertheless, and it demanded a high-level meeting to sort out the options. General Sibert was there, along with three or four others with stars on their shoulders. Of course, Major Branch Rickey was there. There were officers from the medical branch, experts from ordnance and chemical weapons units, and assorted others.

And, too, there was Baseball royalty in the house. Ban Johnson, president of the American League was there, as was his National League counterpart, former Congressman and Pennsylvania Governor John Tener. There was even a federal judge there down from Chicago, named Kenesaw Mountain Landis. Nobody quite knew why he was there, but Ban Johnson had been insistent on the point. Landis, he knew, was a friend of the game, by which he meant the Establishment of the game, and a smart, devious operator – all traits that might come in handy in the current situation. A couple of years earlier, he had been on the bench to hear a dispute in which a new league, the Federal League, was challenging the two existing major leagues in a way that could have put at risk their so-called "reserve clause" – some standard language in the player contracts they wrote that legally bound players to their teams so they couldn't just move from team to team whenever they liked, and as a result, held down their potential compensation. Landis had simply sat on his decision until the upstart league had time to fail. Perfect solution. If he could have looked forward a few years, Johnson would have seen that he and Landis would become bitter rivals in their respective quests to control the game. But that was the future, and this was the here and now.

The medical people went first. Major Barrett was commanding officer of the base hospital, but it was a Colonel nobody recognized who handled the briefing. Lieutenant Mathewson had suffered considerable exposure to a gas, almost surely a new, experimental variant of chlorine gas. His lungs were weakened, he was having difficulty breathing, and he was coughing up liquid that suggested he might have an infection. Still, they said, they were optimistic that he would recover, though probably not fully. War or no war, they reported, experience with these things was still limited, and that contributed to the uncertainties regarding both optimal approaches to treatment and the predictability of outcomes. Privates Chance and Stone had less exposure, and were already out of the hospital. Private Armstrong, who had had a much greater and longer exposure to the gas, had died within minutes of reaching the base hospital.

Ordnance went next. Once again, the local commander, Major Gaugler, was replaced as briefer by an unknown Colonel who had arrived in camp the day before. They were not sure what sort of foul-up had led to this incident. Customary practice was that, when new forms of ordnance were obtained to be examined, as was the case here, dummies or blanks were used exclusively, unless none were available. In this instance, the ordnance in question was new, but an ample supply had been captured and sent to the camp, and Private Armstrong had every reason to expect he could work freely to develop a system for dismantling the device. Yet, somewhere along the line, there was obviously a slip-up. Cannisters got switched around. It was impossible to tell just where for sure, or by whom.

An administrative officer followed, summarizing the personnel records of everyone in the unit, and everyone outside the unit known to have handled the device. He had found that Lieutenant Mathewson was an extraordinarily well-regarded officer, with no known enemies. The only unsettled item, the significance of which was unclear, was that there had been a confrontation within the Company some days before in which one of the celebrity members, Corporal Cobb, had verbally and physically assaulted a local orderly who was cleaning up his tent, and whom the Corporal accused of having been spying on him by riffling through his papers. Cobb was effectively restrained and talked down by other members of the unit. The incident was reported up the line per regulations, and Lieutenant Mathewson and Major Rickey had investigated and had admonished Corporal Cobb. This is possibly germane because other members of the unit have speculated that Cobb may have blamed Private Armstrong for having reported him to Lieutenant Mathewson. Cobb, as you may already be aware, has a reputation for physical altercations and ill humor. That said, we have no definitive proof of any kind at this time that Corporal Cobb was directly implicated in the death of Private Armstrong.

Then it was Sibert's turn, and it was clear to all that day why he wore those stars.

"Gentlemen, thank you for those summary remarks. You have done an excellent job of framing the issue before us. But let me restate what we know and what we suspect from a somewhat different perspective.

"We have in Ordnance Depot Company Number 44 an elite military unit comprised of volunteers who mostly happen to be highly prominent major league baseball players. Among them, for those who follow the sport but may not have reviewed the roster of the Company, are Corporal John Franklin Baker, better known as Home Run Baker, Private Max Carey, Private Frank Chance, Corporal Ty Cobb, Corporal Davy Jones, Private Ed Walsh, and Ordnance Sergeant Honus Wagner. I believe that Private Henry Jones, another member of the unit, also had some limited major league time. These men have agreed to serve their country in a dangerous undertaking, and they have all performed to a satisfactory, or in some cases an exemplary, standard. The unit is, or was until a few days ago, commanded by Lieutenant Christy Mathewson, another baseball great. He in turn reported to Major Branch Rickey, also from major league baseball, who is here with us today.

"From the perspective of the Army, this unit was put together by Major Rickey at my specific request, in order to show our young men that even these prominent athletes are able and willing to serve their country in any way needed, even in the Chemical Warfare Service. These are brave men all, and genuine patriots. We need to bear that in mind.

"I will defer to Mr. Johnson or others, if they so choose, to speak on behalf of Baseball. But as I see it, the major leagues have been under considerable pressure from the public, and in turn from the War Department, to encourage their players to take on a bigger role in fighting this war. So, from their perspective, the prominence of this unit and the dangerous task it has taken on is equally essential to them as it is to the government.

"Mr. Johnson, Mr. Tener, is there anything you'd care to add?"

Tener deferred to Johnson. "Just one thing, General. I am sure that everyone in this room is familiar at some level with the principal surviving victim in this incident, Lieutenant Mathewson. But what you may not appreciate is just how much admiration this man receives from his teammates and competitors alike, and from the fans of our game. Christy Mathewson has done more than any other man to establish baseball as a respectable, nay a highly valued, sporting activity in our society. He is an educated man, a Christian man who will not don a baseball uniform on the Lord's Day, a friend to all and an enemy to none. Even Corporal Cobb, whose name and reputation were mentioned earlier, is known to like and respect this man. He exemplifies the best in our game and the best in our nation. That this fate should have befallen this man in particular is a tragedy of the first order." And he sat back down.

"That is all true," resumed General Sibert. "And it is the very reason that we are meeting today. The question, as you all know, is this: What do we do about this terrible situation?"

There was a slight delay in resuming, as JT returned from the privy, happy, he thought, that he had gone there only for the stated purpose and not the alternative, only to find that Abner was out in front of the station pumping gas for a customer and checking his tires. But a moment later Abner was back, ready to pick up his tale in mid-telling, needing only to first wrap his hand around one iconically-shaped bottle of warm soda and to offer a second to JT, which he accepted. The two tops were popped using an eponymously labeled opener hanging on the door frame of the office.

"So I was tellin' ya 'bout what ol' Johnny tole me, all private like. He said that he was there takin' notes for the Gen'ral at this meetin' of officers, and they was a bunch of the local ones there. An' that Gen'ral, he was layin' down the law, sayin' how they all was gonna git in deep serious trouble if any of 'em ever be tellin' anybody 'bout what happened. An' he says sump'n about it bein' national security at stake 'cause this accident it happened with some captured German munitions, and how they don' want the Hun to know they have it, and also 'cause, as the accident shows, they ain't yet figured out how to deal with it. An' that jes' cain't get out or it'll hurt morale. So, jes' shut up 'bout the whole thing.

"An' I know that was true, so now we're back on me. I know it 'cause 'bout the very next day this bird colonel come over to the Company, an' ain't none of us ever seen him b'fore. An' he says gentlemen – tha's what he called us – gentlemen, I have here a paper for each of you to sign that says you take an oath on your life that you will never mention in any way or reveal any details about the incident that occurred in this unit earlier this week. And you will sign this paper. And you will keep your mouths shut tight. This is a matter of gravest national security, and the penalty for violating this oath is death. We are at war, and the government is not fooling around. Do I make myself clear?" Abner was doing his best impression of a bird colonel in control.

"An' we all go, Sir Yes Sir! Jes' like we trained to do. An' we all signed that paper. An' wouldn't ya know it, but maybe two or three days later a stack o' orders come down, and a bunch o' them boys, they tole they now all trained up and they shippin' out for France. And by god, off they went. Or some was tole they ain't trained enough, and off they go to some other camp somewhere. An' I think they sent a bunch o' them ballplayers on home.

"'Course, I stayed behind to clerk for the next bunch o' fellas that come in. But before that happened, that same bird colonel, he pulled me aside, and he said, Corporal, as the Company clerk, I order you to go back into the daily records of Company Number 44 and re-do them to show that Private Armstrong transferred out of the unit three days before this incident occurred. That would be June 3. And Lieutenant Mathewson returned to the unit today. June 9. Fill out the forms all new, and sign them just as you normally would. Is that clear, Corporal?

"An' all I says was Sir Yes Sir! An' that's what I done."

"Gentlemen." The word was spoken quietly by the unassuming man in the gray suit who had been sitting alone in a rear corner of the room. No one seemed to know him, except perhaps General Sibert, and no one had much noticed him, either. He walked slowly to the front of the room.

"My name is George Creel. I am the Chairman of the Committee on Public Information, and I join you today as the representative of the President of the United States. President Wilson has taken a personal interest in this matter."

This got their attention, one and all.

"I agree with General Sibert. This is a serious threat to public support for the war effort, it is irreversible, and it challenges us to develop a strategy for managing the situation. That is my area of expertise, and it is the reason the President has dispatched me here.

"There is an essential truth to this situation. Lieutenant Mathewson has been grievously injured in an accidental discharge of poison gas from German ordnance. There is no way around that truth, nor any reason to circumvent it. To the contrary, we must find a way to use it to the advantage of our country and all the lesser interests represented in this room." At that last, he glanced toward Judge Landis and the baseball executives present.

"Here is what we are going to do. First, we are going to eliminate any ambiguity about the cause of this accident. I know, for example, there has been speculation locally that Corporal Cobb may have had some role in creating the circumstances that led to the accident. I am telling you definitively that he did not. That determination comes directly from the President. Any such question or speculation is to cease from this moment. Is that clear?" Nods all around.

"Second, as it turns out, Private Armstrong actually transferred out of Ordnance Depot Company Number 44 three days before this incident even occurred. He was not present, and thus could not have been involved in any way, something he is, unfortunately, in no position to dispute. General, can I assume you can make that happen?" Another nod.

"Third, effective immediately, Lieutenant Mathewson will be promoted to Captain. In order to avoid any suspicion, Corporal Cobb will also be advanced to the rank of Captain. The official rationale for his rapid advancement, if one is required, will be his courage in running toward the scene of a training accident and rescuing a fellow soldier whose identity was not recorded. General, again I expect you to handle that. Given his prominence, I doubt anyone will really question it.

"Fourth, this Company is to be broken up immediately. Send some of the men home. Send some of them to other units to continue their training.

177

And send some elements to their theater assignments in France. We will arrange proper care for Captain Mathewson, who will be among those assigned to the war zone. In a few weeks, he will travel incognito in a special area of a troop ship that will assure his comfort insofar as possible. It is my understanding that General Sibert and Major Rickey have spoken personally with Captain Mathewson, and that he has agreed to this procedure. Cobb should go as well. The two are friends, and that may be useful at some point. Cobb knows what's what; I'm sure he'll do and say whatever we ask.

"Fifth, this entire base will be sanitized. Any officer or enlisted man who has any knowledge of this matter whatsoever will be required, upon penalty of death, to sign a national security oath agreeing never to disclose any information of any kind related to it. The first to sign will be all members of Ordnance Depot Company Number 44, which should be accomplished by the end of today since many of them will be shipping out shortly afterward.

"Sixth, it has come to my attention that one of the local newspapers, tipped to the presence of these athletes on the base, has planned a special issue featuring Camp Hancock to be published later this week. That was excellent work by Major Brandt here, who has been in charge of public information. But it is now highly problematic. Major, I will expect your team to redirect the emphasis of that publication, perhaps even publicize an event such as a baseball game that will supplant any idea that such prominent athletes have been assigned here. My advice would be that, rather than deny or even discuss the original expectation, you simply bury that newspaper under so much information they will forget the matter on their own. I have considerable personal experience in providing, shall we say, 'guidance' to the press, and I will take the lead on that. But I would ask that you arrange for the baseball contest. Admiral George up in Charleston is expecting your call, and I think you'll find him cooperative. A good interservice contest should be just the distraction we require.

"Seventh, at the outset of the voyage to France, Captain Mathewson will contract a case of the influenza that will be raging aboard ship. That will require that he travel in isolation, which will allow both for his comfort and for additional days of improvement. He will recover from the flu, but this illness will account for any lingering effects of the training incident on his breathing and stamina. Captain Mathewson, however, is star-crossed, because as soon as he is able to move freely on his own, he will become the victim of an accidental discharge of poison gas in a combat training setting in France. That, of course, will be a ruse – one that will allow us to transfer him back to the United States as a true hero demonstrating bravery in the cause of freedom. This outcome will comport with the Army's initial objectives in establishing this elite unit, and as well, I should think, with the interest of professional baseball.

"As was noted earlier, Captain Mathewson is a most honorable man. I am given to believe that he understands the need for these measures, and that they are consistent with his patriotic and other personal reasons for having volunteered to serve his country. Gentlemen, in following this course, he is a true patriot and will be worthy of any accolades that he may receive upon his return from France. In fact, we will make sure that happens. Lastly in this regard, and I am sure most difficult for him, he has agreed that his wife should not be informed of his condition at this time, but only after his exposure to the gas 'actually' occurs, which is to say, once he is in France. The resultant impact upon his health in the long-term will be the same in any event, and as he himself noted, this will give her far less opportunity to worry.

"Lastly, Mr. Johnson, Mr. Tener. It may be the case that certain official records of baseball games or performances beginning with the month of June may need to be amended to include the participation of individuals who might otherwise have been presumed to be elsewhere, or other reasons identified for their absences. I trust you will find that within your powers to achieve.

"I do know that the events of your sport are covered in the press. If it is useful to add the names of any of these players – or managers, as in Mathewson's case – to already published accounts of games in early June, so that it is clear they were participating in the normal manner, please contact me at once. I see no need to be concerned about the thousands of copies of such papers that may already have been replaced as birdcage liners; no one will remember them. But for those copies in archives and libraries, where they are on permanent display, we may need to substitute certain pages with necessary corrections. I have all the authorities required to accomplish that.

"As for the newspapers more generally, I can assure you that no mention of either the events that have brought us to this pass nor any steps we might take to address them will see the light of day. This I guarantee.

"Those are the President's wishes in this matter, and they are to be carried out to the letter. To accomplish those wishes will be a complex undertaking, but I have confidence in the ability of those in this room to carry that out successfully. And if I may say it, though the tasks may be complex, the result in the near term is simple.

"And gentlemen, remember. For the good of the Nation, for the good of the Army, and, of course, for the good of Baseball, *this never happened.*"

Mr. Jason Drumm
Drumm Farms
DeKalb Falls, NY

Dear Mr. Drumm:

I am Professor of English and Linguistics at Columbia University in New York City. I believe Adam Wallace has told you to expect this letter. Please forgive me for not employing university letterhead, but since this is a response to Adam's private and unofficial request, I thought that inappropriate.

I have now had an opportunity to examine the journal identified on the first page as belonging to Jocko Drumm, whom I understand to be your grandfather. According to Adam, you and he believe that the journal pertains in some way to items in a suitcase that you discovered recently in a barn on your farm. He did not specify what those contents were, nor do I require that information.

I understand that your grandfather was something of an itinerant traveler during at least some years of the Great Depression. Not only does that fact comport with the contents of the journal as I have interpreted them, but it is central to the interpretation itself.

During the Depression there were thousands of hoboes roaming the land on foot, as hitchhikers, or by rail. They were sufficient in number to have developed a subculture of sorts, complete with its own language and symbols. The former was employed as a sort of slang or verbal shorthand known primarily to those in their ranks, and largely unknown to others. The latter, the symbols, were typically chalked or carved into fenceposts, trees, gates, or other similar places, and conveyed messages to those who followed (and knew how to read them) about such things as safety, the availability of handouts, and the types of people living nearby.

Your grandfather's journal is written in a combination of the language and symbolic markings of this hobo subculture. On the attached pages, I will provide the original text from the journal and a translation of each key term or symbol. At the conclusion, I will provide you with a summary narrative that represents my interpretation of the content of the journal.

I hope this proves to be of assistance.

Sincerely,

Maria Faye Hoffbert
Professor

ROADWISES
NAPPERRI
G 2/10
CHASEFORT
HEVARNISHN
AILEDSTRE
AMLININGB
LINDBAGG
AGETOURIS
TMISSEDTH
ESKIPPERG
RABDUCKEt
FROMSLEEP
ER
RIDINGTHE
CUSHIONSSI
TBYBOSTON

Roadwise	Knew how to survive
Snapper Rig	Second-hand clothes
2/10	Thieves in the area
SYM	Man with a gun
SYM	Police on the lookout
SYM	Get out fast
Chase for the Varnish	Run to catch passenger train
Nailed	Successfully hopped train
Streamlining	Traveling with no pack or gear
Blind Bag Tourist	Riding as if with a ticket
Missed the Skipper	Avoided the Conductor
Grab Ducket from Sleeper	Took ticket from person asleep
SYM	Gentleman
Riding the Cushions	Riding in a passenger train
Sit By Boston Bum	Sit by a highbrow poseur

BUMWILLET TWHITECOL LARWITHCA NDYJOBCAL IFORNIABL ANKETSGLA DRAGSSTO GIESBIGW HIFFLE (eye) WHITECOLL ARCAUGHT THEWESTBO UNDJACKRO LLEDPOKE ooo TOADSKINS/ //// LE	Willett	Apparent name, no translation
	White Collar	Businessman
	With Candy Job	With a pleasant job
	California Blankets	Newspapers
	Glad Rags	Nice clothes
	Stogies	Cigars
	Big Whiffle	Passed the time (long)
	SYM	Sleeping
	White Collar	Businessman
	Caught the Westbound	Passed away
	Jack Rolled	Took his money
	Poke	Wallet
	SYM	Wealthy man
	SYM	Lots of money
	Toadskins/////	Paper money (slashes indicate large amount)
	SYM	Worth robbing

183

Left 4 Nickel Notes	Left 4 $5 bills
Took Keister	Took the suitcase
SYM	Afraid
Captain	Conductor
SYM	Left quickly
Ditched	Jumped off
Drifting Train	When train was slowing
SYM	Safe camp
Check Roll	Checked the wad of money
And Keister	And suitcase
Glad Rags	Nice clothes
Sheets	Papers
Stake	Money
In kick	In trouser pocket
Padding the hoof	Walking
SYM	Good road to follow
Yonder Walk	Slipped out of one place, showed up in another

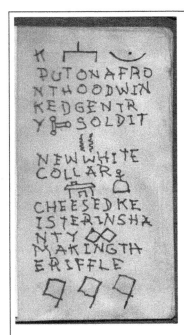

	SYM	Here is the place
	SYM	Cops Inactive
	Put on a Front	Put on all new clothes
	Hoodwinked	Deceived
	Gentry	Social elite
	SYM	Easy mark
	Sold It	Made someone believe
	SYM	Sky's the limit/ anything goes
	New White Collar	New businessman
	SYM	Unguarded house
	SYM	Woman
	Cheesed	Hid something
	Keister	Suitcase
	In Shanty	In a ramshackle or hastily built building
	SYM	Keep quiet
	Making the Riffle	Succeeding
	SYM (Repeats)	Keep your mouth shut

SUMMARY: It is my considered opinion that the narrative that unifies these symbols runs more or less as follows:

Jocko Drumm knew how to survive on the road. He wore second-hand clothes, suggesting he was not prosperous. Mr. Drumm stole some unspecified object, and was being chased by a man with a gun. The police were on the lookout as well, and he had to get out of town quickly. He hopped aboard a moving passenger train, but had no kit with him. He was not riding outside the train as a hobo would, but inside as if he were a paying passenger. He avoided the conductor and stole the ticket of a sleeping passenger, a gentleman. He then sat down by another gentleman, one who looked highbrow. That gentleman may have been named Willett.

He was a businessman with a nice job, and either worked for or was reading newspapers. He was well-dressed, and smoked cigars, or alternatively shared a cigar with Mr. Drumm. They talked a long time. The man, and/or Mr. Drumm, fell asleep. It then appears that the businessman died. No reason is offered, nor is there any indication of foul play. At that point, Mr. Drumm took the money from his wallet. He was a wealthy man and there was a great deal of paper money. The robbery was worthwhile, or profitable. Mr. Drumm left twenty dollars in the man's wallet, then took his suitcase. He was afraid the conductor would come, so he left quickly.

When the train slowed, he jumped off and found a safe place to camp. He counted the money and checked the suitcase, in which he found nice clothes and some papers. He put the money in his trouser pocket and started walking. He found a good road, and was able to travel a considerable distance in a short time.

He came to a place he thought was safe, one where the police would not be looking for him. He dressed in the nice clothes from the suitcase and fooled one or more prominent locals. They were easy marks, and he made them believe he was the person he now looked like. It worked very well, and he saw unlimited opportunity. He became a businessman himself, found a safe place to live, and found a woman. He hid the suitcase in an old building and kept quiet about it. He became a success.

The journal ends with a strong admonition (indicated by larger and repeated use of the relevant symbol) to keep your mouth shut.

I acknowledge that this summary is broadly interpretive, and that at places the text and symbols in the journal could yield alternative meanings. In my best judgment, however, the actual meaning of the journal content would not vary greatly from the indicated narrative.

This leaves one issue unresolved. On the first interior page of the journal, just below the signature of Jocko Drumm, are found a series of dots or points. These were not typical of the hobo codes of the 1930s, so their interpretation must come from elsewhere.

I first considered that these dots might serve some purely decorative function for the first page, or in the alternative, that they were nothing more than doodles. It is impossible to reject that explanation outright at this distance in time and without consulting the author or having other exemplars of his writings for comparison.

Next, I considered whether they might be a form of Braille writing. However, I did not isolate any specific combinations of dots that seemed to convey a relevant message. The dots were not raised, but they did produce impressions on the reverse that might have been detected by a skilled reader. If there was any evidence that Mr. Drumm had a friend or a family member who was not sighted, suggesting that he might have had some occasion to learn Braille writing, it might be worth revisiting this possibility.

Finally, I considered the possibility that these dots were some sort of numeric code. Specifically, if one rotates the book 90 degrees in a clockwise manner, it is possible to see here the following numbers: 1, 9,

> 3, 6. Given the provenance of the book and the use of hobo lingo and symbols, the simplest answer might be the best. That would suggest that this journal was written in 1936.
>
> I have no idea how well any of this fits the facts that are known to you. But I do hope it can be useful to you.
>
> MFH

JT was literally... what's that odd word he'd heard someone use just recently... gobsmacked. He had more story than he could ever have dreamed of. As he had left Abner last evening, he did everything he could think of to express his appreciation. He could not pay for the story. *The Sporting News*, after all, was not *The Journal*. The newspaper had a firm policy not to pay for stories. Or where would it stop, he thought. But he now had Abner's address, and would make sure that something nice arrived there in the near future.

He also had his work cut out for him. Obviously, he would need to go back and have a long conversation with Jane Mathewson. Now that Abner had told JT his tale, she might be willing to add some details from her end. But he also had some new leads to follow. It's always best if you can find more than one source for a story with meat on it, and he would dearly like to cut the risk to his own reputation by finding as much corroboration as he could for what Abner had relayed. Abner had been willing to part with one of his purloined unit rosters and the daily record, and that was an excellent start. He had also given JT some leads to track down the two other (surviving) members of Ordnance Depot Company Number 44, Privates Stone and Simpson. He was not sure what they knew, let alone whether they would do what he had done – break their solemn oath. After all, unlike Abner, they had not read Cobb's obsequious comments to the Georgia papers back in 1925. (Maybe, JT thought, he could track down some clips. Grantland Rice had been at the Atlanta paper sometime back then, and might have something. But no, he thought, I'd have to tell him why I was asking, and next thing you know he'd break the story himself in his *New York Tribune* column or even, god forbid, in the Paramount newsreels. No, best to keep this to myself until I can break it.)

He had an actual address from Abner for Stone, some little town up in Indiana. Simpson would be harder - somewhere in New England was the best Abner could do. So, Stone was the obvious next - no, don't even think it - stepping stone. You need some rest!

But not quite yet. JT had a plan. Head up toward Chicago and over to Indiana and talk to Stone. See if he by chance has a way to find Simpson. He'd be next, and then Jane. At that point, he'd have the story nailed down. Then he would backtrack to St. Louis and see what, if anything, Branch Rickey would tell him. Rickey was now the President of the Cardinals club, and they had talked some over the years about the state of the game. There was a chance. Then, at the very end, he'd have to go back down to Augusta and talk with the man himself. That would not be a pleasant conversation. He might need a witness, or perhaps a bodyguard.

The one thing he was sure of was that he was done writing columns on the train. He needed to bang out one new column - a new lead-in piece using some of this new information - and reorder things a bit while he was waiting in the station, but that was it. Not only was it difficult physically to write on the trains, with all the noise and rocking and distractions. Normally he could just bang them out regardless. But not now. He was tired. Absolutely exhausted really. And he still had work to do on the road. After Jane, he would go home, sleep for three or four days, have some good meals at his favorite restaurants in the City, and then sit down, clear his head, figure out what he had and what he wanted to say about it. Then, and only then, would he wrap up this series.

This was some story he'd stumbled on. Maybe it would be his last one. He was certainly at an age where he could slow down and take it easy. Maybe go to some ballgames just for the pure enjoyment of it. No deadlines. He'd never really thought much about that before, but now, after breaking the story of a lifetime? Now might be the time. And what a way to go out.

"Jesus Christ, Adam! He stole it! The old man stole the damn suitcase from some dead guy. Took all his money, too! And then he stashed it away in that old barn because he knew he couldn't risk selling it. Can you believe it?"

"Well, he must have been a hell of a guy, your old grandfather," Adam replied, smirking a bit on his end of the line. "But everything she said fits, doesn't it?"

"Yeah, it does. But you know what else? I mean, think it through. Forget about the suitcase and the papers and all that. I think what this means is that back in the day, and we are talking eighty some years ago, Jocko Drumm, my dear grandpa, bought this farm where I live with the money he took off a dead body. I mean, holy shit. What am I supposed to think about that? What am I supposed to do with that information?"

"Honestly? I don't think there's much you can do, and I don't think you should worry about it. There is no reason to think he killed this man. In fact, we know from his Wiki bio that JT Willett died of natural causes on that train. The worst your grandfather did was steal some money and property.

"Now granted that's a bad thing, it has been eighty years, as you said, and the statute of limitations has long-since run out. Possession is nine-tenths of the law, or whatever that old saw says. But more to the point, you are jumping to conclusions. You don't really know if the place he talks in his journal about settling down was DeKalb Falls, though I'll grant you it would surely seem to be. And you don't know for a fact that he bought that farm with the proceeds of the robbery. In fact, you don't even know for sure there was a robbery. What you have is a story told in code. Maybe he just liked to tell tall tales – isn't that what you told me? – and this is just one more, elaborate though it may be.

"But I'm glad you called, because I have another piece of news for you, only it's one I need to deliver face-to-face. Are you going to be around up there for the next few days?"

"Where else would I be? I'm busy breaking in a new farm hand, name of Rooster, if you can believe it. And damned if it's not right there on his Social Security Card. I mean, what kind of mother names her son Rooster? Anyway, name fits the job and he seems to be an okay guy, so yeah, I'm here. Come on up when you can."

JT was an experienced rail rider, but even he could find the separate and overlapping schedules of the multiplicity of railways and rail alliances thoroughly confusing. Over the years, though, he'd made a practice of getting to know some of the passenger agents at the major hubs and stations. If he was near a telephone, he could often reach out and get some guidance.

He passed through Chicago frequently, so it was natural that one of his contacts was R.C. Caldwell, the Division Passenger Agent for the Pennsylvania road. JT remembered passing a phone booth on his walks out to Abner's place, and headed directly for it, several dollars' worth of quarters in hand. He lifted the receiver, dialed zero, and soon heard the familiar voice on the other end.

"Operator. How may I help you?"

"Long distance, please."

Three rings, and then, "Long Distance Operator. How may I help you?"

"I want to call Chicago, Illinois, CENtral 7200. Person-to-person for Mr. R.C. Caldwell. My name is JT Willett."

"And the number you're calling from?"

JT looked at the center of the dial. "That would be DIXie 5731. It's a pay phone."

"Thank you. I'll put that call through and call you back at this number. The lines appear to be fairly open at the moment, so it shouldn't be more than six or seven minutes."

"Thank you, Operator. I'll be here waiting."

It was closer to ten minutes, but the phone did ring.

"This is the Long Distance Operator. I have Mr. R.C. Caldwell on the line for you. Please deposit $3.75 for the first three minutes." JT dropped fifteen quarters into the appropriate slot atop the phone, each followed by a subtle "ding."

"I'll connect you now."

"Thank you, Operator."

A switching sound, followed by the voice of Mr. Caldwell. "Hello? JT, is that you?"

R.C. was always a friendly fellow, even though he was responsible for all of the passenger agents in Chicago and the surrounding area. JT explained his situation and asked which might be the best way to get up to Chicago. Caldwell took just a moment to confirm what he was about to suggest with a glance at the master timetable. What he told JT was a little surprising.

"Okay, JT, what you want to do is take that Southern line you're on there in Waycross, but don't go back up to Atlanta. And don't come all the way up here to Chicago. Your better bet is to go the other way, down to Jacksonville. We've got a through train, the *South Wind*, that leaves Jacksonville for Chicago right around noon tomorrow. It runs up through Birmingham, not Atlanta, and it makes a stop in Indianapolis at around noon the next day. Usually runs within an hour or two. And I'm thinking that Indianapolis will get you a lot closer to that little town you're looking for than coming all the way up here will do. The whole train is reserved seat coach, but there's plenty of room tomorrow. I can book you right now, and I'll call down to the agent in Jacksonville to make sure there's not a problem."

"If that's the best, let's do it. Thank you, R.C. Next time I'm through town I'll drop you off some tickets. Was it Cubs or Sox?"

"Cubs for sure. I always like a winner. And thanks."

Just before he hung up, JT heard the familiar voice of the Operator. "Please deposit $2.00 for an additional three minutes."

JT simply hung up the phone.

Once again JT's luck held. The twice-a-week train from Atlanta to Jacksonville was due to pass through Waycross just about the time he was ready to catch it. The run down to the coast was uneventful, but slow. Southern Railway. In Jacksonville he found himself with time to kill before he switched over to his old favorite, the Pennsylvania. He fell asleep on a bench in the depot, something he did not usually do. Luckily, he woke up with a half hour to spare. Florida weather must have been good, because the *South Wind* that had departed Miami at around 5:30 that morning rolled in right on time. JT settled in for the nearly two day ride up to Indianapolis.

Adam made it up to the farm a couple of days later. He carried the clipping with him. When he turned down the lane to the house, though, he was greeted not by Jason, but by a stranger with a full head of red hair. Suddenly, it made sense.

"You must be Rooster," he said, offering his hand. "I'm Adam. Jason is expecting me."

"Yep, he told me you might be coming by this afternoon. Pleased t' meet ya."

"Where is Jason? Is he around?"

"He had to run into town for supplies. Should be back any time now." The words were timely, if not prophetic, for just then they could see Jason's truck turn toward the house.

"Hey, guys," he said, climbing down from the cab. "Rooster, could you go ahead and unload all that stuff while I catch up with old Adam here?"

"Sure thing."

"Thanks." Then turning to the new arrival, "So what's this big deal that seems to have you in a tizzy, enough that you'd make the drive all the way up here again?"

"I'm not really sure how to start. Remember a couple of days ago, when we talked, you were so shocked to learn that your granddad had apparently stolen that old suitcase?"

"Remember? Are you kidding? And it wasn't only the suitcase. I mean, look around you. And besides, I still can't find the damn thing. And I am sure as I can be that Melvin didn't run off with it."

"Yeah, well, let's stick with the suitcase. He stole it, okay? And you can't find it. I get that. But it's not your problem anymore."

"Beg pardon?"

"It's not your problem anymore. It's been sold."

"Say what?"

"It's been sold. In an auction. And somebody made a lot of money. Look at this." And Adam showed Jason the newspaper clipping that had brought him up here.

Auction of Baseball Memorabilia Sets New Record

By Aubrey Winston III

Special to *The Times*

Until yesterday, the highest price ever paid for an item of baseball memorabilia was $4.4 million for a New York Yankees jersey said to have been worn by Babe Ruth in 1920, his first season with the team. That record was shattered yesterday in a sale at Marbury House auctioneers, where a collection highlighted by a personal 1925 letter from Ty Cobb to Jane Mathewson, widow of pitching great Christy Mathewson, expressing his condolences upon his friend's death, fetched $7.8 million.

The collection also included a letter from Branch Rickey to Mathewson asking him to assist in forming an Army unit for World War I comprised of prominent baseball players. Mathewson, it may be recalled, was exposed to mustard gas while serving in Flanders during the war, which was widely believed to have contributed to his death from tuberculosis a few years later. Also included were artifacts from a prominent early sportswriter, JT Willett, and some other documents.

Bidding opened at $3.7 million, and the Ruth jersey record was surpassed in less than a minute of spirited competition. The winning bid was submitted anonymously, but is widely believed to have been entered by a well-known baseball enthusiast. The auction house declined to confirm the bidder's identity, and *The Times* has so far been unable to establish that independently. Calls to the suspected bidder have not been returned.

Christy Mathewson pitched for the New York Giants in the early years of the last century, and has been regarded as the best pitcher in the history of baseball. The value of the collection is presumed to lie primarily in the two letters, which bookend Mathewson's military service.

Mathewson, Cobb and Rickey are all members of the Baseball Hall of Fame.

Jason took a moment to read the article, and looked up at Adam. He could think of nothing to say. Adam, having had the same reaction himself just a couple of days earlier, let the silence linger for a moment, then said, "I think there's very little doubt about what it is those guys were auctioning off. The question is how they got it in the first place."

"Don't they have to be very careful about things like that? Trace the provenance, or conduct due diligence, or whatever the lawyers call it?"

"You'd think so. Tell you what. Let's head into town and jump on the girls' computer and see if there's anything else we can find out. And then we can get in touch with the auction place. If they sold it, they'll know who bought it. And if it wasn't theirs to sell, either you're going to get a lot of money from somebody, or you'll get your suitcase back."

"Adam, I only see three problems with that.

"First, I'm not sure I have a claim to ownership. What I have is proof of a sort that my grandfather stole the suitcase and hid it away for what ended up being about eighty years. Those guys might just laugh in my face.

"Second, if I were going to pursue this with the auction place and somehow I could be confident that, what with the passage of time and all, I actually had some sort of a claim, the first thing I'd probably have to do is file a police report about the stolen property. I don't know where I'd start. Think about it. "The Police" up here means two county constables, Pete and Rich. They're fine fellows and nice guys and all, and they know how to write a ticket for speeding. But they are not the NYPD. They might not even know how to write up a report of something like this.

"There was this old suitcase my grandfather stole from a dead guy on a train in 1936. I found it a couple of months ago. It was full of old papers. And somebody stole it. And no, I don't have a picture or any other real proof, just my best friend Adam who saw it at my house.

"Pretty weak.

"Then there's the third problem. And now I'm beginning to understand it a little differently. See, we can't use the computer at the girls' store because the store is closed and locked up. Has been for about three days now. And nobody's home across the way, either."

"Oh shit!" was about the best Adam could do.

"Crows Nest. Can you tell me how to get to Crows Nest, Indiana?" It was the fourth time he'd asked that question of a passerby at Union Station in Indianapolis, and the fourth time he'd seen that same, quizzical, are-you-crazy expression.

It was one thing, thought JT, to have trouble finding a person in a town. Only so many people were likely to know the person, and if they weren't in the telephone directory, you needed some luck to find one of those people to help you out. But this was a town. A whole damn town. And Indiana wasn't Texas, for god's sake. How did they manage to lose a whole town?

On the fifth try, his luck turned. "Crows Nest? Oh, sure. You've probably been having trouble finding anybody who's heard of the place, am I right?"

JT nodded.

"Reason for that is it's a new place. Maybe six, seven miles north of where we're standing. Used to be all old farms up that way, but about ten years ago some company came in and paved a couple of roads, built a bunch of houses. Can't be more'n a hundred or so people living up there.

"If you were going to walk it, and you probably could, you'd just go out this exit here, which'll put you on South Illinois Street. Take a right and just keep walkin'. Like I say, it's maybe five, six miles or so. About half a dozen blocks after you cross Westfield, you're going to come to Kessler Boulevard. Big street, can't miss it. Go to your left across the river and you're basically there. I'm sure somebody who knows the place can get you to wherever you're going."

"Out that door. Turn right. Walk a long way. Left on Kessler and over the river. Even I can remember that! You've been really helpful. Thank you." And off he went.

"Marbury House Auctioneers. How may I direct your call?"

Jason had decided to give it a try. Nothing ventured, and all that.

"I'd like to get some information about an item that was sold recently at auction."

"I'll connect you with the Sales Department. One moment."

"Sales, Julie Katznelson. How can I help you?"

"Good morning. I saw the article in the paper and I'd like to get some information about the buyer and seller of the baseball memorabilia that you sold a few days ago."

"You and every other baseball nut in America. I'm sorry, but we don't give out that kind of information."

"I'm afraid you don't understand. My name is Jason Drumm, and I believe that I am, or was, the rightful owner of those items you sold."

After a pause, "I see. Would you mind holding a moment? I'm going to see if I can connect you with Mr. Marchant, our Director of Acquisitions."

Jason held for about three minutes worth of insipid classical music, which he found tedious. Then...

"This is Frederick Marchant. How may I help you?"

"Mr. Marchant, my name is Jason Drumm. I saw in the newspaper that you recently sold a collection of baseball memorabilia for a rather nice price. I'm calling because I believe that what you sold is actually my property, and that you had no right to sell it."

"Mr. Drumm. I know that that sale attracted a great deal of attention. We have been fielding calls, and more than one claim just like yours, all week. The only thing I will tell you is that, before Marbury House sells any high-value item, we do thorough due diligence, which includes convincing ourselves that the seller is the rightful owner. And I can assure you that we did precisely that in this instance."

"Sir, these items were stolen from my house two months ago."

"Do you have a police report to that effect? Did you report the theft?"

"No, I did not file a police report. Honestly, I had no idea that those papers had any value. But I can tell you in detail exactly what was in the collection. There was an old typewriter...."

"Let me stop you right there, sir. As perhaps will not surprise you, we published a complete list of items in the collection in our auction bulletin and on our website. So, the fact that you can recite the list to me is of no probative value whatsoever.

"Do you have a clear statement of ownership from an established authority?"

197

By then, it was clear to Jason just where this conversation was heading. "No, no I do not. What I have...."

"Sir, let me just cut in here. You have no proof of your claim, and we have complete assurance that our seller had the right to offer the property in question. If you think you are being mistreated, sir, then I suggest that you seek legal counsel. For my part, and in behalf of Marbury House, I cannot help you. Good day to you."

The line went dead.

A woman who appeared to be in her forties opened the door and peered out.

"Good afternoon, ma'am. My name is JT Willett. I am with a newspaper called *The Sporting News*. I'm looking for a Mr. Herbert Stone. Do I have the right house?"

"I'm sorry mister, but we aren't buying any newspapers these days. Hard enough to put food on the table without that."

"No, ma'am. I'm not selling newspapers. I actually write for the paper. I'd like to interview Mr. Stone for a story I'm working on. Does he live here?"

"You promise me you're not a bill collector? 'Cause if you're lying to me, you should know we have a dog. Mean dog." JT could actually hear the dog growling somewhere inside the house.

"I promise you. Please tell him that I'm a writer, and that Abner suggested that I talk with him."

"Who's Abner?"

"He'll understand. If you'd just please...."

"Hey! Herbie! There's some guy at the door wants to talk to you. Says somebody named Abner sent him."

There was a shuffling down the hall, and the sound of the dog being closed up behind a door. Unhappily. Then a man JT assumed to be Herbert Stone appeared in the doorway.

"I'm Herb Stone. Who the hell are you?"

"Mr. Stone. I'm sorry to disturb you. My name is JT Willett, and I'm a writer for *The Sporting News*. I'm working on a story about the players who have just recently been elected to the new Baseball Hall of Fame. Maybe you've heard about that. I was just down in Georgia - Waycross to be exact - and I had a chance to talk with Abner Barnum down there. I gather that you and he were in the same unit during training down at Camp Hancock during the Great War. And according to Abner, that unit was mostly filled with a bunch of professional baseball players."

"I've never heard none of this," chirped the woman at the door, whom JT took to be Stone's wife or companion.

Stone stood up a little straighter and puffed out his chest. "That's true. There was a bunch of them fellows in the unit. In Georgia, and then a bunch of us shipped off to France pretty quick after that."

"Well, I don't know if you've been following this, but three of those fellows you were with down there, and I guess *over* there as well, are going to be among the five very first players to be in the Hall of Fame. Honus Wagner, for one. You might have known him as John. Ty Cobb, for another. And then, I think, the officer in charge of the unit was Christy Mathewson, and he'll be inducted as well." JT watched carefully for any reaction as he went down the list, but there were no tells in Stone's face or demeanor.

"You're right. I did know all those boys. Hall of Fame, huh? Three of them from that little group? I kind of had the idea they were special, just the way the Army was treating them back then. But I had no idea they were that good. Never was much of a baseball fan, you know."

"There's a lot of people who'd tell you those three were the best baseball players of all time. Well, plus Babe Ruth, of course."

"Well, none of the guys I knew in those days ever had no candy bar named after them." And he smiled slightly. JT began to take heart that he might be able to engage this man in conversation after all.

"Why don't you come on in here and take a load off? Betty, fetch us some iced tea, would you, dear? How *is* old Abner? Haven't thought of him in a couple of years or more."

"He's fine. I mean, he's having a hard time, what with the Depression and all, just like everybody else. But he's managed to keep the service station going, and he does like his CoCola."

"Yeah, real Georgia boy.... We just have iced tea. I hope...."

199

"Believe me, iced tea will be perfect." And as if on cue, Betty returned with three glasses and settled herself in for a good listen.

"I would say," Jason began, recounting his Marbury House conversation to Adam, "that they were not highly receptive to my call. Did everything but accuse me of trying to con them. They just seemed incredibly sure of themselves, that they had the right owner and that was that."

"Either that or they have lawyers telling them that in situations like this, they need to stonewall, if only to see if somebody has the gumption and the wherewithal to sue them. Times we live in, I guess."

"Do you suppose," Jason again, "that it really was Elaine and Jenna who stole the suitcase? I've just assumed they went off someplace on a vacation and just forgot to say something beforehand. But they've always been pretty good about that, just so no one worries. Plus, they just went on a trip down to New York City a few weeks a...go.... Damn!"

"I'm no detective, Jase, but wow. Two months ago, the suitcase disappears from your unlocked house. Then your cousins, who would have known about the suitcase because, like fools, we told them about it, they take a trip to New York. Which happens to be where Marbury House is based. Then there's this auction that brings in millions, and next thing you know, the shop is closed up and they're nowhere to be found. Nothing incriminating about that."

"Right. But would they really know anything about the stuff in the case? How would they figure that out?"

Things were quiet for a moment.

"We told them that, too," Adam offered. "We didn't even think twice about it, but we did all of that research on their computer at the store. I bet they back-tracked all of our searches."

"Family!"

"But there's one thing they don't know anything about," Adam continued. "The journal. Jocko's journal. Unless you told them about it, that was something we didn't even find until right before we set everything aside, and all the work on figuring out what it said was done down in the

City, and not by us. In fact, that was all done *after* they must have arranged for the auction.

"And if it was them, that might also explain how they got away with it. I mean, this was just an old barn find of stuff nobody was looking for. Probably all they had to do was prove they lived on a farm with an old barn that's been in the family for the right number of years to match up with the contents. Maybe a will to show they had inherited the farm."

"What you're saying is, they had exactly the same paper trail to establish provenance as I did. It's like the perfect crime!"

"Except for one thing. They didn't have - didn't even know about - the journal. And we still have that. We might not have any way of getting the collection back, what with it having been stolen property in the first place and all. But if we went to the police with the journal and the Professor's analysis, I bet we could get them into a shit pile of trouble. At least they wouldn't profit from that they did."

Jason thought a moment, then spoke.

"No. Look, first, there are all the problems we've just been talking about as far as claiming ownership and all that. Then, there's the whole thing with the auction house. I mean, that place is all attitude. They ought to want to be on our side, but from their point of view, I guess, all of the incentives are to try to get me to back down.

"But the real thing is this. I've been really lucky in life. My folks left me this farm, and it's a really good, productive one. Yes, we try to save on expenses here and there, but that's just farming. I'm actually doing pretty well. Of the two farms, back when Jocko split them up, it turned out this was by far the better land. Then, when the girls couldn't make a go of the other parcel, I bought them out, which maybe they took as arrogance, who can say. And then I let them stay at the house rent free. To me, that was just being nice, but maybe, again, they saw it differently.

"Bottom line is, they've had it much tougher than I have. Now they've managed to make a big score. And if I step in to try to stop it, well, it's quite possible that nobody will get anything out of it. Everybody could end up losing out. I don't want to do that. And like I say, I don't really have to. I'm comfortable just like things are, and I have nobody to leave it to when my time comes.

"Now, if there were any actual victims of this set of circumstances, like if old JT Willett had had a wife and kids he'd left everything to, well, then I could see how maybe they, or by now their descendants, might have a valid right to the proceeds of that sale. But we know from that profile we read that the man was like me. He didn't have any family to leave it to, either.

"So, I'm going to let this go. If Elaine and Jenna have the money, and if they figured out a way to get it, then more power to them. Maybe that makes them well and truly the real heirs of Jocko Drumm."

"Mr. Stone," JT began.

"Herb. Just call me Herb."

"Thank you. Herb, when I was down in Georgia, Abner told me a remarkable story about an accident at Camp Hancock that involved Ty Cobb and Christy Mathewson, Lieutenant Mathewson. He said that...." JT went on to relay the barest outlines of the story he'd been told.

"Abner told you that? Honestly? That never happened. That *never* happened."

"Herb, let me tell you how that came about, his telling me. Captain Mathewson—he was a captain by the time he left the service—died back about ten years ago. He died from the consumption, and everybody said that it was because of an accidental exposure to poison gas over in France during the war. Not sure if you realized it, but Mathewson was a really important man in baseball circles, plus he was something of a national hero after being gassed in the war.

"Well, when he died, a lot of the players who knew him back in the day went out of their way to tell the local papers wherever they lived stories about Mathewson and how great he was and how sad they all were. Real heartfelt kind of stuff. Well, Cobb, he lived down in Georgia, not so far from where that old camp was. And I guess he was doing the same thing as the others, but for him the local papers were all Georgia papers.

"As I understand it, Abner saw Cobb's comments in some newspaper down in Waycross - probably the Atlanta paper - and he got really angry about it. So, he wrote a letter to Mathewson's wife... well, widow, Jane.

And apparently, he told her the story he just told me the other day. Said he'd taken an oath of silence and all, but he'd seen what Cobb said and thought after almost twenty years she had the right to know what really happened.

"I went to interview Jane Mathewson for this same story about the Hall of Fame, and she told me I needed to go down and talk to Abner. Wouldn't tell me the story herself so as to honor his oath. And I went down there last week and I talked to Cobb, and then I talked to Abner. And now I'm sitting here in your living room talking to you.

"I understand that you took an oath, and that talking to me can have consequences, although I have to say, at this point, I'd be surprised if the government still cared one way or the other. But I do understand.

"Still, I wonder if there is some way that you can help me. It's a heck of a story Abner told me, and I want to tell it to the world. But I'll feel better about doing that if I can just confirm some of the basic facts."

"Well, Mr... Willett was it? Mr. Willett, I'd like to help you. I surely would. But if there was an oath taken, and I'm not sayin' there was, but if there was, well, I'd have to say I take oath-takin' pretty seriously. Yes sir, I do."

"Herb, I understand that, and I appreciate that. But maybe there's a way we can do this that doesn't require that you violate any oath that you may or may not have taken.

"Let's focus on Mr. Cobb. He was a great baseball player in his time, but he didn't have very many friends on or off the field. He was an irascible sort of a fellow. In very general terms, and without thinking about any particular incident, would you say that was your impression?"

Herb smiled. "Yes, sir. I would say that word about captures Mr. Ty Cobb. If it was me, I'd have just said he was an asshole."

Now it was JT's turn to smile. "Fair enough. And there are some who say he had kind of a short fuse. Didn't take too much to set him off. Sometimes let his anger get the better of him. Does that sound right to you?"

"Yeah, I think you could say that, too."

The give and take went on like this for a while, Willett never quite asking what he wanted to know, and Stone dancing around what he really didn't want to say. Then JT tried a change of direction.

"Let's talk for a minute about some of the men in that unit who weren't ballplayers. There was you and there was Abner. And I think there was a fellow by the name of Armstrong, is that right?"

"Armstrong... Armstrong.... Oh yeah, I remember him. Tall, skinny guy from somewhere up north. I want to say Pennsylvania, but I'm not sure about that."

"What ever happened to Armstrong? Think I could track him down somewhere."

Stone was quiet for a long moment. JT could almost see the wheels turning.

"I don't honestly remember what happened to Armstrong. I know he didn't ship out with us. I think his mom was took ill or some such. I'm thinking he transferred out of the unit a few days before... before we got our orders. He could be anywhere by now, if he even made it back from the war."

"And there was another guy," JT went on. "Simpson, I think. Any idea what ever happened to him?"

"Oh, yeah. That'd be Will Simpson. Williston Perry Simpson. Used to joke about that name. From back east, y'know. We actually kept up writin' letters and such for a long time after we got back from France. We just sort of gradually slowed down to nothin' after a while. But he's probably still doin' what he was doin'. Will was a plumber. I think that's why they put him in the, in that unit we were in. Plumbing-type skills were just real valuable. He set himself up in business with his brothers when he got back. Someplace outside of Boston... let me think... Chickpea?... no... Chicopee. It's somewhere over there in Massachusetts. Simpson Brothers Plumbing, I think. Should be easy to find old Will."

JT started up from his chair. "Herb, Mrs. Stone, thank you so much. You've been very helpful to me. And you have also been able to keep the oath you took. I appreciate your hospitality."

"This has been about the craziest damn two months I can ever remember," Adam said with a wry smile on his face.

"First you call me to rush up here and look at some barn find. Then the barn find turns out to be golden. Then your cousins steal the barn find right out from under your nose, and they manage to pawn it off to a high-end New York auction house. Still don't have that one figured out completely. Then it turns out the barn find was stolen goods, and the fact that you have this big, successful farm might in a sense be the same. Then the auction goes off, and somebody - we assume Elaine and Jenna - pockets almost eight million bucks. Then you decide to just let them have it.

"Wow! This is like something you'd read in a novel."

"Welcome to my life, I guess," responded Jason. "If everybody wins something, nobody really loses, and all the players go home happy, what the hell. I mean, I'm as old as you are, and for all of those years except for the last two months or so, I might as well have never had any of that contraband because I never knew that I did. Way it goes, man, way it goes.

"Want to stick around for dinner and head back in the morning?"

"Thanks for the invite, but no. I'm actually feeling kind of washed out from all of this. I think I just want to get back down to the City, order a pizza, and kick off my shoes. See ya when I see ya."

"Alright take care. Drive safely. And don't be a stranger."

Adam pulled out of the graveled parking pad, moved slowly down the lane to the main road, made a left and headed home. It was only when he got an hour or so away that he realized how right he was. This was like something you might read in a novel.

Perhaps, at long last, he had his next project.

As Adam headed down the drive to the main road, Jason was suddenly overcome with an urge to do something he had not done for many years.

Down what was now an overgrown path and off in a remote corner of the farm was the family's private burial ground. It's where he and Uncle Paul and his parents had laid Jocko to rest, and then a few years later Grandma Julie. They would all come back down the path once or twice a year and take some time to share memories. Then it was the place where he'd laid his own parents to rest following the accident. And he had not been back since. Those memories were either still too fresh, even these many years later, or simply too terrible to bring back to consciousness.

But now he knew the time had come. So, he donned some boots for the high grass and weeds, grabbed a walking stick just in case, and off he went.

The graves were pretty much as he remembered them. He paused for a long time to think, first about his mother, then about his dad. Then he moved on to his grandmother. Finally, he came to his grandfather's grave, and there, he had to smile.

He'd forgotten old Jocko's sense of humor, which he'd kept right to the end. The tombstone read simply:

John O'Connell Drumm
1890-1956
He Took It With Him

You old goat, he thought to himself. What the hell did you do?

JT had his confirmation. He was sure as he could be that Herb Stone had understood the little verbal game they had been playing, and had been careful to answer the question that JT was avoiding asking while remaining true to his sense of honor about oath taking. In his way, he'd even confirmed the incident involving Cobb and that young veteran, Petey. The story was there to be written. But Willett was thorough, and he hated surprises. He still needed to track down the plumber, Will Simpson, before going back to Jane, perhaps with parts of the story she did not already have.

JT headed east.

The smart thing to do would be to head up to Chicago, then grab a Pullman berth on one of the overnight expresses like the *Manhattan Limited* or the *New Yorker* back to the city, then head up toward Boston on one of the New Haven trains. Then he could double back to Springfield, which was the closest rail service to Chicopee, his destination. But that meant hanging around Indy, then Chicago, probably overnight in both. Instead, he did the less smart thing. He grabbed a handful of rail timetables at Union Station, and settled on a local heading northeast, up to Cleveland, then across through Buffalo and across New York State to Massachusetts. The advantage was that this one actually ran through Springfield, rather than up the East Coast from New York. It was, basically, a trade-off between relative comfort with lots of connections, or relative discomfort with a more direct route of travel. He chose the latter.

He was either fast or lucky yet again. He climbed up into the third coach from the end of the train, a trick he'd learned years ago. For some reason, people were less likely to choose that car than any other on the average train. That, in turn, meant the car would be less crowded, and thus quieter. Plus, he managed to snag one of the four tables in the car, seating himself facing forward. He hated riding backwards across the country more than almost anything. JT hoisted his suitcase into the overhead rack, and settled in for a very long ride.

Not too long after one of the early whistle-stops, an interesting-looking fellow entered the car and sat down facing him across the table. Looked a bit shopworn, but that was more the rule than the exception these days.

"Jocko Drumm. How d'ya do?"

"Name's Willett. Nice to meet ya. Headed for Boston?"

"Appears so. I decided to get on a train and go where it goes. Guess this one goes to Boston."

Bottom of the Ninth

Six weeks had passed since Adam had last visited the farm or spoken with Jason. As much as the "Jocko Papers," as he'd come to think of them, had fascinated him, after three false starts he found himself unable to follow through on his plan for writing a book about them. He'd read what other books he could find that talked about players participating in the War, and a selection of player biographies, but all of them seemed incomplete. Company Number 44 had either been written out of the history, or had never been written in to begin with. Adam could not find a way to add that piece back in. Moreover, most of the biographies were basically puff pieces about this or that great man, typically skin deep and fawning (except, perhaps, for Cobb, who was even moved to write an *auto*biography in self-defense). He wanted to write a book about people – that's what he did best. But all he saw here was a story about papers, first a couple of old Army records and JT Willett's handiwork in the suitcase, and later Jocko's abbreviated and coded confession. And the story just went around in circles but never led anywhere, or at least never led *him* anywhere. There was simply no closure to the story. There was no drama, no arc, no real plot.

Yes, JT Willett was an interesting, and in some circles, a famous person. Yes, Jocko himself was an intriguing and complex character. Yes, the papers told an alternative history of baseball, one in which one icon of the game *may* have unintentionally shortened the life of another, and in which the mortal gods of Baseball, the US Army, and even the President of the United States *may* have been complicit. And yes, the collection of papers had sold for an astronomical sum.

And yet, Adam didn't have the papers, or have any access to them. And yet, whoever *did* have them had chosen to remain anonymous. And yet, so much was unknown, perhaps unknowable, about them; so many unanswered questions remained. And yet, even the origin or validity of the documents rested in some measure on a set of assumptions and a latter-day interpretation of a coded journal that was itself more than eighty years old. A stack of unknowns about two sets of inanimate objects. With all of that, how could he tell the story?

The only solace Adam found was in knowing that no one else could tell it either. Well, not exactly. He supposed it was possible that some other *writer* might actually have acquired the papers, and at that moment could be hard at work telling the story his own way. George Will's name kept coming to mind – Will, or someone like him with a history of producing respected books on the sport, and perhaps with the money or the contacts to have spent nearly $8 million to own JT Willett's story of a lifetime. Of course, he mused, Will, or any would-be Will emulator, would not have Jocko's journal, or even know about it. But would that matter in the least? After all, the papers had sold at auction, with Marbury House authentication, without that piece of the puzzle.

As he was rolling over these thoughts in his head for about the hundredth time, Adam's phone rang. "Adam? Hey, it's Jason."

"Man, I was just thinking about you. What's up?

"How's the writing coming?"

"I thought this was a friendly call!"

"Sorry. Understood."

"I do owe you an apology, though. About three weeks ago, I finally got the original of your grandfather's journal back from the professor. I've been meaning to send it to you, but you know me. I promise I'll do that this week."

"Hey, no rush. What am I going to do with it anyway except put it back in the box."

"Elaine and Jenna ever show up?

"Nope. Actually, earlier this week one of their friends, May Appleton, if you can believe that name [the pun sailed far above Adam's head, urban creature that he had become], anyway May opened the store back up. Noticed it when I was at the feed and seed and thought maybe they'd come back. Turned out my dear cousins had mailed the keys to May along with a letter transferring ownership of the place to her. May was one of their suppliers, and I guess they thought she could make a go of it. Point is, the store's back open, and the girls are in the wind."

"Well, that really is the end of it then."

"Yeah, but that's really why I called you. With everything that went on, there was one small thing we never did. No real reason to, but we never did it. You're more of a baseball fan than I am. You ever actually been to the Hall of Fame?"

"No, no I haven't. Funny, huh?"

"Well, I haven't either. Never felt the urge. What say we remedy that? Cooperstown is sort of halfway between you in the City and me in Dekalb Falls. How about we meet there for lunch tomorrow and check the place out?"

"Hold on a sec.... Okay. I like that idea. I need to clear my head anyway and find something to keep me busy. I was just looking at Google Maps, and there's a flagpole right in the center of town, almost next door to the Hall of Fame. How about we meet there at noon tomorrow? Work for you?"

"Perfect. See you there at noon."

"Deal. And I promise I'll bring the journal along. Making a Post-It and sticking it on my phone as we speak."

The flagpole was hard to miss, and both Adam and Jason found it at about the same time. About a block down Main Street, they found a hole-in-the-wall diner that seemed to be drawing a lot of the locals, so they went in and had a quick lunch. Then they crossed Main and headed to the Hall of Fame.

The Hall was in a red brick building with a couple of ramps and some steps leading up to the entrance. Looked pretty much like a big auditorium. Through a door cleverly labelled "General Admission" they found a couple of ticket counters and paid their way in. The collection was housed on three levels, but rather than start at the bottom and work up, or even the top and work down, both the staff and the brochure showing a map of the place suggested starting in the middle, on the second level. And that's what they did.

The second level housed what seemed to be the permanent collection of the Hall, or at least of the museum that was the part that the public typically visited. And almost from the moment they entered the display area, they were struck by three displays. There was a case devoted to Ty Cobb, complete with a uniform, statistics, and even a letter that he'd written to another player, Bobby Doerr, about autographing a bat. The handwriting looked very familiar. Just around the corner was a mock-up (they assumed) of Honus Wagner's Pittsburgh locker. And to their left was an entire small room devoted to Babe Ruth, complete with uniforms, a mannequin, photos, and even running audio of old broadcasts. It was like The Babe got a walk-in closet, and everyone else got a coat hook. Old JT may have been right on point – Ruth did seem to be the *raison d'être* for the Hall's very existence, at least in the early days. It took a little longer to find some of Christy Mathewson's memorabilia, but they were there, along with a small photo of Frank Chance and his double-play colleagues, Tinker and Evers. There was a relatively significant space devoted to Moe Berg, a catcher who'd doubled as an agent of the OSS in World War II, but nothing comparable on the Gas and Flame Division of World War I. Jason and Adam both noted the contrast.

They finished touring the second floor, then moved on to the third, which was smaller and took less time. That level was devoted more to ballparks than to players, or as the Hall preferred to call them, the sacred grounds. Sounded like a ritzy coffee shop. The main exception was an area devoted to Hank Aaron. Why Aaron? Well, the standard answer, evident from the captions and surroundings, was because he was a great African American player. But was it an accident, cynical Adam wondered, that the only player with a space that rivaled Ruth's was the player who, by besting The Babe's home run total, had reinvigorated the homage afforded to Ruth himself? Just a passing thought. Then, it was back down to the lower level and on to the portion of the Hall many fans have in their minds as the image of the place, the so-called Hall of Fame Gallery.

The Gallery was a long, brightly lit room, with the walls lined with plaques commemorating each of the 300 or more players and others who have been inducted over the years since 1936. At the very entrance was a large portrait of Stephen Clark, who was described as having founded the Hall and selected Cooperstown as its site, all with the "help" of Ford Frick, then-National League president. Across from that was a comparable portrait of Mr. Frick, who was credited with initiating the idea of a Hall and selecting Cooperstown as its location, all with the help of Stephen Clark. Go figure. (Oh, yes. Coincidentally, Adam had discovered in his reading, while a reporter, Mr. Frick was also a paid ghostwriter and publicist for a player named Ruth.)

Adam and Jason spent some time walking down one side of the long Gallery, then the other. They noted plaques honoring several of the by-then-familiar players in JT's truncated narrative: Home Run Baker, Max Carey, Frank Chance, Branch Rickey, Ed Walsh, and even Ban Johnson and Kenesaw Mountain Landis. Finally, they made their way to the semi-circular end of the Gallery, where the plaques of the first five inductees, the Class of 1936, were on display. And sure enough, there they were: Christy Mathewson, Babe Ruth, Honus Wagner, Walter Johnson, and, right in the middle of the display, with pride of place, Ty Cobb.

Looking more closely, Adam noticed something odd. Under the plaques for Mathewson and Cobb were small bronzes indicating that each had served in the military in World War I. But there was no such added recognition beneath the Wagner plaque. Isn't that interesting, he thought. There had been some other, similar bronzes under some of the plaques up and down the hall, but neither he nor Jason remembered off-hand having seen any for the other members of the Camp Hancock contingent. So, they back-tracked, only to find that they were wrong. There was, in fact, a similar recognition bronze beneath the plaque for Branch Rickey, who had recruited and commanded the players during their service and was part of the established narrative. But for Baker, Carey, Chance, and Walsh, as for Wagner, no such recognition. It was as if they had never served.

"They don't know," mused Adam. "Mathewson, Cobb, and Rickey – they're the players in the mainstream story of players in the War. Mathewson went off to war in August of 1918, or September, or December and was gassed. Cobb was there with him. Rickey recruited them, and he was there in France, too. That's what's in all the books. Nothing else. They must not even know those other guys served. They must not know that all of them were in Georgia being trained in June of 1918. They must not know that Mathewson may have been collateral damage when Cobb possibly tried to exact revenge on someone else. They surely know about Cobb's letter to Jane Mathewson, because that was openly displayed by the auction house, and chances are they heard about the auction from somebody. But they must not know what that letter was really all about. They must not know about the story JT Willett was writing. And without those papers from your barn, they never will." And with that thought, they continued their meandering tour of the Hall.

There was not much left other than the massive museum store, but they were determined to see it all. So, they climbed a long, circular ramp to the last area of the museum toward something called the Bullpen Theater.

Along the way they passed a display showing the paperwork behind Babe Ruth's sale from Boston to New York. There's Ruth again, thought Adam. Then, at the top of the ramp, just to their right, they found something unexpected: an area labelled Scribes and Mikemen, a small space devoted to the sports reporters who have covered or broadcast baseball over the years. Though not members of the Hall, they obviously merited its appreciation.

Both guys stopped short in front of the first display case in this little area, struck by the same thought. There in the middle of the display was a small, black portable typewriter that looked for all the world just like JT's Royal. It was a Corona, but the similarity of size and appearance caught their eyes. It was Jason who first looked to the left, to the small section of wall that inset the display. What he saw there chilled him for a moment. It was a smallish plaque, different in style from those in the Gallery. It read:

> **This plaque honors JT Willett (circa 1870-1936), widely recognized as the first "baseball writer" in history. He began his career with the *New York Journal*, but spent the greatest portion of it as the principal baseball columnist for *The Sporting News,* where he is widely credited with earning that newspaper the title of the Bible of Baseball for the quality and extent of its coverage of the sport. Willett was a founding member of the Baseball Writers' Association of America, and chaired the selection committee for the First Class of Hall of Fame inductees. He was said to be preparing profiles of the first inductees when he passed away. Those profiles, if they existed, were never located.**
>
> **Willett never married and had no family. In a will written shortly before his death, he directed that all of his papers and other professional materials be donated to the Hall of Fame. Those papers, comprising Willett's columns published in *The Sporting News* over the course of his career and a few supporting notebooks, are maintained in the Hall of Fame archive.**

"Adam, we have to tell these people. I mean, when I decided to let go of all of this Jocko stuff, I did it because I didn't care about the money. I have nobody to leave it to, and I don't need it myself. Let the girls have it. But that was when I thought that their crime – and I guess that's what it was, a theft – had no other victim. Let it be. But looking at this, it seems that there is a victim. And we're standing in it. Those papers don't only belong *in* the Hall of Fame. They belong *to* the Hall of Fame. We need to talk to somebody."

Just who that might be became immediately obvious as they stepped away from the journalism display and back out into the main passageway. There, just to the right, they noticed a doorway with a big sign overhead that read: Giamatti Research Center. And that's where they headed.

Opening the door to the Research Center, they found themselves in a smallish library of sorts. There were two double rows of work spaces and a couple of public computer terminals off to their right, and a long mural depicting a baseball game on a nineteenth-century village green, presumably Cooperstown itself, lining the wall to their left. Directly ahead were two or three shelves of books and documents, and in front of those a librarian's desk behind a counter. A librarian of perhaps twenty-five looked up, smiled, and asked, "Can I help you gentlemen?"

"Actually," Jason said, "we're here to help you. We saw just down the hall that an old-time sportswriter, JT Willett, had left all of his papers to the Hall."

"That's correct. Let me just look here on our ABNER database, and I can tell you what we have." She typed something into her workstation and, turning her display so they could see it, reported on the results. "You can see here, we have all of Mr. Willett's columns that were published in *The Sporting News* from... the middle of 1910 through the end of 1935. We also have the original manuscript from a 1925 feature he wrote for *Time Magazine* looking back at the 1919 Black Sox scandal. And a few old notebooks, mainly from the '20s. And that's about it. You can search through the holdings on ABNER online if you like."

"Well, that's very interesting. Because we know of some important Willett documents that aren't listed there. That means you don't have them, right?"

"Right, unless there's been a cataloguing error sometime over the years. But with documents this old, that seems unlikely. All of these older items were entered in the system when the database was established about twenty years ago."

"If you had the documents we are talking about, someone would know it. And some of the exhibits in the museum and the gallery might have to be changed as a result."

"The thing is," Adam chimed in, "we believe these documents are actually the property of the Hall of Fame, and no one here knows it. And we can prove it. Is there someone here we can talk to about this?"

"One second," she replied. She walked over to the large glassed-in office that occupied about a quarter of the entire library space and spoke to the man seated at the single desk inside. He arose with a quizzical look on his face and walked over to Adam and Jason.

"Good afternoon," he said, offering his hand. "I'm Peter Marwick, the Library Director for the Hall. I hear you have some of our documents?"

Jason took the lead. "No. We don't have them. But we know they're yours." And the duo began to recount the story of the Marbury House auction a couple of months earlier, how the papers that were sold had been purloined from Jason, and how their contents would fundamentally alter the history of baseball as it is commonly understood. When Jason got to the part about having proof that the papers actually belonged to the Hall of Fame, and either they or the proceeds of the auction were rightfully property of the Hall, Marwick held up his hand to stop them in mid-sentence.

"Would you hold on a second? There's someone I need to call."

They watched as Marwick returned to his office, closed the door, and reached for the telephone. He was back in a flash.

"Gentlemen, could I ask that you come with me? I'm afraid what you're telling me is a bit above my pay grade. The person you should really be talking to is Magda Bloomsbury, our Chief Archivist. Please follow me."

With nods to the librarian behind the counter, the three left the Research Center, took a right turn across a small lobby area toward a structure that looked like a concrete cube that had been jammed into the side of the building in a collision with a spacecraft from the planet Picasso, entered through a door labelled "Staff Only" and climbed an open stair to the top level. Marwick punched in a security code, and opened the door.

"This is the Hall's archive area. And this, gentlemen, is Ms. Bloomsbury." Handshakes all around once again, and Peter Marwick took his leave.

Once seated in her office, Adam and Jason proceeded to repeat their account of the papers, how they'd been found in the old barn and then stolen, and their amateur assessment of their significance. When they came to the part about all of these items actually belonging to the Hall of Fame itself, the Chief Archivist sat up a little straighter in her chair.

"And how is that the case? What makes you think they belong to us?"

At that, Adam pulled out Jocko's journal, which he had brought along as promised, but thus far forgotten to return to Jason. He handed it over to Ms. Bloomsbury. "This is a journal that Jason's grandfather wrote back in the 1930s, and that we found recently. Looking at it, it makes very little sense. But we had a linguistics professor at Columbia go through and interpret the journal. Basically, it tells how his grandfather was on the train with Willett when he died, and how he essentially stole Willett's suitcase that turned out to be full of all these papers."

Then Jason picked up the narrative. "I had pretty much figured there was nothing I could do about any of this, and since I was the only victim of the theft, that was the end of it. But a few minutes ago, we were over in the museum and we came across the plaque you have in the journalism area that said old Mr. Willett had left all of his papers to you. So, that meant you, that is, the Hall of Fame, actually was a victim of the theft and illegal auctioning of the papers. Either the papers or the $7.8 million they brought at auction belong to the Hall. And that's before your lawyers start talking to Marbury House about what they've done."

"Wow. That's quite a story." She paused for nearly two minutes, clearly lost in thought. "Here's what I'd like to do. First, I'd like to hold onto this journal for a little while and have a chance to look through it more closely. Is that alright with you, Mr. Drumm?"

"I don't see why not. I mean, if you decide to do something about all this, you're going to need it. It has some obvious sentimental value to me. But the truth is, that book sat on a shelf or was packed away in a box for decades. It would be good to see it put to proper use."

"Thank you. But what I would really like to do is to have you meet with several members of our senior staff to make sure that we have all the facts here. It's going to take me a little while to arrange that. Would you gentlemen be able to stay in town overnight and meet with us first thing tomorrow morning? We can arrange a couple of rooms over at the resort. All at our expense, of course."

That sounded like a good plan, and was quickly agreed.

"Excellent. The executive offices of the Hall aren't actually here in the main building. But if you were to stand out front facing the main entrance, then turn left and walk down the sidewalk past the electronic board with the major league standings, you'll come to another building with a big white door. Those are the offices. I will meet you out in front of that door at nine tomorrow morning. And again, thank you."

"The resort" turned out to be the Otesaga Hotel, a sprawling building that occupied the land surrounding the very tip of scenic Lake Otsego. It was fronted by a large circular drive, and backed by lakefront terraces and a well-manicured golf course that swept around to the left as you faced the lake. Terraced water views provided ample places to walk, think, eat, or drink. Everything was landscaped and maintained with care.

Adam had been to a few places like this before, back when he was still doing book tours and conference presentations. But Jason had never seen the like of it. "Good lord," he muttered. "So this is how the other half lives. I half expect to see Jay Gatsby and Daisy Buchanan walking down the hall."

"Thought you weren't a reader," Adam deadpanned.

"High school," replied Jason. "Mrs. Barrett. Freshman English. The woman was obsessed with that book."

Check-in went smoothly, both Adam and Jason being assigned rooms with views of the lake. After scoping out the accommodations, they wandered outside and soon found themselves seated around a fire pit with a pair of hoppy local drafts in hand.

On the way out of his room, Jason had grabbed a reproduction of something called *The Otsego Farmer*, a reprint of what must have been the local paper back in the day. It was dated July 16, 1909, and told the story of the opening of the hotel earlier that week.

"Hey! Look at this. This place was owned by the Clark family. Wasn't Clark the guy that came up with the idea for the Hall of Fame? I remember that JT thought he did it so he could fill up the rooms in his hotel during the Depression. This has to be the hotel!"

"Wonder if JT ever stayed here. Probably couldn't have afforded it," offered Adam.

"You know," he continued, "the whole Cooperstown thing is a myth."

"What are you talking about?"

"When I started to write – well to try to write – about Jocko and the papers you found, I did some reading up about how all this got started. It turns out that the whole story about Abner Doubleday inventing the game of baseball here was made up, mostly by a guy named Albert Spalding. Used to be a player, but then he started this sporting goods company and he was looking for some way to promote the game. So, he and some other guys made up this story about how this Doubleday fellow had laid out the first diamond on a field here. One of them was from the town here, and that had something to do with how they settled on the location. Then they picked this big Civil War hero, Doubleday, as the inventor as a way of legitimizing the story. He's the guy Abner was named after. Nobody knows if he ever even visited Cooperstown, and he was dead by then, so nobody could ask him. Anyway, Spalding was apparently this very famous fellow, and he created his own commission to determine the origins of baseball. Then he essentially told them what they would find. And lo and behold, that's just what happened. Abner Doubleday invented the game of baseball from whole cloth in Cooperstown, New York, in 1839.

"Then the folks who lived here figured out there was money to be made from being the home of baseball. And they went with it. By the time old Mr. Clark, and maybe Ford Frick, or even, from one thing I read, a guy named Cleland who worked for Clark, came up with the idea for the Hall of Fame, it was like piling on to the myth of creation. I mean, it all had to start somewhere. And the fact that the Hall would open in 1939, basically on the hundredth anniversary of the 'invention' of the game and almost on that very spot, well that was pure genius."

"Who was this guy Clark? Maybe somebody around here knows something about him."

After a second beer, the duo started back through the hotel lobby when Adam had an inspiration. He saw an older, distinguished-looking fellow sitting at the concierge desk and thought he might know something about that. Probably wouldn't be the first time someone had asked the question.

"Oh, Mr. Clark. You know, the Clarks still own this hotel. Important local family. Way back when, old Mr. Clark – he was a New York lawyer – he was partners with Isaac Singer. Not the writer, the guy who invented the sewing machine. That was back when an invention was an invention, and the pair of them made a lot of money. A lot. Well, Mr. Singer, he was a strange duck, and pretty irresponsible. Hard to get along with, supposedly, and he had something like five or six wives and a couple of dozen children. All at the same time. Had to leave the country, I think.

"But Mr. Clark – that would be Mr. Edward, Sr. – he was very different. Saved his money, invested wisely, and bought up thousands of acres of land around here. Very philanthropic, too. Loved it here. You know, James Fenimore Cooper grew up here. Town is named for his family. But back to the Clarks, Mr. Edward, well he was a pretty aristocratic fellow. But nicer, I guess, than the Coopers, and the people here just took to him. And the Clarks have been good to this whole area ever since. You won't find many folks with much bad to say about them.

"It was the sons, Stephen and Edward, Jr., who built this hotel. But Edward left town shortly after that, and it was Stephen who built the business. He picked up where his father left off. Helped found the Museum of Modern Art down in New York City, and the Fenimore Museum just down the road, and, of course, the Hall of Fame."

Speaking of the Hall of Fame, Jason and Adam walked the half mile or so from the hotel grounds to the building housing the executive offices, down a Main Street lined with shops that must have housed every baseball card and autographed baseball in America. The histories were right. Folks around here had obviously seen the potential. And when they reached the entrance to the executive offices, Magda Bloomsbury was waiting for them out front as promised.

"Good morning. I trust you found the accommodations to your liking?"

"That's quite a place!" Jason replied.

"You know, when the new inductees to the Hall come to town for their ceremonies, they all stay at the Otesaga. Chances are several of them once stayed in the same rooms you did. The history here is just everywhere.

"Please, let's go inside."

She led Adam and Jason through the entrance and up some stairs to a second-floor conference room. Already seated there were three men, each of whom rose as they entered and offered their hands.

"Good morning. Roger Coppersmith. I'm the Chief Operating Officer of the Hall. Thank you for coming."

"Hi. Dave Russell. I'm the Director of Security."

"Good morning. I'm Eugene Seyforth. I'm General Counsel for the Hall of Fame."

Coppersmith took the lead. "And you've already met Magda. Please, everyone, take a seat.

"Magda has shared with us the gist of what you have told her, and I must say, that's quite a tale. And we appreciate your bringing it to our attention. We'd all like to hear it direct from you in whatever level of detail you like. But before that, there's one technicality we'd like to take care of. Gene?"

"Right. Magda passed along this remarkable little journal from... [consulting the journal] ... Jocko Drumm. I must say, I've never seen anything quite like that. And I'm not sure how it will play in court, if we ever get there. But before that, we do need to establish ownership so that we can protect the journal. Magda said you were not averse to turning it over to the Hall. Is that correct?"

"Yes. I mean, I guess so," Jason responded. "It seems only right, since my grandfather basically stole property that rightly belongs to the Hall of Fame."

"Thank you," Seyforth again. "That being the case, I'd like to ask that you read over a little document I've prepared, and if it looks okay, go ahead and sign it. We'll get you a copy. You'll see that it's pretty standard boilerplate. We use it all the time."

To Whom It May Concern:

I, JASON DRUMM, do hereby transfer to the NATIONAL BASEBALL HALL OF FAME ownership of a document which I represent to be the journal of my grandfather, Jocko Drumm, and which I believe to date to 1936, and transfer as well all rights and claims appurtenant thereto. Transfer is made effective by my natural signature below.

The NATIONAL BASEBALL HALL OF FAME does hereby accept ownership of the aforementioned document, in exchange for which it agrees to compensate Mr. Drumm in the amount of $1. In addition, Mr. Drumm is granted one lifetime membership in the NATIONAL BASEBALL HALL OF FAME. Transfer is made effective by the natural signature below of ROGER COPPERSMITH, Chief Operating Officer.

Mr. Drumm agrees to participate upon request as a fact witness in any legal action brought by the Hall as it may pertain to this document. Should Mr. Drumm be called upon to offer, in either deposition or testimony, an account of the discovery of this document in any legal proceeding that may be brought by the Hall, the Hall will compensate him for his time at a rate commensurate with the hourly rate of its lead outside legal counsel.

This contract is made under the laws of the State of New York, and constitutes the entirety of the agreement between the parties.

Roger Coppersmith

_____   _____
        Jason Drumm   Roger Coppersmith
              National Baseball Hall of Fame

DATED This _____ Day of _____ , _____

Jason read over the document, noticing that Coppersmith had already signed it, and decided it looked okay. He signed his name and added the date, then passed the paperwork back to Seyforth. In turn, the lawyer produced a crisp dollar bill and a laminated membership card made out in Jason's name.

"Excellent," said Coppersmith. "And again, thank you. We are grateful for your cooperation in this. Now please, do tell us about these papers."

Jason and Adam proceeded once again through the details they recalled from the time they had spent with JT Willett, his columns and his interview notes. They tried to be as thorough as possible, each filling in gaps as the other offered portions of the story they had pieced together. As they were wrapping up, Adam offered his interpretation of the find.

"When you take this material in its totality, and having just taken a walk through the museum and the Gallery here at the Hall of Fame, it seems to me there are some fairly important anomalies.

"First, the papers clearly show that it wasn't just Mathewson, Cobb, and Rickey, among players in the Hall of Fame, who served in the Chemical Warfare Service. At the very least, Home Run Baker, Max Carey, Frank Chance, Honus Wagner, and Ed Walsh are also deserving of their place in history, and each of them would seem to merit one of those little military service plaques you have under the others.

"Second, and again going by the papers, the date everyone uses for Mathewson and Cobb entering the military, which seems to be August of 1918 or later, is wrong. Clearly, they, and all the others, were in a training camp in Georgia in June of that year learning how to deal with poison gasses and other weapons.

"Third, Mathewson was certainly a hero for his service, but the details of his exposure to poisonous gas may well be mistaken. Willett's research, if we take it as solid journalism, indicates he was exposed in Georgia in June, not in France months later.

"Fourth, one cannot be sure, but it would appear from the papers that Cobb may have had a hand, unintentional though it may have been, in Mathewson's exposure. Or at least the company clerk, Abner, seemed to think so. That's the same Ty Cobb who holds the centermost spot in the featured display of plaques from the first group of players admitted to the

Hall. If you accept Willett's research and Abner's reported supposition, you might conclude that one of your first five inductees was in some measure responsible for the premature death of another of your first five inductees, and more especially, that the guy who did that was one of the surliest and most feared ballplayers of his era, and the victim one of the most respected and revered figures of those same early years of baseball, one whose reputation and actions helped to legitimize baseball itself at a time when that was most needed.

"And finally, not only was organized baseball complicit in a coverup of all of this, but, if the papers are correct, baseball actually conspired with the Army and even the President of the United States to exploit it. They went to elaborate lengths to hide what had really happened, and then they took the one man who had the most to do with making the game socially acceptable by virtue of his personal character, and the one man whose fame and standing they had all most relied on to generate support for the war, and a man who had volunteered for the most dangerous kind of military assignment – working with poison gas on a daily basis – out of a sense of duty, and they shipped him off to France in what they knew was a weakened condition, extended his suffering for weeks or months, staged or invented a second incident to explain his condition, and only then brought him home. And in the long run, it killed him.

"In sum, these papers have a very significant story to tell. They will change the way everyone thinks about the game of baseball. Jason and I have spent enough time here to know that this is the principal repository for that history. And yet, there are these anomalies. These documents, when you get a hold of them, will address them all. And as you said, Mr. Coppersmith, what an interesting story they tell."

As Adam and Jason were clearly finished with their narrative, all eyes turned to the head of the table.

"That, gentlemen, is quite a tale. We clearly need to look into all this. Before we go any further, though, let me just nail down a couple of things.

"Do you have any copies of any of these papers? Even a few pages? Pictures? Anything someone could use to track them down? Or even to prove they exist?"

"No," Jason said. "I suppose we should have done that. But they were all in a suitcase in my house. It never occurred to me they would simply disappear like they did."

"Okay. And do you have any idea who might have taken them?"

Jason paused at that one. "No," he said. "Not really. I have some suspicions, but I have no evidence whatsoever for any of them. For all I know, it could have been anyone."

"And did you show the papers to anyone else before they were taken? Did anyone besides the two of you see them?"

"No. We were the only ones who saw them, at least that we know of. Now as you know, they were recently auctioned off by Marbury House down in New York City. I have no idea who saw what in that process. And I don't know who has them now."

Adam chimed in at that point. "I did see a news story after the sale. In fact, that's how we found out that the papers had reappeared and been auctioned off. But the story just described the papers in general terms; it didn't say anything about what was in them. Which makes me think no one actually read them. But that's just a guess."

"Tell you what," said Coppersmith. "It's nearly noon. Magda, why don't you run Adam and Jason over to the hotel and buy them a nice lunch. And while you're doing that, the rest of us will spend some time thinking about what our next steps might be. Let's plan on reconvening at about two, if that's agreeable to you fellows."

It was, and off the threesome went for a buffet lunch overlooking the lake.

It was closer to three by the time the group got back together, minus one. Seyforth took the lead.

"Roger sends his apologies. He'd forgotten that he had an important meeting at two that he simply had to take.

"On his behalf, I want to thank you two again for bringing all of this to our attention. You're right. If this was the true story of baseball during World War I, this is the place it should be told.

"But we have some issues with what you've told us."

Something in the lawyer's tone seemed suddenly to bend the light and suck the very air out of the room.

"To begin with, all that we have to go on here is your recitation of what you claim was in these papers. No one else has seen them, or at least what's in them. And you must admit, your story has some of the elements of a tall tale.

"We don't know why you might make up something like this. Perhaps you are looking to get a piece of the $8 million from the auction or a reward of some kind. Perhaps you are playing a very indirect game of extortion. Perhaps it's something deeper or more complicated that we haven't figured out. Perhaps you're just after publicity. And please, I am not suggesting that any one of those possibilities is the case. But at the moment, all we have is your word. No documents, no pictures, no other witnesses. And that is a curiosity.

"And what you are suggesting, if it's true, well it undermines an important part of popular beliefs about our national pastime, of known and accepted truths. We can't tell a damaging story like that, and in the process risk the credibility of the game, and of the Hall itself, on the basis of hearsay and supposition, which at this point is all we have.

"Now, you do have a claim to credibility in the form of that journal, which you say was written by your grandfather in the 1930s. But honestly, fellows, there is nothing in that journal that could not have been produced last week. And those random words and squiggles could mean just about anything. Or nothing at all. Maybe your grandfather was just getting senile when, and *if*, he wrote that.

"In addition, Marbury House, which sold some items at auction, whatever those might have been, has a stellar reputation, and they would not have conducted a sale and certified the provenance of the items in it unless they had clear and convincing proof that the seller was legitimate and had proper evidence of ownership. You, sir, on the other hand," he said, looking straight at Jason, "have come in here with nothing more than a little book of gibberish and a last name that ties you to nothing more than that very book, and not at all or in any way to the documents which, in any event, as I said, you do not possess.

"Finally, there is this. Your visit yesterday and today is not the first time we have heard about these so-called papers. As you might have realized, had you thought things through a bit more, one of the very first places that Marbury House would have contacted when they were commissioned to sell that collection was the Hall of Fame. As you said, we are the principal repository of baseball's history, the keepers of the flame, as it were. Our opinion is valued, and in point of fact, we tried privately to discourage that auction. We were obviously not sufficiently persuasive in this instance, or that public sale would not have proceeded.

"Consistent with our fiduciary responsibility to the game, to its legacy, and to this institution, we looked over those papers very carefully, and we considered every aspect of the story they purported to tell. It is a twisted and distorted view of the history of our game, one that is at variance with truths we do regard as established and essential, and one that attacks the character of men we regard as icons of the game. In our view, the papers in question *cannot* be genuine. And this story *must* be a fiction; it *cannot* be accepted. Accordingly, gentlemen, I can tell you straight out and without contradiction, it is the position of the National Baseball Hall of Fame that...

"This never happened.

"Dave, would you escort these gentlemen out? Good day to you." And he left the room.

Quick as that, Adam and Jason found themselves on the sidewalk outside the big white door, both in a state of shock. "What just happened?" asked Jason.

There was a moment of silence. Then another.

And then a thought occurred to Adam. "Now I get it. Now I understand. You know, this would make a heck of a book. I should write it."

Of course, This Never Happened.

When I staggered out and gulped in fresh air, I didn't know how badly my lungs had been damaged.... I remember Mathewson telling me, "Ty, I got a good dose of the stuff. I feel terrible."

Ty Cobb

My Life in Baseball: The True Record

Men occasionally stumble over the truth, but most of them pick themselves up and hurry off as if nothing had happened.

Attributed to Winston Churchill, 1936

Extra Innings

POSTSCRIPT: Some Notes on Persons, Places, and Things.

The Players

John Franklin Baker, better known as Home Run Baker, was a third baseman for the Philadelphia Athletics and the New York Yankees over a major league career that spanned the years 1908-1922. He was born in Trappe, Maryland, in 1886, and died in the same town in 1963. Baker led the American League in home runs for four straight years, 1911 through 1914, though he never hit more than twelve in any one season and hit only 96 over his entire career. Baker played during what came to be known as the "Dead Ball Era." He earned his appellation during the 1911 World Series, in which he hit home runs in successive games, an unprecedented feat at the time. He is a member of the Hall of Fame, and served in Ordnance Depot Company Number 44.

Max Carey was an outfielder, mostly for the Pittsburgh Pirates, and later the manager of the Brooklyn Dodgers. He led the National League ten times in stolen bases. Carey was the son of a Prussian soldier, and emigrated to the United States after the Franco-Prussian War. He was studying to be a Lutheran minister when a career in baseball beckoned in 1909. He, too, was a member of Ordnance Depot Company Number 44, and of the National Baseball Hall of Fame, to which he was elected in 1961. Carey passed away in 1976.

Frank Chance was a first baseman for the Chicago Cubs, where he anchored the famed double play combination of (Joe) Tinker to (Johnny) Evers to Chance. He later played for the New York Yankees. He was known to teammates as "Peerless Leader," a sobriquet he later put into practice as manager of the Cubs, the Yankees, and the Boston Red Sox. In his case, it was a planned career in dentistry that was interrupted by baseball. Chance was a member of Ordnance Depot Company Number 44, and of the Hall of Fame, to which he was inducted in 1946. He passed away in 1924 at the age of 47.

Ty Cobb was perhaps one of the most complex men ever to play the game. Davy Jones, who played beside Cobb for several years, used that very word to describe him. He was disliked by many of the other ballplayers of his time, both teammates, who regarded him as surly and thin-skinned, and opponents, who thought him dangerously aggressive. Yet there are others, players and some biographers, who suggest that Cobb was misjudged, and that his main flaw may simply have been the lack of a sense of humor that led him to misinterpret the normal byplay of the game as personal affronts. Christy Mathewson, Branch Rickey, Davy Jones, and others regarded him as a friend. Cobb was as intelligent a player as he was intimidating, and the one may have led to the other. He was the dominant hitter in the American League much as Honus Wagner was in the National. Cobb held the rank of Captain during World War I, and served in Ordnance Depot Company Number 44. He served with Mathewson in France, both as volunteers, and was, by his own account and to a lesser extent, a victim of the same chemical weapons accident that so affected his friend. Cobb, a savvy investor and something of a philanthropist, spent much of his retirement in Augusta, Georgia, where he was a beloved figure. The son of a school administrator, he valued education; in later life he endowed a college scholarship fund for needy Georgia students, and even helped to select the scholars. Cobb built a hospital in Royston, Georgia, as a memorial to his parents, and was also known to provide assistance to down-and-out former ballplayers. He passed away in 1961.

Walter Johnson, known as Big Train, was a pitcher for the Washington Senators who compiled 417 wins, more than 3500 strikeouts, 110 shutouts, and 531 complete games out of 666 that he started over his eighteen seasons. He was widely regarded to have had the fastest fastball ever seen. It was so fast, in fact, that Johnson feared that he would inadvertently hit a batter someday and kill him. He was among the first class inducted into the Hall of Fame.

Davy Jones was a major league outfielder between 1901 and 1918. He was not a member of the Hall of Fame, but played with many who were. Of particular interest, he was the very first batter ever to face Walter Johnson in a big-league game. And he was a teammate and friend of Ty Cobb who seemed to have the ability to talk Cobb down when he went into one of his rages. Today we might describe Jones as the Cobb-Whisperer. Jones was a member of Ordnance Depot Company Number 44. He died in 1972.

Henry Jones pitched five games in the major leagues for the Pittsburgh Alleghanys, a predecessor of the Pirates, in 1890. With his 2-1 record, he was actually the only pitcher on the team that year with more wins than losses. Decimated by defections to a rival league, the team finished with a record of 23-113, only 66 ½ games out of first place. Jones is not a member of the Hall of Fame, but he, or someone with the same name, was a member of Ordnance Depot Company Number 44.

Christy Mathewson has been regarded by many as perhaps the best pitcher in the history of the game. Mathewson was an educated man, and by all accounts a gentleman. Indeed, one of his principal contributions to baseball in its early years was to confer upon the game, by virtue of his participation, an aura of respectability. He played most of his career with the New York Giants, then the final three years with the Cincinnati Reds. Mathewson was also a genuine war hero. He did serve in Ordnance Depot Company Number 44 and later as a Captain in the Chemical Warfare Service, and according to the established history, it was in Flanders (or on the way there) that he was the victim of both the influenza that was sweeping the ranks and a mustard gas accident that permanently weakened his lungs. He died of tuberculosis in 1925. He was a member of the first class inducted into the National Baseball Hall of Fame. He and his wife, Jane, were major donors to Bucknell University; their names are prominent on several campus landmarks.

Babe Ruth (George Herman Ruth, Jr.) is, arguably, the most famous baseball player of all time. He began as a pitcher for the Boston Red Sox, then was traded to the New York Yankees, where he moved to the outfield so that he could bat more regularly. He was for many years the most prodigious home run hitter the game had known, hitting 60 home runs in a single season (1927, breaking his own previous record of 59) and 714 over the course of his career. He was also a large personality; everyone in America knew who he was. Ruth played twenty-two seasons, from 1914 to 1935, and his many exploits both on and off the field are the stuff of legends. Ruth was inducted into the Hall of Fame in the first cohort, and is honored with his own gallery in the Hall's museum. Ruth did not serve in the military in World War I. He died in 1948.

Honus Wagner was described by his peers as the most athletic and versatile man ever to play the game. Wagner was a true great at shortstop, but over the course of his career also played every other position except pitcher. He was an awkward looking fellow whose bow-leggedness was reportedly quite striking, but his large, soft hands allowed him to make plays routinely that others were unable to complete at all. He was a league leader in hitting, and a prolific base stealer, playing almost his entire career with the Pittsburgh Pirates. Wagner was a member of Ordnance Depot Company Number 44, and of the first class of inductees into the Hall of Fame. He passed away in 1955.

Ed Walsh was a star pitcher for the Chicago White Sox from 1906 to 1912, one of only two pitchers in the modern era of baseball to win 40 or more games in a single season. His career ERA was just 1.82, still the lowest on record. Walsh pitched an average of 375 innings per season during his prime, which had the effect of cutting short his career because his arm went dead. Walsh is a member of the Hall of Fame, and also served in Ordnance Depot Company Number 44.

The Baseball Executives

Ford Frick was a sportswriter for the *New York American* – and a paid ghostwriter for Babe Ruth – who became director of public relations for the National League, then served from 1934 to 1951 as the League's president. From that year until 1965, he served as Commissioner of Baseball. He shares credit with Stephen Clark for conceiving of the Hall of Fame and bringing it to fruition, and his portrait shares pride of place with Clark's in the Hall of Fame Gallery. Frick was himself elected to the Hall in 1970.

Byron Bancroft (Ban) Johnson was the moving force in establishing the American League, which he ruled with an iron hand as its president from 1900 until 1927 when, coming out on the short end of yet another of his many conflicts with baseball's first Commissioner, Kenesaw Mountain Landis, he was unceremoniously cast aside. That dispute centered on allegations by former major leaguer Dutch Leonard that Ty Cobb and Tris Speaker had been involved in gambling on a game several years earlier. Johnson, a self-declared enemy of wagering on the game, paid Leonard $20,000 to remain silent, then quietly informed Cobb and Speaker that they were to resign from the managerial positions each then held, one with Detroit, the other with Cleveland. Cobb and Speaker complied, but were later reinstated when in 1927 Landis, seeing an opportunity to enhance his own power and embarrass Johnson, after a seemingly staged open "hearing" before the press, declared that no offense had occurred. In effect, both Johnson and Landis, each in his way, acted to cover up (if the incident did occur as evidence offered by Leonard appeared to indicate) or dispel any doubts about (if it did not), a threat to the reputation of baseball. Johnson was elected to the Hall of Fame in 1937.

Kenesaw Mountain Landis was the first Commissioner of Baseball, serving from 1920 until his death in 1944. Landis, appointed to the bench by Theodore Roosevelt, was a federal judge with a reputation as a trust-buster and a hard-liner, particularly in cases involving draft resisters and opponents of World War I. In the wake of the 1919 Black Sox Scandal, in which members of the Chicago White Sox were accused of conspiring with gamblers to lose the Series, baseball needed to improve its image and, through an intensely political process, turned to Landis to both do the job and symbolize it. He was aggressive in the role, particularly in purging gamblers from the baseball scene.

Branch Rickey had a brief career as a major league baseball player and a lengthy and historically significant career as a baseball executive. After playing with limited success for three seasons with the St. Louis Browns and the New York Highlanders, Rickey obtained a law degree from the University of Michigan, where he also learned about sports administration from the school's athletic director. He returned to major league baseball in the Browns' front office in 1913, and served as their manager for a couple of years. It was shortly after he was fired from that position that he accepted an invitation to join the Chemical Warfare Service with the rank of Major. His first assignment was to recruit major league players into the service. The roster of Ordnance Depot Company Number 44 is a testament to his success. Rickey then enjoyed a long career as a manager, general manager, and club president with three teams, the St. Louis Cardinals, Brooklyn Dodgers, and Pittsburgh Pirates. It was Rickey who developed the concept of the minor league farm system, set up the first permanent spring training facility, and even introduced the batting helmet to protect players from the fate that Walter Johnson had feared his fastball might inflict. But his place in the history of the game, and of the civil rights movement, was assured when, in 1947, after four years of planning and preparation, he brought Jackie Robinson to the Dodgers – the first African-American to play in the major leagues in the modern era. Rickey, a member of the Hall of Fame, died in 1965.

The Hall of Fame Personalities

Stephen Clark (1882-1960) was an heir to the fortune his father, Edward Clark, made as half-owner of the Singer Sewing Machine Company and as an investor in New York real estate. The Clark family was, and remains, the most influential force in Cooperstown and the surrounding area, much of which remains in family hands. Clark and his brother founded the Otesaga Hotel in Cooperstown in 1909, and it was in part because of hard times in the hotel business during the Great Depression that he was motivated to establish the Hall of Fame mere walking distance from his property. He served as chairman, president, and CEO of the Hall until the time of his death. Clark was a patron of the arts and a major philanthropist, both locally and nationally. He was, among other things, a founding trustee of the Museum of Modern Art in New York City.

Alexander Cleland is perhaps the least known real person on this list, so little-known that he barely even made it into the story. He was a senior executive working for Stephen Clark, and in 1934 wrote Clark a letter proposing the establishment of a baseball museum in Cooperstown to draw what he thought might be hundreds of tourists to the town annually. That is to say, it was Cleland who initially proposed the concept to Clark, who immediately appreciated its merits. On Clark's behalf, Cleland then negotiated creation of the Hall with Ford Frick, who represented organized baseball, and he later traveled the country soliciting artifacts for its collection. Cleland is not a member of the Hall, nor even mentioned prominently in its displays. But copies of his correspondence are included in the collection of the Hall of Fame Library.

Abner Doubleday (1819-1893) was a Union general in the Civil War. A native of New York State (though not of Cooperstown) and a graduate of West Point, Doubleday seemed to possess a history magnet of sorts. It was he who fired the first shot in defense of Fort Sumter, i.e., the first Union shot of the Civil War, and he also played a central role in the Battle of Gettysburg two years later. Doubleday is memorialized in a monument on the Gettysburg battlefield, and is buried in a hero's grave at Arlington National Cemetery. After he left the military, he proved to be an inventive fellow as well, having obtained the patent for the cable cars in San Francisco. The one thing he did *not* invent, though, appears to have been baseball. Doubleday was singled out by Albert Spalding long after his death as a legitimizing name to establish the American roots of the game, a choice later confirmed by the Mills Commission, whose members were named by... Albert Spalding. While the Doubleday myth has long been questioned, it was not until quite recently that the Hall of Fame itself began to move away from it. When the seventy-fifth anniversary of the Hall came around in 2013-14, it issued a press release that stated, "On June 12, 1939, the National Baseball Museum opened its doors for the first time, in honor of the 100th anniversary of the mythical 'first game' that allegedly was played in Cooperstown on June 12, 1839." Even George Creel might have enjoyed that one.

The Media, Military, and Government Personalities

George Creel (1876-1953) was an investigative journalist and politician who was selected by President Woodrow Wilson to chair the Committee on Public Information (CPI). CPI was created for the dual purposes of countering enemy propaganda, a newly significant component of warfare in World War I, and disseminating effective American propaganda abroad. Under the first of these portfolios, it conducted propaganda operations within the United States to generate and maintain popular support for the war. The Committee developed a scheme for characterizing propaganda that stood as a standard for many years. CPI began its activities just a week after the country entered the war, and terminated them upon the signing of the Armistice Agreement that ended it. But during this short period, CPI served as a training ground for a generation of prominent practitioners of the emergent profession of public relations, among them Edward Bernays, often regarded as the father of American public relations.

William Randolph Hearst, a child of privilege, was fifteen years younger than Joseph Pulitzer, with whom he is often linked. Upon moving from San Francisco, where he published *The Examiner*, to New York, he purchased the *New York Journal*, the second of almost thirty newspaper holdings he would gather. The *Journal* employed the same approach to sensationalized journalism as Pulitzer's *New York World*, and the two papers became circulation rivals as well as competing to see which could claim the greatest influence on such world events as the opening of the Spanish American War. Hearst was a Progressive and an isolationist and, following World War I, a critic of the League of Nations. Hearst outlived Pulitzer by four decades, as a result of which his influence on American journalism was deeper and more profound. He is generally regarded as the inspiration for Orson Welles's portrayal of a newspaper publisher in the movie *Citizen Kane*. Hearst died in 1951.

Joseph Pulitzer was a Hungarian-born newspaper publisher best known for his ownership of the *New York World*, where he led in the development of what came to be known as "Yellow Journalism." Pulitzer pioneered the inclusion of color comics in the newspaper, and it was one of the characters in the comics, the Yellow Kid, who gave his name to the newspaper's overall style. Pulitzer's paper covered crime in colorful ways, crusaded against corruption in government and business, and emphasized sex, sensational writing, and graphic presentation. Following the example of Alfred Nobel, the inventor of dynamite who established a prize for peacemaking in his own name as a means of essentially laundering his image, Pulitzer established the eponymous prizes in journalism, rewarding high professional achievement, through an endowment at Columbia University. Born in 1847, Pulitzer suffered from ill health for many years, and passed away in 1911.

William Luther Sibert, born in 1860, was a civil engineer who participated in the construction of the Panama Canal, Soo Locks, and Hoover Dam. He was educated at the University of Alabama and West Point, and received his commission in the Army in 1887. With the outbreak of World War I, Sibert was given command of an infantry division, a job for which his engineering training did not prepare him. Later, on the recommendation of General John J. "Blackjack" Pershing, he was named to head the newly established Chemical Warfare Service. In 1920, when the Service faced elimination, Sibert testified before Congress to urge its continuation on a permanent basis, then resigned his commission. Congressional acceptance of his recommendation was reflected in its passage of the National Defense Act of 1920. It was at Sibert's initiative, working through Perry Haughton, President of the Boston Braves, that Branch Rickey was recruited to the war effort.

George Will is a political columnist noted for his love of baseball. His 1990 book, *Men at Work: The Craft of Baseball*, based on hundreds of hours of player interviews, is regarded as a classic treatment of the sport. Mr. Will did not purchase the JT Willett papers at auction, but if they had really been available, he would surely have coveted them, and appreciated them for what they were.

Places and Things

The National Baseball Hall of Fame and Museum, located in Cooperstown, New York, about an hour west of Albany, is regarded by those who love the game of baseball as a national treasure. It was conceived in the mid-1930s as a repository for baseball history and memorabilia, a mechanism for remembering the greats of the game, a tourist attraction for an area hard hit by the Depression, and a potential promotional and legitimizing bonanza for organized baseball, principally the major leagues. The location was selected based on an apocryphal origin myth: that Civil War hero Abner Doubleday had laid out the very first baseball diamond in a field in this quaint little village. Today the Hall comprises an extensive museum collection, a research facility, a gallery of bronze plaques recognizing the contributions to the game by more than 300 players and executives, and, not to be overlooked (as if that were possible), an extensive museum store. Responsible for preserving and advancing the legacy of the game, the Hall of Fame has more than 35,000 paid members, and more than a quarter of a million visitors annually. The adjacent Doubleday Field, which hosts numerous baseball games during the year, is operated by the Village of Cooperstown.

Camp Hancock, Georgia, was a National Guard training facility that opened in 1917 and closed upon the conclusion of World War I. As an overlay map prepared by historian Joe Lee and shared with the author, and a tour of the site provided by local journalist Bill Baab, make clear, Hancock was a sprawling facility covering a large swath of what is today part of the city of Augusta. That footprint encompasses Daniel Field, the general aviation airport where uncounted corporate aircraft line the outer taxiways during the week of the annual Masters Tournament at Augusta National Golf Club, a golf course (not Augusta National), a massive Veterans Affairs medical center named for the late Congressman Charlie Norwood, shopping centers, housing developments, parkland, and more.

Ordnance Depot Company Number 44 was apparently a real unit of the Chemical Warfare Service, and did train at Camp Hancock, Georgia, in June 1918. It was commanded by then-2nd Lieutenant Christy Mathewson, under Major Branch Rickey, and its members included a substantial cohort of then-current or retired major league baseball players, seven of whom were eventually inducted into the Baseball Hall of Fame (eight if you include Rickey himself), including three of the first five elected to the Hall: Mathewson, Honus Wagner, and Ty Cobb.

AUTHOR'S DISCLAIMER

(Wherein the author exits his flight of fancy and returns to reality.)

To be entirely clear, this never happened. It is a work of fiction.

The central, documented, and apparently *true* fact behind this narrative is that in 1918 a brave cohort of professional baseball players, most of them future members of the Baseball Hall of Fame, volunteered for service in a unit assigned to dismantle unexploded ordnance, including chemical weapons, to deploy chemical weapons, and to train soldiers in the use of gas masks. They served together in a National Guard company that trained at Camp Hancock in Georgia, which was a real place. The author learned of this fact from an episode of the PBS series, *Antiques Roadshow*, which featured documents from that unit. The remainder of the story is a yarn spun from that single thread of truth, and nothing more.

John Tyler (JT) Willett was not a real person, and any resemblance the character may bear in name or otherwise to any real person, living or deceased, is purely coincidental. *The Sporting News* was a real weekly newspaper, then a magazine, and is now a real digital platform, but at no time, to the author's knowledge, did it employ JT Willett as a baseball columnist (since he did not exist). Nor, for that matter, did the *New York Journal* in any of its various appellations. Any thoughts, observations, actions or interactions, opinions, experiences, claims of credit, employment, relationships, or words associated here with JT Willett are purely fictitious.

Similarly, any resemblance between the other purely fictional characters in this book, including but not limited to Jason Drumm, Jenna and Elaine Drumm, and Adam Wallace, and any real persons is purely coincidental. And any and all documents, including letters ostensibly written by Ty Cobb, Jane Mathewson, and Branch Rickey; other correspondence; Jocko's journal; and others ~ with the exception of the modified versions of the two Camp Hancock documents presented here ~ are fictional creations designed to advance the narrative.

To the extent that this story references people who were real – baseball players, newspaper and magazine publishers, family members, military officers and enlisted personnel, or any others – the author has endeavored to ground the respective characterizations of these individuals in fact and/or common perception to the extent these are known, but great liberties have been taken to advance the story. Words and actions that go beyond well-established facts are thus to be regarded as fictional, as are things that could have happened or been said in the circumstances, but did/were not.

Specifically, there is no reason whatsoever to believe that Ty Cobb or anyone else was implicated in any purposeful act that resulted in the exposure of Christy Mathewson (or anyone else) to the poisonous gas that by most accounts eventually led to his death. Both Cobb and Mathewson were patriots who volunteered to serve their country. And while the records show that the entry for June 3 was postdated by two days, while the real Private Armstrong did transfer out of Company 44 on June 6, while Lieutenant Mathewson did spend four days in the base hospital from June 5 to June 9, while the records also show no daybook entries of any kind after June 10 (the day following his release) even though the (original) pay roster runs until June 20, and while other records that might be used to support or contradict the story as recounted were lost many years ago in a fire at a National Archives storage facility, there is no reason to associate those facts with the fictional events presented here. All of the latter were figments of the author's imagination.

Several characters in this story were assigned names based on, but modified from, those of real persons who were members of the Chemical Warfare Service company that is its focus. This was done to preserve continuity with the real, factual payroll document that gave rise to the tale, while at the same time respecting their privacy and that of their descendants. The author does not know the full and true identities of any of these individuals. This includes, among others, both Abner Barnum and Herbert Stone. All actions, words, and other treatments of these characters are entirely fictitious and an invention of the author. No claim is made as to their accuracy or correctness. The one underlying truth is that the actual men in question were heroic in having joined the Chemical Warfare Service and served in Ordnance Depot Company Number 44.

The National Baseball Hall of Fame and Museum is, of course, a real institution. The core facts of its establishment and history, and of the election of its honorees by the Baseball Writers' Association of America, are true. But any treatment or interpretation here of the context, purpose, history or significance of the Hall by the fictional characters in this story, including the fictional officers and staff of the Hall itself, is, by definition, fictional. It is not intended to suggest in any way the nature of past actions by the real officers of the Hall, or the ways in which they might respond to hypothetical situations in the future. Nor were the fictional characters themselves based in any way on the persons or behaviors of any actual officers or employees of the Hall. The same is true of the Baseball Writers' Association, of which JT Willett was never a member, let alone a founder. Also, it should be noted that Camp Hancock was not an Army training facility, but a National Guard one, and Company 44 was a unit of the National Guard. This may account for the differential treatment by the Hall of the military service of its various inductees.

The town of DeKalb Falls is a fictional location, but if you believe that you live there, perhaps you do.

Then, there is this: In response to the growing public perception that organized baseball was insufficiently patriotic, and at the specific request of General William Sibert, who commanded the Chemical Warfare Service, future Hall of Famer Branch Rickey appears to have recruited for purposes of propaganda a military "show" unit comprising, among others, it seems, seven more future Hall of Famers, including three of the most iconic players of all time – Christy Mathewson, Ty Cobb, and Honus Wagner – to train in the use of poison gas. Yet the existence of this unit was never publicized. It appears in no histories of either baseball or World War I. It is not recognized by the National Baseball Hall of Fame, an institution that exists primarily to sing the praises of the game. And it received no contemporaneous media coverage. Even the local newspapers from the community nearest the training camp, *The Augusta Chronicle* and *The Augusta Herald*, carried no mention of the fact that so many prominent ballplayers were training just outside of town, this despite the fact that one of them, *The Herald*, ran a lengthy profile of the camp as well as a roster of the Camp Hancock baseball team during the very period when the Company 44 documents show the major leaguers to have been present. And at the time, Augusta was a baseball town, one that regularly hosted major league spring training camps. The *only* surviving reference to the unit is apparently found in the pay roster, daybook, and other documents revealed on *Antiques Roadshow*. So the question remains: If *this* never happened to explain the total silence regarding Ordnance Depot Company Number 44, *what did?*

J. B. Manheim

ACKNOWLEDGMENTS

This story is based on a hopefully seamless blending of fact with fiction. For this reason, the listing of references below is limited only to those portions of the narrative that can be distinguished in significant measure as true. This is an effort to give broad credit for factual information where it is due, even though multiple alternative sources might have been cited for many of the same facts. However, because fact and fiction are often comingled here even within sentences, except for those pertaining to the provenance of direct quotations, the reader should not treat these acknowledgements as true footnotes to be cited in any other work. They are not. Rather, they represent the author's best effort to acknowledge his intellectual debt to the previous work of others within the spirit of a work of fiction.

Verisimilitude is central to the dramatic arc of this book, and I thought I knew what the word meant ~ until I saw John Payne's renderings of the several letters and other documents, real and imagined, that are so central to this tale. Even I was so taken in by them that I sometimes lost track of the line between fact and a fiction I had myself created. On the chance that you may have done the same, let me offer this guidance. With two exceptions, all of the purported documents presented here are fictitious. That includes, but is not limited to, all of the correspondence, Jocko's journal, and the columns attributed to JT Willett. The exceptions are the two documents from Ordnance Depot Company Number 44. But even those are not quite true. Working from very fuzzy images of these genuine documents as shown on a 2003 television program, we have presented a general likeness of their content that is completely true to the originals with respect to the roster of baseball players and their activities as recorded at the time, but has been modified in some ways to enhance legibility and to protect the privacy of other members of the Company. Some unintended errors may have also been introduced because the original documents themselves, in the form in which they were available, were not fully legible.

While the reproductions of these documents here are not real, the underlying original documents from June 1918 do seem to be. The author engaged in an extensive effort over several months to locate the original documents so that they might be photographed. The search included queries to the appraiser who presented the papers on the 2003 television broadcast, to WGBH (producers of *Antiques Roadshow*), to Georgia Public Television in both Savannah (where the 2003 program was recorded) and Augusta (where Camp Hancock was located), to editors of the local newspapers in both cities, to the Georgia Historical Society and military museums, to a Georgia baseball historian, and to the members of the Society for American Baseball Research. The search proved fruitless. Perhaps publication of this book will help bring these papers into the public arena so that they can be studied and evaluated by historians.

Special mention is due to Wikipedia. This open source reference can be frustrating to use, and is not always entirely complete or, perhaps, reliable. But for simple, basic facts, and often for more complex treatments, it is a go-to source of first impression in this age of Internet-based research. In preparing this work, the author touched base with The Wiki in connection with the following topics, among others, finding in a number of instances essays that were deep, textured, and highly useful: Alfred Henry Spink, Augusta Fire of 1916, Babe Ruth, *Birmingham Special*, Branch Rickey, Camp Hancock, Central Park, Doubleday Myth, Ed Walsh, George Creel, History of Advertising, History of the New York Giants (baseball), Home Run Baker, Honus Wagner, Joseph Pulitzer, Land Speed Record for Rail Vehicles, Max Carey, Michael J. O'Farrell, National Baseball Hall of Fame, *New York Journal*, North River Tunnels, *Pelican* (train), Pennsylvania Station (New York City), Polo Grounds, *Sporting News*, Streetcars in Washington, D.C., Southern Railway (U.S.), Trenton, N.J., United States Department of War, Walter Johnson, Washington Union Station, William Randolph Hearst, and Winfield Scott Hancock. Alphabetization here is by first word as is the presentation style of Wikipedia.

Since this is a book about baseball, it is unsurprising that two baseball-specific references were especially valuable as well, though in different ways. The first was the searchable database maintained by Major League Baseball and accessible at mlb.com that includes every player who ever wore the uniform. The author made good use of this resource, particularly in confirming player identities and certain basic information. A second valuable resource is found in the biographical articles published by the Society for American Baseball Research on SABR.org. Some of these are cited in the list of sources consulted.

As with any project of this type, many people have contributed, knowingly or otherwise, to the final product. I would like to single out for special mention:

- Paul Kuhn, a local historian of note and, not incidentally, the real, long-time concierge at the Otesaga Resort in Cooperstown, who was a fount of knowledge on the local scene and the history of the hotel, and who may have met more Hall of Fame inductees than almost any other living person;

- Cassidy Lent, a reference librarian at the National Baseball Hall of Fame Library, who provided some insights into the operation of that entity and of the ABNER database; Craig Muder, Director of Communications for the Hall of Fame; and Scott Mondore, Marketing Coordinator, for their assistance;

- Simeon Lipman of Simeonlipman.com, appraisers, who presented the Camp Hancock papers on the 2003/2018 broadcasts of PBS's "Antiques Roadshow"; Allison Dillard, Reference and Cataloguing Librarian at the Georgia Historical Society; Gordon Blaker, military historian and Director of the U.S. Army Field Artillery Museum at Fort Sill; Ben Baughman, Curator of the Southern Museum of Civil War & Locomotive History; Bill Baab, long-time Outdoor Editor of *The Augusta Chronicle*, who actually lives on the site once occupied by the hospital at Camp Hancock, who took a deep dive into the *Chronicle*'s archive in my behalf to search out the contemporaneous local coverage, and who then, foolishly, volunteered to proofread the manuscript, and later provided a tour of the camp's contemporary footprint; writer and baseball historian (and Ty Cobb expert) Lamar Garrard, an Augusta native who now lives in Lincolnton, Georgia, who educated the author on Cobb and his place in Augusta history; Covington, Georgia, historian (and Camp Hancock expert) Joe Lee, who shared his map overlaying Camp Hancock in 1918 on present-day Augusta; Terry Sloope, Assistant Director for Research at the Burruss Institute at Kennesaw State University (and a former student of the author's in another life), who started the Atlanta Chapter of the Society for American Baseball Research back in the 1990s; and Susan Catron, Executive Editor of the *Savannah Morning News*, as well as Chuck Mobley and Steve Bisson, both of whom covered the 2003 Roadshow visit for that paper; for their general insights and their assistance in trying to locate the originals of the Camp Hancock documents;

- John Payne, already credited above, for his extraordinary ability to capture and bring to life documents that were in part little more than collections of fading electrons and in part mere figments of the author's imagination;

- Alexis Valentine and Paul Hogroian of the Library of Congress, and, especially, John Horne of the National Baseball Hall of Fame and Museum, for their assistance in tracking down photographs;

- Beverly Ford for giving the author a tour of the Ty Cobb House in Augusta and for sharing her collection of Cobb memorabilia and photos;

- good friends Neal Chalkley, Ned Lebow, Marguerite Ralston, and Irv Rockwood for their reviews of early drafts of the book;

- Luke Amato, Al Arrighi, Henry Berman, the late Mike Burrows, Reynolds Cafferata, Chick DeThomasis, Eric Dezenhall, Ken Janda, Alan Lincourt, Colin Mustful, Hubert O'Hearn, Deborah Schneider, Mark Schraf, Amity Shlaes, Nancy Wilcox, and Juan Williams for their advice and assistance;

- and publisher Walt Friedman, with special kudos to Gary Cieradkowski for the cover design.

Thanks as well to my wife, Amy, who has steadfastly lived through many drafts of many books, and had surely hoped there would be no more.

NOTES

5	origins traced to England – More specifically, some have since argued, to a game played by Frederick, Prince of Wales and Lord Middlesex on the estate of Grace Boyle, the Earl's wife, at Walton-on-Thames in Surrey, in 1749 – Hoyle. Leeke (*Nine Innings*) tells the story of American doughboys taking the game back to those shores during the Great War, including an exhibition for the royal family.
6	of the National Archives – Rosenberg.
6	men of the highest intelligence - "Three Crack Regiments Make Up The Ordnance Camp At Hancock; Men Soon Ready For Service Over The Waters," *Augusta Herald*, June 9, 1918, p. 1. Found through online searches, November 25, 2020, at https:// gahistoricnewspapers.galileo.usg.edu/regions/east/.
6	More to the point ~ "Soldiers To Meet Sailors Saturday," *Augusta Herald*, June 7, 1918, p. 10; and "Camp Hancock Nine Meets Charleston Navy Yard Team At Warren Park Today," *Augusta Herald*, June 8, 1918, p. 3. As a comparison, in the paper's special issue on Camp Hancock, the *Herald* published the entire roster of all military police officers on the base. See "Military Police At Hancock Are Live Body Of Men, Although Leader Has Had Only Brief Period For Training Them," *Augusta Herald*, June 9, 1918, p. 19. All articles found through online searches, November 25, 2020, at https:// gahistoricnewspapers.galileo.usg.edu/regions/east/.
7	cover up large-scale outbreaks of influenza – Desjardin, passim.
7	just two years before his appointment ~ Bachman
9	See Charlie Chaplin, *My Autobiography*. New York: Simon & Schuster, 1964.
32	failing enterprise – Topping.
33	in the paper's newsroom – O'Neil.
36	the part that counted ~ It was just a few years later, in 1898, that the five boroughs we know today as New York City, were combined into a more or less unified political entity.

38   one of his Harvard classmates – Thorn, p. 229.

40   photos by Conlon – McCabe & McCabe, pp. 9-15.

41   "Hey, Barney" – "The Dreyfuss Incident," *Minneapolis Journal*, June 8, 1905, p. 9, quoted in Williams.

50   hard for him ever since – Deford, p. 224.

52   Fictitious letter rendered by John Payne.

55   The letter ostensibly signed by Branch Rickey is fictitious.

62   This illustration by John Payne is a modified rendering based on a genuine military document that was appraised on the PBS program, *Antiques Roadshow*, recorded in Savannah, Georgia, on July 12, 2003. Please see the related discussion above. A 2018 repeat of the episode showing the document in its original form can be found online at http://www.pbs.org/wgbh/roadshow/season/8/savannah-ga/appraisals/1918-wwi-baseball-player-documents-200301A28/.

71   Serial number information found online at https://typewriterdatabase.com, March 7, 2019.

72   Photograph of typewriter by the author.

74   Photograph of Camp Hancock. Shulman, Isaac, Copyright Claimant. *Looking down Tyler Ave. from 108th Field Artillery, Camp Hancock, Augusta, Ga., Feb.* Augusta Camp Hancock, Georgia, United States, 1918. February. Photograph. www.loc.gov/item/2007664095/. Found online March 7, 2019.

80   his rookie season – Baseball's Greatest Sacrifice: World War I Deaths, found online at http://www.baseballsgreatestsacrifice.com/world_war_i.html, October 1, 2018.

81   All served their country – See Leeke for a detailed discussion of all the professional ballplayers who served during the Great War.

86   They're too much fun – quoted in Baseball Almanac, found online at http://www.baseball-almanac.com/quotes/quoruth.shtml, October 1, 2018.

96   proximity to the Capitol itself – Charles Moore, *Daniel H. Burnham: Architect, Planner of Cities*. Boston: Houghton Mifflin, 1921, p. 160, as cited by Wikipedia.

104   hissed with danger – Cobb, p. 65.

112   that was his fault – quoted in Baseball Almanac, found online at http://www.baseball-almanac.com/quotes/quocobb.shtml, October 1, 2018.

113   I can't scare – quoted in Baseball Almanac, found online at http://www.baseball-almanac.com/quotes/quocobb.shtml, October 1, 2018.

126   About ten years ago ~ Kahanowitz, passim, offers the definitive account of this incident.

134   Fictitious journal rendered by John Payne.

142   Fictitious letter rendered by Jon Payne.

156   This illustration by John Payne is a modified rendering based on a genuine military document that was appraised on the PBS program, *Antiques Roadshow*, recorded in Savannah, Georgia, on July 12, 2003. Please see the related discussion above. A 2018 repeat of the episode showing the document in its original form can be found online at http://www.pbs.org/wgbh/roadshow/season/8/savannah-ga/appraisals/1918-wwi-baseball-player-documents~200301A28/.

161   There was no part ~ Creel, pp. 3-5.

162   lead others during gas attacks – quoted in Ceresi.

172   Once Landis became Commissioner of Baseball and assumed powers and responsibilities that Johnson had held for years, the two became arch rivals. Kahanowitz, especially pp. 191-223.

172   Major Barrett was commanding officer ~ For the entire roster of officers assigned to the hospital during this period, see "Commander of Base Hospital and Members of His Staff," *Augusta Herald*, June 9, 1918, p. 17. Found through online searches, November 25, 2020, at https://gahistoricnewspapers.galileo.usg.edu/regions/east/.

173   replaced as briefer by an unknown Colonel ~ Though there is no reason to associate the fact with the fictional events described here, it is interesting to note that at or around this same period in time, there was a change in command of the ordnance units at Camp Hancock, with Colonel J.W. Benet replacing Major R.L. Gaugler. "Three

Crack Regiments Make Up The Ordnance Camp At Hancock; Men Soon Ready For Service Over The Waters," *Augusta Herald*, June 9, 1918, p. 1. Found through online searches, November 25, 2020, at https://gahistoricnewspapers.galileo.usg.edu/regions/east/.

178   excellent work by Major Brandt ~ "Post Commander at Camp Hancock and Members of His Staff," *Augusta Herald*, June 9, 1918, p. 1. Found through online searches, November 25, 2020, at https://gahistoricnewspapers.galileo.usg.edu/regions/east/. While it is highly likely that Major Brandt cooperated closely with the newspaper for its special issue on Camp Hancock, there is no evidence that he did so for the purpose of promoting the presence of the prominent major leaguers.

180   *this never happened* ~ While this may strike readers as an unlikely plan of action, Desjardin devotes the better part of his book to an exploration of the lengths to which both Mr. Creel and the military were prepared to go to sustain popular support for the war in 1918, including explicit efforts to hide from the civilian population of the Boston area in precisely this manner the fact that there was an emergent and deadly influenza epidemic in their community centered in the local military training camps. The deliberate and systematic masking of a high-leverage accident associated with a unit of prominent baseball players established for the purpose of encouraging recruitment to the Chemical Warfare Service would have been of a piece with this strategy. Moreover, as Kahanowitz argues (pp. 209-241), just a few years later, in 1926, both Ban Johnson and Kenesaw Mountain Landis were involved in a similar, though far more limited, coverup to protect the interests of baseball in the face of allegations that certain prominent players, including Mr. Cobb, were involved in an alleged gambling incident. Cobb and Tris Speaker were publicly absolved of guilt in this incident, but privately, for a time, both were forced to resign from the game. Indeed, if the supposed events of 1918 had actually occurred, one could speculate that Mr. Johnson, in particular, used the subsequent gambling

allegations, which came to his attention just a year following the death of Christy Mathewson in 1925, as an opportunity to even the score with Mr. Cobb, while at the same time maintaining the image of the game. Mr. Creel's promise to suppress any mention in the newspapers of these events or the resulting "corrections" was not, in context, a boast.

181 The correspondence from Professor Hofbert to Jason Drumm is fictitious.

191 My name is JT Willett — name and phone number of the passenger agent recorded in the roughly contemporaneous Pennsylvania Railroad system timetable found online at http://streamlinermemories.info/PRR/PRR46TT.pdf, October 12, 2018.

214 Ruth did seem to be – for a detailed take on the financial impact of Babe Ruth on the game using contemporary analytics, see Leavy, pp. 388-392. Wehrle makes the same point more anecdotally, but offers a compelling argument that Ruth, because of his great popularity and also his oft-expressed working class views, was unpopular with the baseball establishment throughout his career. He was at once a prime ticket window draw and a threat of potentially immense consequence. Interestingly, many sportswriters of the era shared that complex view. It is reflected in JT Willard's own appraisal of The Bambino.

214 player named Ruth – Leavy, pp. 28, 79-80, et passim.

221 Cooperstown, New York, in 1839 ~ John Thorn, *Baseball in the Garden of Eden*, devotes several early chapters to debunking this myth, and others at the end to explaining its origin from a uniquely insightful perspective.

221 Cleland who worked for Clark – Chafetz, p. 29.

223 Photograph of entrance by the author.

231 I feel terrible – Cobb, pp. 189-192.

231 as if nothing had happened – found online at https://quoteinvestigator.com/2012/05/26/stumble-over-truth/ October 14, 2018.

236   used that very word ~ quoted in Ritter, p. 41.

241   June 12, 1839 ~ "Hall of Fame to Mark 75th Year with Special Events, Commemorations for Diamond Celebration," Press Release, National Baseball Hall of Fame and Museum, June 12, 2013, as cited by Wikipedia.

LIST OF SOURCES CONSULTED

About North Georgia. "Ty Cobb." N.D. Found online at http://www.aboutnorthgeorgia.com/ang/Ty_Cobb, September 23, 2018.

Achorn, Edward. *The Summer of Beer and Whiskey: How Brewers, Barkeeps, Rowdies, Immigrants, and a Wild Pennant Fight Made Baseball America's Game.* New York: Public Affairs, 2013.

Bachman, Rachel. "When Women and Politics Took Over Baseball," *The Wall Street Journal* (October 18, 2020), found online November 1, 2020 at https://www.wsj.com/articles/when-women-and-politics-took-over-baseball-11603029600.

Ballparksofbaseball.com. "MLB Ballpark Attendance, By Year." Found online at https://www.ballparksofbaseball.com/baseball-ballpark-attendance/, September 23, 2018.

Barnes, Alexander F., Peter L. Belmonte, and Samuel D. Barnes. *Play Ball!: Doughboys and Baseball during the Great War.* Atglen, PA: Schiffer Publishing, 2019.

Baseball Almanac. "Ty Cobb Quotes." Found online at http://www.baseball-almanac.com/quotes/quocobb.shtml, September 23, 2018.

Brandon, Ruth. *A Capitalist Romance: Singer and the Sewing Machine.* Philadelphia: J.B. Lippincott, 1977.

Breslin, Jimmy. *Branch Rickey: A Life.* New York: Penguin, 2011.

Brunt, Larry. "Christy Mathewson: The First Face of Baseball." Baseballhall.com. Found online at https://baseballhall.org/discover-more/stories/short-stops/christy-mathewson-first-face-of-baseball, September 23, 2018.

Carey, Charles. "Walter Johnson," *Society for American Baseball Research,* N.D. Found online at https://sabr.org/bioproj/person/0e5ca45c, September 23, 2018.

Ceresi, Frank. "Chemical Warfare Service: World War I's House of Horrors: The Little Known Service of Branch Rickey, Ty Cobb and the Great Matty," *Baseball in Wartime,* June 18, 2008. Found online at http://www.baseballinwartime.com/chemical_warfare.htm, September 23, 2018.

Chafets, Zev. *Cooperstown Confidential: Heroes, Rogues, and the Inside Story of the Baseball Hall of Fame.* New York: Bloomsbury, 2009.

Chapman, Kit. "Gas, flame and baseball," *Chemistry World,* N.D., found online at https://www.chemistryworld.com/opinion/gas-flame-and-baseball/3007037.article, September 23, 2018.

Cobb, Ty with Al Stump. *My Life in Baseball: The True Record.* New York: Doubleday & Company, 1961.

Creel, George. *How We Advertised America: The First Telling of the Amazing Story of the Committee on Public Information That Carried the Gospel of Americanism to Every Corner of the Globe.* New York: Macmillan, 1920.

Deford, Frank. *The Old Ball Game: How John McGraw, Christy Mathewson, and the New York Giants Created Modern Baseball.* New York: Grove Press, 2005.

Desjardin, Skip. *September 1918: War, Plague, and the World Series.* Washington, DC: Regnery, 2018.

DeValeria, Dennis and Jeanne Burke DeValeria. *Honus Wagner: A Biography.* New York: Henry Holt, 1995.

Finkel, Jan. "Honus Wagner," *Society for American Baseball Research,* N.D. Found online at https://sabr.org/bioproj/person/30b27632, September 23, 2018.

Foster, John B. "Base Ball and the Service," *Spalding's Official Baseball Guide 1919.* New York: American Sports Publishing, 1919, pp. 175-223. Found online at https://archive.org/details/spaldingsbasebal07chic/page/174, February 23, 2019.

Frierson, Eddie. "Christy Mathewson," Society for American Baseball Research, found online November 1, 2020, at https://sabr.org/bioproj/person/christy-mathewson/.

Fountain, Charles. *The Betrayal: The 1919 World Series and the Birth of Modern Baseball.* New York: Oxford University Press, 2016.

Gallico, Paul. "A Great Moral Lesson," *New York Daily News,* September 3, 1927, p. 20.

Glen Echo Park. "History of Glen Echo Park." N.D. Found online at https://glenechopark.org/history, September 23, 2018.

Gurtowski, Richard. "Remembering Baseball Hall of Famers Who Served in the Chemical Corps," *Army Chemical Review*, July-December 2005, pp. 52-54. Found online at http://www.wood.army.mil/chmdsd/images/pdfs/Jul-Dec%202005/Gurtowski.pdf, September 23, 2018.

Halfon, Mark S.. *Tales From the Deadball Era: Ty Cobb, Home Run Baker, Shoeless Joe Jackson, and the Wildest Times in Baseball History*. Lincoln: University of Nebraska Press, 2014.

History.com Editors. "William Randolph Hearst," December 15, 2009 and August 21, 2018, found online at https://www.history.com/topics/early-20th-century-us/william-randolph-hearst, September 23, 2018.

Hornbaker, Tim. *War on the Basepaths: The Definitive Biography of Ty Cobb*. New York: Sports Publishing, 2015.

Hoyle, Ben. "Baseball's coming home... to Surrey," *The Times* (June 26, 2019). Found online February 11, 2021, at https://www.thetimes.co.uk/article/baseball-s-coming-home-to-surrey-x77xwdft2.

Kahanowitz, Ian S. *Baseball Gods in Scandal: Ty Cobb, Tris Speaker, and the Dutch Leonard Affair*. South Orange, NJ: Summer Game Books, 2019.

Kelly, Matt. "On Account of War," *National Baseball Hall of Fame*, N.D. Found online at https://baseballhall.org/discover-more/stories/short-stops/1918-world-war-i-baseball, September 23, 2018.

King, Gilbert. "The Knife in Ty Cobb's Back: Did the baseball great really confess to murder on his deathbed?" Smithsonian.com, August 30, 2011. Found online at https://www.smithsonianmag.com/history/the-knife-in-ty-cobbs-back-65618032/, September 23, ,2018.

Kirk, William F. "The Dreyfuss Incident," *Minneapolis Journal*, June 8, 1905, p. 9. Quoted in Phil Williams, "William F. Kirk," *Society for American Baseball Research*, N.D. Found online at https://sabr.org/node/32382, September 23, 2018.

Lasswell, Harold D. *Propaganda Technique in World War I*. Cambridge, MA: M.I.T. Press, 1971.

Leavy, Jane. *The Big Fella: Babe Ruth and the World He Created*. New York: Harper Collins, 2018.

Leeke, Jim. *Nine Innings for the King: The Day Wartime London Stopped for Baseball, July 4, 1918*. Jefferson, NC: McFarland & Company, 2015.

___. *From the Dugouts to the Trenches: Baseball During the Great War*. Lincoln, NB: University of Nebraska Press, 2017.

Leerhsen, Charles. *Ty Cobb: A Terrible Beauty*. New York: Simon & Schuster, 2015.

Lennon, Frank. "MLB Hall of Famers: Military Service You May Not Have Known About (Part 2)," *Bleacher Report*, November 11, 2011. Found online at https://bleacherreport.com/articles/934267-mlb-hall-of-famers-military-service-you-may-not-have-known-about-part-2#slide0, September 23, 2018.

Library of Congress. "Topics in Chronicling America – Baseball's World Series, 1903-1922." Found online at https://www.loc.gov/rr/news/topics/baseball.html, September 23, 2018.

Lowenfish, Lee. *Branch Rickey: Baseball's Ferocious Gentleman*. Lincoln, NB: University of Nebraska Press, 2007.

McCabe, Neal and Constance McCabe. *Baseball's Golden Age: The Photographs of Charles M. Conlon*. St. Louis, MO: Harry N. Abrams, in association with *The Sporting News*, 1993.

McGeehan, W.O. "Babe Ruth's Drawing Power," *New York Herald Tribune*, June 6, 1927, reproduced online at https://1927-the-diary-of-myles-thomas.espn.com/babe-ruths-drawing-power-aae4d5d212f6. Found April 12, 2020.

Murphy, Cait. *Crazy '08: How a Cast of Cranks, Rogues, Boneheads, and Magnates Created the Greatest Year in Baseball History*. New York: Harper Collins, 2007.

National Baseball Hall of Fame. "Hall of Fame Veterans," N.D. Found online at https://baseballhall.org/discover-more/stories/hall-of-famer-facts/hall-of-fame-veterans, September 23, 2018.

O'Neil, Tim. "Looking Back: The day Post-Dispatch editor killed his adversary in the newsroom," *St. Louis Post-Dispatch*, October 13, 2016, found online at https://www.stltoday.com/news/archives/looking-back-the-day-post-dispatch-editor-killed-his-adversary/articleff1c78ed-5804-5797-86be-c156e2194b0c.html, September 23, 2018.

Original Hobo Nickel Society, "Hobo Terminology." Found online at http://www.hobonickels.org/terms.htm, September 23, 2018.

Osoba, Stella. "MLB World Series: 11 Most expensive Baseball Memorabilia," GoBankingRates.com, October 25, 2015, found online at https://www.gobankingrates.com/saving-money/entertainment/mlb-world-series-11-expensive-baseball-memorabilia/, September 23, 2018.

Pennsylvania Railroad. "Passenger Schedule." March 15, 1946. Found online at http://streamlinermemories.info/PRR/PRR46TT.pdf, September 23, 2018.

Raycroft, Joseph E. "The Athletic Division of the War Department Commission on Training Camp Activities," in *Reach Official American League Base Ball Guide for 1919*: Philadelphia, A.J. Reach Company, 1919, pp. 45-54. Found online at https://archive.org/stream/reachofficialame19181phil#page/45/mode/1up, February 23, 2019.

Richter, Francis C. "Review of the 1918 Season," in *Reach Official American League Base Ball Guide for 1919*: Philadelphia, A.J. Reach Company, 1919, pp. 8-17. Found online at https://archive.org/stream/reachofficialame19181phil#page/8/mode/1up, February 23, 2019.

___. "Players Who Served Their Country," in *Reach Official American League Base Ball Guide for 1919*: Philadelphia, A.J. Reach Company, 1919, pp. 38-42. Found online at https://archive.org/stream/reachofficialame19181phil#page/38/mode/1up, February 23, 2019.

Ritter, Lawrence S. *The Glory of Their Times: The Story of the Early Days of Baseball Told by the Men Who Played It*. New York: Harper Perennial Modern Classics, 2010.

Rosenberg, Howard W. "Did Baseball Great Christy Mathewson Die of Chemical Warfare?" *Inside Sources* (October 24, 2018), found online at https://www.insidesources.com/did-baseball-great-christy-mathewson-die-of-chemical-warfare/, July 6, 2019.

Rosengren, John. "Baseball's Newspaper: The *Sporting News* Reigned as the Bible of Baseball for Almost a Century," in *Memories and Dreams: The Official Magazine of the Hall of Fame* 40, Number 3 (Summer 2018), pp. 16-18.

Rushin, Steve. *The 34-Ton Bat*. New York: Little Brown, 2013.

Seib, Philip. *The Player: Christy Mathewson, Baseball, and the American Century*. New York: Thunder's Mouth Press (Avalon), 2003.

Shexnayder, C.J. "William Sibert," *Encyclopedia of Alabama*. Found online at http://www.encyclopediaofalabama.org/article/h-3371, September 23, 2018.

Sparks, Barry. *Frank "Home Run" Baker: Hall of Famer and World Series Hero.* Jefferson, NC: MacFarland & Company, 2006.

Stevens, Julia. "Online Exclusive: A Hero in the Field and in the Trenches: Christy Mathewson's WWI service in the Chemical Warfare Service led to his untimely death," *Bucknell Magazine*, N.D., found online at https://www.bucknell.edu/x123747.xml, September 23, 2018.

ThemeTrains.com. "The Story of the Rexall Train of 1936." Found online at http://www.themetrains.com/rexall-train-main.htm, September 23, 2018.

Thorn, John. *Baseball in the Garden of Eden: The Secret History of the Early Game.* New York: Simon & Schuster, 2011.

Topping, Seymour. "Biography of Joseph Pulitzer," *The Pulitzer Prizes*, N.D. Found online at http://www.pulitzer.org/page/biography-joseph-pulitzer, September 23, 2018.

Tye, Larry. *The Father of Spin: Edward L. Bernays and the Birth of Public Relations.* New York: Henry Holt, 1998.

Vlasich, James A. *A Legend for the Legendary: The Origin of the Baseball Hall of Fame.* Bowling Green, OH: Bowling State University Popular Press, 1990.

Weber, Nicholas Fox. *The Clarks of Cooperstown: Their Singer Sewing Machine Fortune, Their Great and Influential Art Collections, Their Forty-Year Feud.* New York: Alfred A. Knopf, 2007.

Wehrle, Edmund F. *Breaking Babe Ruth: Baseball's Campaign Against It's Biggest Star.* Columbia: University of Missouri Press, 2018.

Williams, Phil. "William F. Kirk," *Society for American Baseball Research*, N.D. Found online at https://sabr.org/node/32382, September 23, 2018.